P9-CQX-627

Today with my Father

Today with my Father

Noelene Johnsson

This book is published in collaboration with the Youth Department as an enrichment of the Morning Watch devotional plan.

Review and Herald Publishing Association
Washington, DC 20039-0555
Hagerstown, MD 21740

This book was
Edited by Gerald Wheeler
Designed by Richard Steadham
Cover art by Richard Steadham
Type set: 10/12 Century Schoolbook
Printed in U.S.A.

Library of Congress Cataloging in Publication Data

Johnsson, Noelene, 1938-
Today with my father.

"Published in collaboration with the Youth Department as an enrichment of the Morning watch devotional plan."
Includes index.
Summary: Devotions for each day of the year include a Scripture passage followed by an illustrative anecdote.
1. Devotional calendars—Seventh-day Adventists.
2. Children—Prayer-books and devotions—English.
[1. Prayer books and devotions. 2. Christian life]
I. Title.

BV4811.J59 1984 242'.2 84-9939

ISBN 0-8280-0240-1

MEET THE AUTHOR

Noelene Johnsson, as a typical "preacher's kid," grew up in various cities of Australia and New Zealand. At Avondale College she met William G. Johnsson, and ten days after their marriage they sailed for mission service in India.

The Johnssons first served at Vincent Hill School—a boarding academy nearly seven thousand feet up in the Himalayas. Noelene was matron for the small boys and taught music. Her husband was boys' dean. Later the family moved to Spicer College, where Noelene finished her college degree and eventually taught kindergarten. The Johnssons lived in India for fifteen years, and their two children, Terry and Julie, were born there.

In 1975 the Johnssons moved to the United States, where Dr. Johnsson taught in the Seventh-day Adventist Theological Seminary. Noelene completed her Master of Arts in teaching at Andrews University and taught third grade in the Berrien Springs public school system.

Since 1980 the Johnssons have lived in Washington, D.C., where Dr. Johnsson edits the *Adventist Review* and Noelene edits the *Mission* quarterlies.

Noelene's hobbies include stamp collecting, sewing, walking (and sleeping). She loves children—especially the primaries of Sligo church, who listen spellbound to her stories.

FACE TO FACE

For now we see through a glass, darkly; but then face to face: now I know in part; but then shall I know even as also I am known. 1 Corinthians 13:12.

Joan Marie Cook's friends felt sorry for her. She had the smallest, least attractive room in the dormitory. But Kelly knew Joan Marie's secret. The room had a large window with a perfect view of a stately silver maple tree. Looking from the window, Joan Marie felt almost *in* that tree. Kelly sensed the special magic of the tree just as Joan Marie did. They often stood in their darkened room watching as moonglow bathed the tree. Both girls loved the comfortable silence of a starry night. But sometimes they talked together about their secret selves.

Kelly had been born in South America, but her parents divorced soon after, and mother and daughter returned to the United States. After her mother remarried, the family discovered a wonderful new religious faith. Kelly loved her family, but somehow she missed her real father. The few letters he had written her over the years were all that she knew of him.

"I just want to *see* my father," Kelly whispered one evening as they stood before the window tree.

"You might not recognize him," Joan Marie cautioned.

But Kelly was sure of herself. "Something inside me just longs to meet him," she said. "I feel sort of lonely for him. Do you think he would love me?"

One winter evening as the two girls returned to the dorm from a shopping expedition they heard a pleasant, deep voice call Kelly's name. Turning, the girls saw a tall, deeply tanned stranger standing by the fireplace. "Kelly," he said again.

After a moment of silence Kelly suddenly came to life. "Father," she said with calm assurance as she flew into his arms. As Joan Marie continued up to her room and stood before the window tree she thought of her heavenly Father. "I feel kind of lonely for You," she whispered. "And I will be certain as Kelly was when at last I see You face to face."

TEACH US TO PRAY

And it came to pass, that, as he was praying in a certain place, when he ceased, one of his disciples said unto him, Lord, teach us to pray. Luke 11:1.

Napagi accepted Jesus in the African country of Uganda. Convinced that he should take the good news of Jesus to his own people of neighboring Sudan, he moved to the city of Juba and found work in a boat-building company. Here he shared his faith with his workmates.

Ismail studied the Bible lessons Napagi brought to work and quietly made his decision. "On Saturday I will not come to work," he said. "I will come to your church. I want to see how you pray."

Sabbath turned out to be a wonderful day. Ismail witnessed a baptism. "It was as if I were with Jesus in heaven," he commented later. "I want to worship with you every Sabbath." At work on Monday he told everyone of his experience and his decision to follow the Lord. "Seventh-day Adventists will go to heaven," he declared emphatically. "They know how to talk to God in heaven."

Could people say that if they heard you pray? Or are you like the disciples who asked, "Lord, teach us to pray"? The disciples were God-fearing men. Surely they knew how to pray! But they had heard the Master's prayers. They thrilled to hear Him open His heart to God as to a best friend. And Jesus did not use the loud, pompous tones of the Pharisees addressing the stern God of their understanding. His prayers brought God close to those humble fishermen. How they longed to pray like that!

And so they asked the Master to teach them to pray. Scripture records the model prayer that Jesus gave them. We know it well and love its words. Each morning this year let us consider some aspect of that prayer so that we too may learn to pray.

DOODLES

For whom the Lord loveth he correcteth; even as a father the son in whom he delighteth. Proverbs 3:12.

"What is your one secret wish?" Joan Marie asked one evening. Secret wishes are fun because nobody cares how impossible or fanciful they sound. So I thought of our one impossible wish—to have a little poodle to take the place of the one we left in India. A few days later Doodles bounced through our front door and into our hearts.

Have you ever tried to train a puppy? Doodles needed lots of help. We forgave him endlessly for each breach of good manners we found on the kitchen floor, and tried all the harder to train him. As he learned self-control we praised him and loved him all the more. But Doodles needed to learn obedience. One day the poor little pup developed a respiratory problem. As we waited to see the veterinarian, Doodles barked and yapped and coughed endlessly. "You should really take Doodles to obedience classes," the vet said. "You would enjoy him much more." But our budget could not stretch around obedience classes. We must teach him ourselves. But all our efforts failed—until the day he chewed my pocketbook. I punished Doodles with a rolled newspaper and added a few extra whacks for the benefit of his memory.

Five minutes later that little mutt sat chewing on my pocketbook again. Who would ever love such a badly behaved dog? Again I administered the rolled newspaper. If only Doodles would learn to obey! This time, however, a miracle occurred. Doodles practically asked permission to sniff anything lying about the house after that. He stayed beside us as we walked down the street and came the minute we called him. We were proud of this dog we loved, and he seemed happy and secure with us. Even the veterinarian began to approve of Doodles.

Doodles taught me much about being a child of God—"For whom the Lord loveth he correcteth; even as a father the son in whom he delighteth."

FIRST STEPS

It was I who taught Ephraim to walk, I who had taken them in my arms . . . and led them with bonds of love. Hosea 11:3, 4, N.E.B.

For a baby he was long and thin—not the plump, cuddly mite I expected. "He's like Memsahib (the wife)," our servant remarked. (I had not known how low he rated me!) But to my husband this red, wrinkled little creature was the longed-for son and heir—the future tennis partner, football buddy, and right-hand man. As Terry filled out and tiny dimples appeared, our dormitory students pronounced him cute—looking more and more like his father!

It's just so much jabber, we said of his first da-da's. But there was no denying that first "Dad'n" as he held out his arms to his father. Never was a father more proud! And no father watched with more fascination as his son learned to scoot about on his tummy. Often during that cold north Indian winter, a little yellow, snowsuited figure rode on Daddy's shoulders to inspect the campus. Then Terry learned to balance himself and took off at a run, his daddy sitting on the floor yelling encouragement. There followed the discovery of bat and ball. "More, more," Terry would cry as Daddy patiently threw ball after ball at the little bat. It was difficult to know who was happier—proud father or growing son.

When Terry tests the limits of his father's patience, he often wonders if his dad really loves him. But if he could see a video replay of those long-ago days when his proud daddy taught him to walk, he would glimpse his father's love. He would understand that love requires a father to teach his child not only to walk, but to walk straight. "It was I who taught Ephraim to walk," God said when His wayward people refused to accept His love. "They did not know that I had lifted them like a child to my cheek, that I had bent down to feed them." God's love never changes. He loves you and me like that too.

LIKE A MOTHER

Can a woman forget her sucking child, that she should not have compassion on the son of her womb? yea, they may forget, yet will I not forget thee. Isaiah 49:15.

Recognizing that humans think of mother love as the safest of warm feelings, our great God tells us: Though a mother may turn against her instinct to love and protect, I will never desert you.

What is a mother? "They are wonderfuler than anything else," said 8-year-old Jon. "Mothers are the best thing that could happen to you. They always stay home from work to take care of you even if they get fired for it," adds Julie. And Lori sums it all up by saying, "My mom is best at being a mother." Paul thinks of his stylish mother as "always dressing up," but he loves her for everything she does. "I don't love her for what she *does,"* Jon chimes in. "I just love her."

You understand mother love because you experience it every day. But have you ever thought about children like Jerry whose mothers neglect them? Jerry looks after himself most of the time. And though he is now 10, he wears a baseball cap in school—even in winter—because he doesn't want anyone to see that his hair is not combed.

And how can God reach Erin, adopted three times before she turned 6, only to have her third set of parents divorce a year later? And what of the thousands of battered children in our land? What does mother love mean to them? God wants them to know that He cares for them more deeply than the world's best parents. But He reaches them only through a caring person. Perhaps someone you know needs that touch—to know that somebody cares. Ask God to help you touch that person with kindness and caring today.

MALI'S GIFT

He who did not spare his own Son, but gave him up for us all—how will he not also, along with him, give us all things. Romans 8:32, N.I.V.

Ever since I was tiny the more I liked something the more tightly I held onto it—except once when I was 10. I let go of my new purse while riding the bus. When I remembered it, the bus was miles away and my purse was gone forever—which only served to remind me to hold on tightly to the things I loved. But I have learned a new law of love. Sometimes people show their love for something by giving it up—deliberately letting it go. That is how it was with Mali the gardener.

Every morning at seven Mali came to work. Carefully he swept up the leaves under the rain tree and pulled weeds in the lawn. He dug and cultivated the vegetable garden. In the afternoon he returned to water the garden and run errands for the missionary. And often he brought one of his small children to enjoy the cool of the pretty yard.

One evening the missionary stopped to cuddle Mali's daughter. In jest she exclaimed, "Oh, Rani, you are so cute. I could take you home and keep you!" Mali thought about that for many days. It made good sense. On his humble wages he could not afford to buy Rani pretty clothes or send her to high school. But the missionary could.

"Oh, Mali, I couldn't," she exclaimed at his idea. "You need Rani—she is yours. How could you give her to me to take to America?" The tears in the father's eyes told the answer. Mali would not let his tender father's love stand in the way of his daughter's future. He showed the depth of his love when he offered to give her up.

Can you imagine how much it pained God to give up His dearly loved Son to come to earth and rescue the human race? And can you imagine how hard it is for Him to stand back and allow you the freedom to choose whether or not to love Him? He knows He might lose you forever if you choose it to be that way. But as long as you live He goes on loving you whether or not you love Him. That is how true love works. Don't you love Him for it!

LASSIE

When Israel was a boy, I loved him; I called my son out of Egypt; but the more I called, the further they went from me. Hosea 11:1, N.E.B.

Van dearly loved Lassie, his collie. He gave her all the food, love, and care any dog possibly could need. Also he allowed her freedom to wander in the yard without tying her up. And Lassie knew her master expected only that she protect the house, come when he called her, and love her master.

Lassie had long enjoyed Van's attention. She liked the way he stroked and praised her. But one day while walking through the woods with her master, Lassie saw a rabbit dart across the path. Instantly she took off after it. But, when the master whistled for Lassie to leave the chase and return, the dog refused. She resented having to obey her master. Only after much coaxing did she finally return.

After that, Lassie often slipped away to the woods on her own. The only way Van could keep his collie home was by tying her up. But the more he tied Lassie up, the less she loved her master, until one day, after walking with him in distant woods, she ran away for good. The master called after her. But Lassie ignored his pleading voice. The more he called, the farther she ran. Finally, after searching and calling for two hours, Van gave up and drove home without her.

Van often thought of his dog as he sat beside the fire on cold winter evenings. He knew Lassie would be cold and lonely, her coat matted and dirty. No doubt she was also hungry, having discovered that chasing rabbits for fun is quite different from hunting for survival.

Sometimes I am like Lassie when I resist God's love. I know that for my own good He wants me to stay away from certain places. But I still prefer to do as I please, pretending that I don't hear His voice. However, I find that without Jesus, life is hollow, lonely, and cold. I'm glad that, no matter how far I have strayed, Jesus waits to wrap me in His loving arms again. I want to enjoy the warmth of His love today. Don't you?

BLOOD BROTHERS

Be devoted to one another in brotherly love. Honor one another above yourselves. Romans 12:10, N.I.V.

"What's it like being the only girl?" Patti whispered to me from behind her geography textbook.

"Awful," I groaned, unable to pass up an opportunity to gain sympathy from someone who envied me my three brothers.

"Do you ever fight?" she persisted, hungry for details.

"All the time," I replied. And my conscience pricked me for overlooking all the good times my brothers and I enjoyed. I felt sorry for Patti, though. She needed brothers and sisters. Maybe then she could learn to give and take like the rest of us.

"What about your cousins?" I hissed. "They're really cute."

I knew I shouldn't have said it. Patti had five cousins of various ages, all belonging to one family. They attended the same public school, and two of the boys were a couple of years ahead of us. Sometimes they stopped to tease Patti on the playground. Once they had acted like pals, and she had looked guilty about it.

"My parents must never find out we spoke," she explained later about the incident. "Our two families aren't speaking to each other."

I felt sorry about that and often fantasized ways to bring them together. "Suppose you do what the American Indians sometimes did," I challenged her once. "You and your cousins could secretly cut a cross in your hand and their hands and mix your blood. Then you'd be blood brothers and nobody could keep you apart."

Patti liked the idea, but I don't know if they ever tried it. Soon afterward I moved to an Adventist school and lost touch with her. But I've always wished that I could have told her a secret that I discovered a few years later. I didn't need to cut myself to have blood brothers. My own brothers were real blood brothers—and so were Patti and her cousins. But best of all, we have a relationship with one another through Jesus, the best blood brother of them all. He gave all His blood on the cross to reunite our families with His.

THE WORLD'S BEST STORY

For God so loved the world, that he gave his only begotten Son, that whosoever believeth in him should not perish, but have everlasting life. John 3:16.

The first day of second semester I surveyed the class—26 kindergarteners, half of whom understood little or no English, and many of whom were non-Christians. Six months remained in the school year, so I determined to make every day count.

One morning during Bible class Kishore interrupted me. "Tell us about how God died," he begged. Now our Bible book did not include the crucifixion story, but I decided to add it anyway. "You wait," I teased. "I'll tell it when we are ready."

Every day after that someone would clamor for the story about how God died. When at last the children had progressed sufficiently in English, I told the story in all its glorious detail. For two or three weeks we lived and relived it. And each retelling held the children spellbound, until the wonder and concentration in their eyes almost made me cry.

What is there about that story that so attracts people—Christian and non-Christian alike? Is it that Someone so good and so loving died for us when we least deserved it?

Maybe we all should follow the story to Calvary more often and see again the great God of the universe stumble under the weight of the cross, blood stinging His eyes as it trickles from His thorn-pierced brow. We should watch as rough hands nail Him to the crude wooden beams. And we should wonder again, Why did He allow them to do it? Why did He die the death that was yours and mine for sins in which He had no share? Was it so that we might someday enjoy the life that He alone deserves? Was it to give us goodness and life forever that He wrapped His gift in love? And our part is simply to accept it, believing that it is His to give.

OUR FATHER

Our Father which art in heaven, Hallowed be thy name. Matthew 6:9.

In Old Testament times the Jewish people were very conscious of the great God they worshiped. They referred to Him by a special name—a name so sacred that nobody actually said the word. I was reminded of this practice recently as I watched a talented Jewish public school teacher guide her fifth-graders through a spelling lesson. The pupils were using their spelling words for the week to compose a short story. As somebody suggested a sentence the teacher wrote it on the chalkboard. Somehow the story involved a reference to God and worship. As if everyone understood what she was doing, the teacher wrote "G" for God and left dashes for the other letters of the word. She even avoided pronouncing it.

The original Hebrew word for God consisted of the Hebrew consonants *YHWH*. Scribes wrote those consonants but, out of respect for the sacred name, they did not pronounce it. Instead, they pronounced another word, meaning Lord. Over the centuries they lost the true pronunciation of *YHWH*. Nobody could remember hearing the vowels of that word. Scholars now think, by the way, that the word was pronounced *Yahweh*.

While the Jews honored the sacred name of God and acknowledged Him as Creator of their nation, they did not really think of Him as their Father. In the Psalms David says that the Lord is *like* a father to the fatherless (Ps. 68:5). Solomon explains in Proverbs how God punishes us *like* a father correcting his children (chap. 3:12). But nowhere does an Old Testament writer address God directly, calling Him Father.

Can you imagine the disciples' surprise as they heard Jesus pray, "Our Father." His loving tone of voice would have left no doubt that Jesus and God were close friends. They were family—Father and Son. I wonder how long it took John, the loving disciple, to notice that Jesus prayed, "*Our* Father." The close family ties included them all. God was John's Father, too. And yours and mine. Isn't it great to have a Father like that!

WE, HIS CHILDREN

Love your enemies and pray for those who persecute you, that you may be the sons of your Father in heaven. Matthew 5:44, 45, N.I.V.

When Jesus began His model prayer, addressing God as "our Father," He gave the disciples a new picture of God. The Jewish leaders proudly named Abraham, Isaac, and Jacob as *their* fathers. In fact, any great man who had earned respect was called Father. But never had anyone addressed God the Father as Jesus did.

Jesus taught His disciples a new way of life. "Love your enemies," He said, "that ye may be the children of your Father which is in heaven." Do your kind deeds privately, "otherwise ye have no reward of your Father which is in heaven."

Love, heaven, rewards, Father. The disciples had pondered the words of the Master. But when He taught them to pray, "Our Father," suddenly it all came together. In His love for us God asks us to treat others in His family with the same loving consideration that He shows us.

Arthur S. Maxwell once told the story of Johnny, who enjoyed throwing smooth round pebbles across the crowded beach. Naturally, the stone-throwing annoyed other bathers, and Johnny's dad forbade his son to pick up another pebble. Tired of always being told what to do, Johnny, with hatred for his father burning in his heart, turned and stalked down the beach. On and on the boy walked, unmindful of time or distance, or of the black clouds covering the sun. When the first driving rain hit the beach, Johnny ran for shelter behind an old breakwater. Shivering and miserable, he wished that he had not acted so hastily. Then he saw a familiar figure walking toward him with an umbrella. An hour earlier Johnny would not have believed that he could feel so relieved to see his dad.

And that's how it is with God. Though we don't always act like His children and though we forget Him for a time, He is always there, forgiving and loving as ever, when we turn back to Him.

WHEN MY STRENGTH IS GONE

Do not cast me away when I am old; do not forsake me when my strength is gone. Psalm 71:9, N.I.V.

"I envy kids who go to visit their grandparents," Brenda says. "They get to leave before the novelty wears off. But mine live with us all the time. And we're no longer on our best behavior."

"Sometimes I try really hard to be good, but it doesn't last," Voight agrees.

"My grandpa monopolizes the conversation at the supper table," Greg adds. "Just when our family has a chance to talk together, he wants to tell one of his stories."

"Tell me about it," Brenda chuckles. "Gramp's stories are funny—the first time you hear them. But they become longer and more detailed with every telling."

Brenda, Voight, and Greg admit to sometimes feeling guilty about their impatience when the pressure of live-in grandparents gets them down.

"But having them around is not all bad," Brenda admits. "They often drive me places I need to go. And sometimes I can tell them things that I wouldn't discuss with anyone else."

"Having to fetch things for them keeps me from getting too selfish with my time," Voight observes. "But sometimes it gets me down. Once when I was watching television I had to get up constantly to take things to my great-grandmother. In the end I got so mad that I locked myself in my room. But later my mother brought in Gran's photo album and her Bible.

"Just leafing through them, I realized that Gran was once young and good-looking. It scared me to think that someday I will grow old too. But the thing that really hurt was when I noticed a text underlined in her Bible: 'Do not cast me away when I am old; do not forsake me when my strength is gone.' "

"I like that," Brenda whispers. "That could be my grandmother's prayer."

"Knowing that God cares so much for me, even when I grow old, helps me feel differently about Gran," Voight adds. "She really isn't so much trouble anymore."

WHAT FAMILIES DO

See what love the Father has given us, that we should be called children of God; and so we are. 1 John 3:1, R.S.V.

Tom Butterfield was an extraordinary young man. His mother died when he was 13, and soon afterward his father announced, "From here on you are on your own!" He never forgot the loneliness of that moment. As a college freshman he worked in a state mental hospital, where he discovered little Joey, abandoned, to be brought up there. Taking Joey home, after much persistence, Tom earned the honor of being the first single person and the first under 21 in that state to be licensed as a foster parent.

Butterfield began a home for boys and in no time was father to nine unwanted lads. The oldest, 16-year-old Duane, came against his will. And at the first opportunity he ran away. Soon the police arrested and jailed him for shoplifting. The sheriff offered to release Duane if Tom would take him back. After hesitating, Tom finally gave Duane a choice: Cooperate like a family member or serve your term.

Reluctantly Duane agreed to cooperate and returned home. His arrest, however, had not escaped the notice of angry townspeople who disliked Tom Butterfield's plan to save unwanted children. One day a truckload of angry men drove to Tom's ranch to beat up Duane. "Anyone who wants to fight him fights me first," Tom Butterfield declared. In the fight that followed Tom was hurt before a friend scared the intruders away with a shotgun.

Duane could not understand why Butterfield fought for him. Tom explained it this way: "That's what families do. They stick together."

You and I belong to the family of God. When sin entered our world, you and I came under a sentence of death. But our Foster Parent came to earth to earn the right to bring us into His family. He took the punishment that we deserved so that we might be His sons and daughters forever. Although He promises never to abandon us, neither does He force us to stay. We must choose to remain in His family each day.

WORTH FIGHTING FOR

"Let us have a feast to celebrate the day. For this son of mine was dead and has come back to life; he was lost and is found." Luke 15:23, 24, N.E.B.

"Will you just listen to all the noise at gate number 2," I grumbled. "How come the people arriving from Cleveland are so noisy?" A woman seated nearby responded that someone was adopting babies at Gate 2, so I wandered across to see.

"Here they come!" a 10-year-old squealed as he broke from his closely grouped family and jumped up and down. And sure enough, two women appeared with four tiny Korean orphans. Another woman with bulging flight bags and large brown envelopes stuffed with official papers bustled around, delivering the orphans to their adopting families.

One ivory-faced 4-month-old, bundled up like a papoose, went to the squealing 10-year-old's family. Flashbulbs popped as each member of the family proudly posed with the sleepy newcomer.

"It's like Christmas, just watching," a middle-aged bystander commented, wiping a tear from her eye while her 13-year-old daughter enviously eyed the 10-year-old.

It's easier to admire a pudgy 4-month-old than a wrinkly blue newborn like Baby Nick. Only a few hours after his birth doctors discovered the symptoms of a blue baby. The child's heart sent steady streams of bright-red life-giving blood on a closed circuit between his heart and lungs while pumping only exhausted blue blood to the rest of his little body.

But as Mr. Leggatt gazed at his son's thin blue body, he cared little for appearance. The helpless infant stole his heart, and he vowed to fight for Nick's life. The Leggatts endured seven years of sleepless nights, caring for little Nick, before his final surgery brought a normal pinkness and energy to his body. But Nick was worth fighting for, they said.

The Saviour loved you right from the start. He is willing to fight to save you from sin. To Him, you are worth the struggle. Aren't you glad?

ABBA, FATHER

And because ye are sons, God hath sent forth the Spirit of his Son into your hearts, crying, Abba, Father. Wherefore thou art no more a servant, but a son. Galatians 4:6, 7.

After the prodigal son came to his senses in the far country, he realized how much better off he had been with his father. Memories of his loving father flooded his mind. Even the servants are better off than I am, he thought. So he resolved to return home as a servant. When his father met him in the road, the boy cried out, "Father, I have sinned against you and against God."

"Dress the boy in the best clothes and place the family ring on his finger," the father ordered. And though the boy had offered to be a servant, he was treated as a son. So it is when we accept Jesus as our Saviour. He sends His Spirit into our hearts as a sign that we are family members. The Spirit brings a sense of belonging so that we don't call God "Father," in a stiff, formal way but we call Him "Abba, Father," or "Daddy."

Johanna lost her parents during the war. Her own life was also in danger until kind Dutch Christians took her into their home. Because Johanna was Jewish and all Jews were supposed to be sent to prison camps, anyone caught protecting her would also go to jail. But in spite of the danger a Dutch minister hid Johanna and several other Jewish boys and girls. But soon that house fell under suspicion. It was not safe to remain. Friends took Johanna to live with a young couple who needed a baby-sitter. But even after the danger to Jews ended, she did not feel at home there. She knew that the man and woman appreciated her work, but she was not part of the family.

"Why don't you come and live with me?" another kind woman asked. And Johanna became part of her family. What made the difference? Johanna was loved and wanted there as family. And Johanna knows that she's loved and wanted in heaven also.

HAPPINESS IS

If God so loved us, we ought also to love one another. 1 John 4:11.

Have you ever noticed that the people who most need our love often are most difficult to love? Like Jimmy. Jimmy's dad had left home before his son was old enough to remember. When other boys were catching fly balls with their dads after supper, Jimmy was still at the baby-sitter's waiting for his mom to get home from work. Nobody had time to teach Jimmy the skills he badly wanted to learn.

Often Jimmy dreamed of helping his team win an important game, but he usually struck out—much to the distress of his teammates. When he did connect with the ball and deserved some praise, nobody felt like complimenting him because he made such a big deal of it. What Jimmy needed more than anything else, his teacher decided, was a true friend—someone to help him feel good about himself.

Miss Fuller spoke to her class about Jimmy. Everyone felt sorry and tried for a day or two to be kind. But nobody wanted to risk losing the respect of his buddies by being a real friend to Jimmy. I often wonder whether Jimmy found the friendship that he so badly needed. I wish he had known Kristie. Unselfish with praise, she knew just what to say to brighten the dullest day.

Victor Hugo once said that the greatest happiness in life is knowing that we are loved. I believe that the greatest happiness is knowing that God loves us. No matter how popular or unpopular a person is at school, he is special to God. Knowing that should give each of us confidence to face today. No matter that we did or said something foolish yesterday, God gives us the courage to try to do better today. In the confidence that His love brings, let's show His love to others. Who knows what a friendly smile or a caring word might mean to someone else! Won't you ask God to help you be a true friend to a lonesome Jimmy today?

NO FEAR IN LOVE

There is no fear in love; but perfect love casteth out fear. 1 John 4:18.

Ever since I can remember, I have dreaded death. One day I heard the adults around me discussing in hushed tones the death of a church member. "Her son heard a loud bang," someone said. "By the time he got there she was gone." I assumed that a loud bang and death always went together. So the next day when I saw a dead bird on the sidewalk, I amused my aunt by saying, "There must have been a bang here last night!" And I felt a chill of fear that someday I would hear the big bang that would take me.

Corrie ten Boom described her own first encounter with death in the book *The Hiding Place.* She and her mother visited a Dutch family whose baby had died. Corrie stared at the still form as it lay in its little coffin. That night she felt a terrible dread—not for herself but for her father. Corrie thought that with his long silver beard he looked almost as old as God and might easily die at any minute. When her father came in to kiss her good night, Corrie burst into tears and clung to him, begging him not to die.

Gently and wisely Mr. ten Boom reminded Corrie of the many trips they had taken together by train. "When do I always give you your ticket?" he asked. Corrie thought of her last trip to Amsterdam. Father had bought the ticket and kept it in his pocket until the train pulled into the station. Then just when she needed it he gave it to her. "That's how it is with God," her father said. Just when we need special strength, God gives it to us. And He promises to stay with us, too. So we never need face death alone.

Whatever worries bother me today—moving to a new school, being liked by other people, the time of trouble, or death itself—I'm going to give them to Jesus. And as I start today I want to place my hand in His, knowing that He will give me my ticket just when I need it. For "there is no fear in love; but perfect love casts out fear" (verse 18, R.S.V.).

MICKEY

It is good to give thanks to the Lord; for his love endures for ever. Psalm 106:1, N.E.B.

Have you had difficulty lately feeling truly thankful for your life, health, and friends? If so, you should meet 9-year-old Mickey Hays. Mickey's body already is growing old because of a rare disease that afflicts one child in eight million. Progeria has stunted Mickey's growth and already left him bald.

Recently Mickey spent a few days at Disneyland with Fransie, an 8-year-old South African boy suffering from the same disease.

"Me and Fransie really enjoyed each other," Mickey later told his tape recorder. "We really, really, really enjoyed each other because we had the same face, because we had the same disease. Finally I had seen someone like me. People are treating me just right, they're treating me fine and dandy. I really don't like my disease. Sometimes I feel sad."

If you could see the photograph of Mickey and his grandfather in the Sunday *Parade,* you would see the deep sadness in Algie Callahan's kind eyes as he carries his grandson on his shoulders. It hurts a grandfather to know that nobody can help his grandson. It hurts God too.

Yet Mickey's story makes me feel good. I like courageous people who can be glad for the way people treat them when they might easily sit around feeling sorry for themselves. Mickey reminds me that God placed deep within each of us a spark of courage such as that which lighted Jesus' life on earth. If we ignore opportunities to use that courage, it eventually may go out. But when we do something brave, we warm our own lives and those of others whom we touch during the day.

I can step out fearlessly to meet this day with Jesus by my side because God gives me courage to live as Mickey does—one thankful day at a time.

THE MIRACLE OF LOVE

Herein is love, not that we loved God, but that he loved us. 1 John 4:10.

"We have a 6-month-old baby, mentally retarded and blind," the nurse told May Lemke. "He needs a home. Would you care for him if he lives?"

"What do you mean, *if* he lives?" May snorted. "If I take him, he will live." And he did.

Although Leslie lay limp in May's arms, she taught him to suck so he could feed without tubes. She bathed him, cuddled him, and sang to him for hours—for years. In all that time Leslie neither moved, nor smiled, nor cried. But May did not give up. Every day she prayed for a miracle and while she waited she tirelessly worked to shower the boy with lasting kindness and love.

With a wide leather belt she fastened the growing boy about herself, clasped his hands to her hips and walked about the yard, hoping that though Leslie had never seen anybody walk, he would absorb the walking motion. At 16 he stood up for the first time, and at 18 he took his first steps.

"Please do something for Leslie. He's like an overgrown baby," May prayed in desperation. "Please, dear God, remember my boy."

Then May had an idea. Perhaps Leslie would respond to music. From dawn to dark she filled the house with recorded music. She bought an old piano and put it in Leslie's bedroom.

Leslie's miracle came that winter in the early morning. May awoke to hear music filling the house. For the first time in his life Leslie had gotten out of bed on his own. Seating himself at the piano, he began to play Tchaikovsky's *Piano Concerto No. 1*. He had not even struck a note on the piano before.

I heard Leslie play that concerto on a nationally televised program and I thank God that He didn't forget Leslie. May's love for that helpless boy reminds me of today's text: "Herein is love, not that we loved God, but that he loved us." He's waiting to make wonderful changes in our lives too, if we'll only let Him.

MOTHER'S TOUCH

"As a mother comforts her child, so will I comfort you; and you will be comforted over Jerusalem." Isaiah 66:13, N.I.V.

Fourteen-year-old Jenny found her first baby-sitting job at camp meeting. The fact that it did not pay anything was immaterial. With 3-year-old Kelly in tow, Jenny need not report her whereabouts to her mother every hour.

They stopped by the Davidson cabin first. "Meet my second cousin-twice-removed," Jenny joked as she proudly presented her blonde, brown-eyed charge. "She's adorable," they all agreed as they fussed over Kelly until time for meeting.

Candy Davidson, Jennie's best friend, helped walk the little girl to the bookstore where the gang often congregated. During the hour that they stood around talking, Kelly grew restless. Occasionally Jenny hoisted her onto her hip. But the child was heavy, and Jenny soon put her down.

"Say, isn't she getting tired?" Candy asked after awhile. But Jenny was too busy trading jokes to notice. "Shouldn't you take her home?" Brett questioned a little later. But again Jenny missed the warning signals. When Jenny started back to the cabin, Kelly was beginning to fret. Soon she began to sob loudly.

Embarrassed by all the attention they were attracting, Jenny picked up the little girl and quickened her pace. But Kelly was heavy and slowed her down. By the time they reached Kelly's cabin the crying was a hoarse wail. "I tried to comfort her," Jenny said, humiliated at being unable to stop the tears. The child's mother took Kelly into her arms, and instantly the crying subsided. Jenny couldn't believe it.

"As a mother comforts her child, so will I comfort you." Even the toughest fellow enjoys the comfort his mother provides when he feels discouraged. Others may have little faith in what he can do, but his mother still believes in him. That's the kind of comfort Jesus offers you today.

MARK FINDS A BROTHER

A friend loves at all times, and a brother is born for adversity. Proverbs 17:17, N.I.V.

One of the big bonuses that comes from accepting God as our Father is our sense of belonging to His family. It is almost as if He created us with a space that only His love may fill, and another space that we need to fill with friendship.

Mark's family had been missionaries in India for many years. Now they were returning to the United States for good, and Mark looked forward to attending a new school and making many new friends. "Don't worry, son," his father advised. "Take an interest in everyone. Listen to them, show them you think they are OK, and you'll soon make new friends." And he did.

The first day of school Mark sat next to Dave. Dave had a wry sense of humor that often made Mark laugh. But the other kids hardly seemed to notice Dave. They were busy trying to chum up with Billy. Tall, worldly-wise Billy wore just the right clothes and treated school with all the seriousness of a circus.

At recess time Billy usually captained one of the softball teams. The first day Mark felt embarrassed when he and Dave were chosen near the last. For the next two days he spent a lot of time trying to impress Billy. And it worked. Before the end of the week Billy chose Mark early in the lineup. "Choose Dave," Mark whispered as he joined Billy's team.

But in spite of the fact that Dave was one of the best hitters, Billy left him until next to last.

"It's not fair," Mark said to himself. "Why does everyone leave Dave out of things?"

The second week of school Mark captained for the first time. He was tempted to score points with Billy by choosing him first in the lineup. I'd have it made for the rest of the year if I were on the right side of Billy, he thought. But when Mark saw the sparkle of expectation in Dave's eyes, he knew he could not let him down.

"Your turn to choose," the teacher called impatiently.

Mark took a deep breath. He chose Dave! And he knew that in a sense he now had a brother.

YOU ARE MINE

I will proclaim the decree of the Lord: He said to me, "You are my Son; today I have become your Father." Psalm 2:7, N.I.V.

Amy liked to visit her neighbor, a college professor. And although she was only 8, they had some deep conversations together. "Dr. Thomas," she asked one day, "could you tell me why my daddy left us?" The professor shook his head.

"No, Amy," he said kindly, "I'm afraid that you've asked a question I can't answer. I don't know why he left."

But Amy did not want to know what had happened the night before her father decided to depart. She wanted Dr. Thomas to assure her that her father's leaving was not because he rejected her.

Brett fooled around his freshman year in academy. He wondered where he should go the day the principal asked him to leave. His father was hard to get along with. Brett didn't want to go to him. So he called his mom. "I have to leave academy," he said. "Do you want me to come to you?"

"Well, no, not really," the mother candidly replied. Brett felt crushed. His own mother did not want him. So he went to his married sister.

There is good news for people like Amy and Brett. God says, "You are My son [or daughter]; today I have become your Father."

Imagine yourself standing on Pennsylvania Avenue in a crowd of people waving American flags. The President drives slowly by in a limousine. As the car pulls abreast of you, it stops. The President steps out and walks up to you. Tapping you on the shoulder, he invites you to come with him.

You feel awkward, standing there in your school clothes, but he assures you that you look great. After you get into the limousine he breaks the big news. He wants to adopt you as part of his family. Unbelievable? Yes and No. Someone far greater than the President said, "Today I have become your Father." And with Him you never need fear rejection. He will never let you go.

KENNY'S PROMISE

Everyone who believes that Jesus is the Christ is born of God, and everyone who loves the father loves his child as well. 1 John 5:1, N.I.V.

Kenny had attended church all his life. Had you asked him when he was 6 if he loved Jesus, he would have replied, "Of course I do!" And had you asked him when he was 12, he would have shrugged and said, "I guess so. Why did you ask?" For that year he did not give the matter much thought.

But something happened the following year. Kenny's Bible teacher involved the class in helping others. They took a real interest in people that Kenny had never known existed before. In the fall, for example, they raked leaves for an elderly couple who lived two blocks from the school. When they were done, the man and woman invited Kenny and his friends inside for cookies and punch. The punch puckered Kenny's mouth a bit, but the old man stole his heart.

Kenny couldn't believe that Mr. B. had once been athletic. He still followed his favorite ball team. Next morning in class worship Kenny was glad when someone suggested that they offer special prayer for Mr. B.'s upcoming surgery. Kenny planned to stop by and look in on Mr. B. once in a while, but somehow he was always too busy. However, he resolved at least to pray for the man each morning.

Looking back on that year, Kenny says, "After I would pray for Mr. B., I took time to talk to God about other things." Kenny joined the baptismal class and discovered that he really cared a lot about God. "Somehow I knew that God cared about Mr. B. and me," Kenny said.

As a child of God, Kenny was really the same person after his baptism, except that now he asked God to help him do things right. To be sure, he occasionally made someone mad at him, and he felt bad whenever he let God down. But after Kenny asked forgiveness, he tried to do better. Do you think loving God has anything to do with loving people? Read today's text again and make it sound like a promise. For that's what it is!

WHICH OF THE TWO?

This is love for God: to obey his commands. And his commands are not burdensome. 1 John 5:3, N.I.V.

"'What do you think? There was a man who had two sons. He went to the first and said, "Son, go and work today in the vineyard."

"'"I will not," he answered, but later he changed his mind and went. Then the father went to the other son and said the same thing. He answered, "I will, sir," but he did not go.

"'Which of the two did what his father wanted?'" (Matt. 21:28-31.)

Suppose we change the story a little. Instead of a father wanting his sons to work in the vineyard, think of a mother requesting her children (as many of them as are at your house) to clean their rooms. You get mad because it is not your turn, and you refuse to lift a finger toward cleaning anything. But later you hear Mother washing the dishes by herself. Suddenly you realize how hard she works for you. And you sheepishly take out the vacuum cleaner and get to work. What one thing would have made you change your mind?

Maybe you know someone—not yourself, surely—who gets up from his favorite breakfast of pancakes and hash browns and says, "Mom, you're the best! I love you!"

"You're pretty good yourself!" she replies. "How about cleaning your bedroom first thing!"

"Sure!" you reply without hesitation as you pick up a book. Four hours later you haven't touched your room, so in the end your mother has to do it. Why did you let her down? Look for the answer in today's text. Which example shows that you loved your mother? The first, second, or both? And which boy chose a better way to show that love? In Jesus' story, the first boy was tempted to put his own feelings first, but love won out in the end. The second planned to show his love by obeying, but in the end he put himself first. Think of the happiness the first son gave his father. Can you think of a better way to say, "I love you"?

WHAT OF YOUR BROTHER?

Then the Lord said to Cain, "Where is your brother Abel?" "I don't know," he replied. "Am I my brother's keeper?" Genesis 4:9, N.I.V.

Both boys knew how to prepare a sacrifice. They had seen Adam do it hundreds of times. But Cain decided to rewrite the rules. Why should he make a deal with his brother the herdsman to obtain a lamb when he might more easily sacrifice a basket of his own produce?

"Why are you angry?" God asked Cain after his plan fizzled. "If you do as I ask, your sacrifice will be accepted. But if not, then sin is crouching at your door; it desires to have you, but you must master it" (verses 6, 7).

You may wonder why Cain acted so rashly when he had the advantage of God's personal counsel: "Sin is at the door; master it." Cain probably wished later that he had taken that advice and set aside his jealousy. But instead he allowed it to rage in his heart until he murdered Abel.

"Where is your brother?" the Lord asked. You know the famous reply: "Am I my brother's keeper?" Cain might have said, "Why should I care?"

Knowing that Cain was too rebellious to hear about love—the best reason for caring—God gave Cain a punishment that touched the things he really cared about: his land, his God, and his life.

" 'You are driving me from the land, and I will be hidden from your presence,' " Cain moaned. " 'I will be a restless wanderer on the earth, and whoever finds me will kill me' " (verse 14).

"But the Lord said, to him, 'Not so' " (verse 15). Although Cain's terrible act deserved punishment, God still loved him. If only Cain had humbled himself and determined to change his ways!

Sometimes jealousy of a brother or sister comes between us and our heavenly Father. Our lack of caring hides His presence from us. But Jesus waits to help us care if we'll only ask Him.

A HELPING HAND

How great is the love the Father has lavished on us, that we should be called children of God! And that is what we are! 1 John 3:1, N.I.V.

If yours is a normal home, sometimes the rafters ring with happy singing and laughter, and sometimes they tremble with angry voices. One of the first lessons of growing up involves getting along with brothers and sisters. It's funny how we don't always appreciate them until the security of one or all is threatened.

Young Bill was glad that he had four brothers. Being the youngest meant that he had plenty of help learning to do things.

For hours at a time he and his grown-up brothers would row down the river to fish. One Sunday Bill and his older brother, Doug, rowed into a long water-circulation tunnel connected to an idle factory. Fish were plentiful, and the boys were so busy with their catch that they did not notice how the water level was rising until they banged their heads on the top. Wondering what had happened, they pushed themselves along to the mouth. But when they reentered the river, they discovered that a storm had blown up. High waves threatened to capsize the boat.

They decided to shelter under the wharves that lined the sides of the river. Bill stood in the boat and propelled it forward by pulling on the wharf above. Suddenly the boat encountered a swift current from another circulation tunnel. The boat shot forward, and Bill landed in the water, where the current dragged him out toward the sea.

But fortunately Doug noticed what had happened. As Bill bobbed within reach Doug leaned out and grabbed his hair. Huddled in the boat as they pulled for home, Bill realized just how much a brother's love can mean.

Appreciating brothers and sisters teaches us to value the members of God's family. Let's take an active interest in the church family and be ready every day to lend a helping hand to someone in need.

PORTRAIT OF A FRIEND

And it came to pass, when he had made an end of speaking unto Saul, that the soul of Jonathan was knit with the soul of David, and Jonathan loved him as his own soul. 1 Samuel 18:10.

"Abby, I don't understand you," Pauline said. "You need a new dress for the junior-senior banquet. You say your folks can't afford it. But you let your mom send this new dress for Jenny. Why?"

"Oh, forget it! You wouldn't understand," Abby said, as she danced down the hall to Jenny's room, wondering all the way why Pauline had never noticed that not a single dress of Jenny's was worth borrowing. "Look, Jen," Abby said, as she burst into her friend's room. "My mom sent it. But it doesn't fit me. I'd like you to have it." Abby's thoughtfulness reminded me of two good friends in the Bible.

When they met, one wore the simple clothes of a shepherd, the other dressed like a prince, but he did not let himself be put off by the shepherd's rough, country clothing. Noticing the twinkle in David's eye and the spring in his step, Jonathan admired his enthusiasm when tackling giant problems. He was glad when his father invited David home. And "the soul of Jonathan was knit with the soul of David." They became best friends.

Jonathan had good reason to be jealous of David. Who did he think he was after all?—walking into the camp of professional soldiers and offering to take on the enemy single-handed. To make things worse, David was as good as his word. King Saul was understandably happy. David's victory took the heat off Saul. But Jonathan, trying to grow up and prove he was a leader in his own right, now had a young hero his own age to compete with. Jonathan could have scored by making fun of David's clothes. But instead he took his own designer clothes, including his sword and bow—the symbols of his manliness—and gave them all to the shepherd. Jonathan was a genuine friend.

THE SEAL OF FRIENDSHIP

And Jonathan said to David, Go in peace, forasmuch as we have sworn both of us in the name of the Lord, saying, The Lord be between me and thee, and between my seed and thy seed for ever. 1 Samuel 20:42.

Patty and Marta were best friends since the third grade. They understood each other perfectly. Patty might begin a sentence and pause. As quick as lightning Marta would finish the sentence. "Your minds run along the same track," Patty's mother often said.

In the eighth grade jealousy threatened to separate the two girls when Patty was elected class president. "Why?" Marta asked herself. "We do all the same things. I am as popular as she is. Why am I never elected to anything?"

Every election must end with winners and losers. As one star leaving the Grammy Awards ceremony said recently, "The problem is that everyone deserves to win. They are all good."

Jonathan had a problem earning recognition if anyone did. He was born heir to the throne. But while still in young manhood he met another with the bearing of a future king. Even the king himself realized that God had chosen David as the next ruler. Did that mean that God rejected Jonathan? I don't think so. Had Jonathan survived that last battle and seen his best friend crowned king, God would have had some other exciting plan for Jonathan's life.

King Saul reacted with jealousy, as some earthly parents do when they see someone outshine their own children. He made no effort to hide his hostility. But nothing he did or said could turn Jonathan from loyalty to his friend. He covered for David at the king's table and then warned him to flee for his life. And as the two saw each other for the last time, Jonathan sent David away with a promise. Jonathan possessed the qualities of true greatness. Secure in the love of God, he swore friendship with David. As you feel the security of God's family won't you trust Him to value you even though you don't always win first place in the popularity polls?

LOVE IN ACTION

Dear children, let us not love with words or tongue but with actions and in truth. 1 John 3:18, N.I.V.

As a child of God, you know that you should love everyone, but sometimes don't you find that hard? Like Charlie Brown's friend Lucy. She loved the human race—it was people she couldn't stand. Lucy loved in words but not "with actions and in truth."

But the boy who offered Jesus his lunch put love into action. And Jesus helped that love feed thousands of people.

Many teenagers put their love into action through summer work camps. One group found Mary living in a house damaged by a tornado. Mary had dragged all her belongings into the living room—the only room where the roof didn't leak. The teen group removed knee-high mounds of moldering papers, and boxes of rags and old clothing to transform the room into a cozy den. They replaced the back door and patched the roof. Their actions changed themselves as well as the house and Mary.

"I can't believe how much I have grown," work camper Cheryl Ferment, of Pennsylvania, marveled. "This experience has brought me closer to God."

I like the way Linda Cherry put it: "We're all living proof that Jesus can love through us. There's a saying, 'Love is like five loaves and two fishes—there's never enough until we start to give it away.' And that's what we did this week."

When you feel unloved and left out of things, remember the loaves and fishes. Find someone else who needs some friendship and share yourself. Like Nancy. She felt envious of the kids at the next lunch table. They always had so much fun. Nancy wished she were part of their group—until she decided to liven up her own table. She began by taking notice of people around her. Soon she had people talking and sharing. Everyone else began wishing that they belonged to Nancy's fun group. As we share our friendship today, maybe the results will surprise us, too!

IN THE BEGINNING GOD

In the beginning God created the heavens and the earth. Genesis 1:1, N.I.V.

Everyone I know, everything that I see and touch, had a beginning. But at the very beginning of everything else God already was. I can't understand this any more than I can see Him. But lots of things happen that I don't understand. Try this experiment and you'll see what I mean.

Take a one-inch ball of steel wool (if you use a soap pad, you might want to wash out the soap so you can see the fibers) and place it in a glass jar. Pour a cup and a half of water into the jar. What happens to steel wool if left in water? You may speed up the rusting action by pouring four teaspoons of bleach and two teaspoons of vinegar into the water. Stir it with a spoon and let it stand a while. The bleach and vinegar will combine to form hypochlorous acid, which reacts with the iron in steel wool to form hydrated ferric oxide, or rust.

Later you may remove the steel wool with a spoon and let the jar stand. The rust will settle to the bottom. Carefully pour off most of the clear solution. The powder and some liquid will remain. Pour in some more water to wash the powder. Let it settle and pour off most of the liquid. To filter out the rust powder, lay a paper napkin over the top of another jar. Pour the remaining rust and water into the napkin. After all the liquid has filtered through, spread out the napkin to dry. You may scrape the dry powder together into a heap. Test it with a magnet. Iron magnetizes easily. Does rust?

If you scrape the rust powder onto an old metal spoon and heat it over a candle, the powder will change color slowly. After the color changes completely, test it again with the magnet.

Unfortunately (or fortunately, depending on how you look at it), we cannot put God into a glass jar or test Him with acids and magnets. We cannot see Him or prove His existence. And nowhere does the Bible try to do this. It simply tells us that in the beginning He was there. But though I cannot see Him, I see the change He makes in people and feel His loving presence.

WHAT IS MAN?

What is man, that thou art mindful of him? and the son of man, that thou visitest him? For thou hast made him a little lower than the angels, and hast crowned him with glory and honour. Psalm 8:4, 5.

Many people do not believe that God exists. They think that man came into existence by a series of accidents. Ever since I was 13 I have been unable to believe in creative accidents. In the seventh grade I struggled for weeks just getting a pair of shorts cut out and the side seams sewn. The work demanded complete concentration. Nothing ever fell into place accidentally. If I didn't pay attention to what I was doing, I had to pull the work apart and start over.

So I can't imagine the parts of a garment coming together by chance or the parts of a watch falling into place without help from the watchmaker. How, then, could I believe that human beings—the most marvelous things ever created—could have happened except as the work of the Creator?

Take my hand, for instance. The twenty-seven bones and more than thirty pairs of muscles that make up its delicate structure were put together in such a way that I can pick up the tiniest pin or deliver a glancing blow.

When I want to impress other people with my knowledge, I ask them how the hands of an animal differ from those of a human. It's not just the fingers, for monkeys also have long digits. But only the human hand has an opposable thumb that works against the fingers to grasp things. One morning I tried taping down my thumb. I thought I'd never get my shirt buttoned.

Believing in the miracle that is God and His creative power makes a difference in the way I think of myself. I want to bring credit to the Creator today. Don't you? That's why I keep a check on my eating, sleeping, and exercise habits. I want to keep my complex system in running order. After all, I'm much more than a marvelous machine—I'm a child of God.

NO EQUAL

"To whom will you compare me? Or who is my equal?" says the Holy One. . . . The Lord is the everlasting God, the Creator of the ends of the earth. Isaiah 40:25-28, N.I.V.

He was a worldly young man, self-satisfied and smug. But his confidence seemed shaken as he sat down to supper opposite my three brothers and me. Having been duly cautioned to be seen rather than heard while at the table, we sat and watched him. We had an advantage where the food was concerned. Since he had never eaten a vegetarian meal before, he appeared nervous over what we might serve him. Our attention was fixed on him.

As if to set us at ease and break the ice, he posed a riddle. "What is it that a poor man often sees, a king seldom sees, and God never sees?" I felt sorry for the man immediately. Did he not know that God sees everything? I smugly asked. The young man laughed.

"He sees all but one thing," he gently corrected me. "Take my word for it. The Bible says so." For two days we wrestled with that riddle. Finally he gave us a clue: Isaiah 40:25.

And I knew that I still had lots to learn about God.

Think how you like being with people your own age—your equals. Don't you dislike potlucks or visits with your parents' friends unless they reassure you that someone your own age will be there? And you'd refuse to go for sure if you heard that only younger children than you would attend. You don't feel as comfortable talking with them as with someone from your own age group.

But I'm glad God does not keep to Himself. He doesn't wait for me to speak to Him before He makes a move toward me. And He is never far away. That makes me feel comfortable, safe, and secure with Him. It also changes the way I treat my equals. I hope I'll grow more like my Father today and put the needs and comfort of others before my own.

FROM ABOVE THE CIRCLE

He sits enthroned above the circle of the earth. . . . He stretches out the heavens like a canopy, and spreads them out like a tent to live in. Isaiah 40:22, N.I.V.

Many people live all their lives under the shadow of a huge mountain, never discovering the view from the top. And in some places people spend all their lives in misty mountain fastnesses, never seeing the sweeping panorama of the plain.

From Vincent Hill School, 6,500 feet in the foothills of the Himalayas, we could look out across a narrow valley to the mountainside beyond. All around we saw the work of human hands, though we could not detect the people themselves. An ugly cut in the opposite mountainside daily grew larger as workmen quarried rock and carted it away. Occasionally we heard the blasting. Once someone saw a truck disappear in a landslide. We also enjoyed the view of terraced paddy fields on a closer mountainside to the southeast. Between the two mountains the valley dropped away to low-lying hills. Beyond, on a clear day, we could see the silver streak of the Roorkee Canal, more than fifty miles away.

Many a balmy afternoon we watched an eagle, wings outstretched, calmly gliding with the air currents below us, as it serenely scanned the valley. If only I could launch myself off the garden wall and glide like that! I often thought. It would have been a great place to learn hang gliding—except that if you sailed downward for an hour it would have taken at least a day to find your way back.

At night one could almost reach out and touch the stars from that mountainside. God seemed especially close up there. Isaiah describes the sky as if it were a protective shell God spread out over the earth. And just as the eagle spotted every movement down the steep sides of that valley, God takes in the whole circle of the earth—the whole sphere, in fact. I'm looking forward to the day when He teaches us to float on the updrafts and shares with us His worldview. Aren't you?

GRASS, FLOWERS, AND PROMISES

The grass withers and the flowers fall, but the word of our God stands forever. Isaiah 40:8, N.I.V.

Tanya thought it would take forever to reach her tenth birthday. Now that she is 14, time seems to be speeding up. Her father says that it will fly when she enters college.

Almost two thousand years have passed since Jesus told His disciples of the home He was preparing for them in heaven. "I will come again," He promised. Recently a friend of mine died. Suddenly I can't wait for Jesus' soon return. Why does it have to take so long?

Isaiah understood the longings of the human heart when He pointed out that all beautiful things on earth wither or fade away. Not so with God. His word, His promises, stand forever. They may not be fulfilled immediately, but they will eventually.

Because something takes a long time by earth standards does not mean that it seems long to God. To Him a thousand years passes like a day does for us. So if you like good news, you'll like verse 9, where Isaiah tells of an announcement we shall soon hear: "Be not afraid. . . . Here is your God."

At Jesus' first coming, most people had given up looking for Him. They missed the angels' announcement of His birth. Soon it will be heard again for His second coming. Can't you imagine the brilliant clouds of angels surrounding your King? Can you hear their trumpets and the triumphant shout, "Here is your God!"?

Wouldn't you like to look into His face and ask Him why it took so long? And when you see the people who would not have made it had He come sooner, you'll probably be glad He waited. Let's use the waiting time to get to know Him better and to help someone else find the way. Meanwhile, "The grass withers and the flowers fall, but the word of our God stands forever."

GOD IN HEAVEN

Guard your steps when you go to the house of God. Go near to listen rather than to offer the sacrifice of fools, who do not know that they do wrong. Ecclesiastes 5:1, N.I.V.

"I really enjoy earliteen Sabbath school," Dana said. "If we get there early enough I like to see what my friends wear. Sometimes we catch each other up on what has happened since we left school at three o'clock the day before. Sometimes when we whisper and giggle too much, the leader frowns and asks us to listen. Once we start listening, we usually enjoy what they do up front.

"In church I have to sit with the family. So I read my *Guide*. That helps the time pass more quickly. But my mother is forever bumping my arm and reminding me to worship. I guess I'm not much into worship. In fact, I'm not sure what worship is. I know that it isn't talking, or chewing gum. I suppose it's not giggling, or reading stories, either. Sometimes I just put my mind into neutral and look around. But I don't feel like that's worship. Usually I end up watching the academy students sitting in front of me and admiring the way they do their hair."

If only Dana knew it, she is close to worship when she admires people. But that's hero worship. In church Jesus is the hero we worship. If we talk and giggle there, we offer the "sacrifice of fools." Listening is an important part of worship. The hymns, prayers, and Bible reading all help us to think of the greatness of God in heaven and to feel thankful for all that He does for us. And that's worship. Singing and praising God is worship, as is bringing an offering.

When you go into the house of God this Sabbath, try to think of Him, the great God of the universe, coming to earth in order to save you. Think of the freedom He gave up to become a babe. Notice the words of the hymns as you sing. Do they describe how you feel about your wonderful God? And which parts of the prayer show that the one praying thinks some of the same thoughts about God that you do? This Sabbath let's "go near to listen."

YOU ARE ON EARTH

Do not be quick with your mouth, do not be hasty in your heart to utter anything before God. God is in heaven and you are on earth, so let your words be few. Ecclesiastes 5:2, N.I.V.

Jesus and three of His disciples toil silently uphill in the gathering gloom, each wrapped in his own thoughts. On reaching the top, the disciples turn to Jesus as if to ask why He has brought them so far. But they suddenly forget their question as a heavenly light illumines the Master's face. His clothes shine a brilliant, blinding white, and Moses and Elijah appear.

His good fortune at seeing the transfigured Jesus with Moses and Elijah, two of the most revered figures in Jewish history, overwhelms Peter. "Let us make here three tabernacles," he says (Matt. 17:4, K.J.V.).

From our vantage point of the 1980s we wonder how Peter could have been so stupid. What kind of shelters could he afford to build on a mountaintop? How long would they have lasted? What purpose would they have served? In the midst of such majesty and glory why did he not follow the example of John and James and button his mouth?

But "while he was still speaking, a bright cloud enveloped them, and a voice from the cloud said, 'This is my Son, whom I love; with him I am well pleased. Listen to him!'" (verse 5).

The disciples fell on the ground and covered their faces from God's glory. "But Jesus came and touched them. 'Get up,' he said. 'Don't be afraid.'" (verse 6).

Jesus, the God-man, allowed the three disciples a glimpse of His Father's glory. Peter quickly realized how far heaven is removed from earth. How insignificant he must have felt! How humbling the experience! In such moments of truth, words are unnecessary. Have you ever walked outside and gazed into the starry sky and experienced God's presence? You may experience it as you sit in worship, too, if you think about Him and give Him your undivided attention. Why not try it today?

THE SERVANT'S PRAYER

But when ye pray, use not vain repetitions, as the heathen do: for they think that they shall be heard for their much speaking. Matthew 6:7.

"Hari Ram, Hari Ram, Hari, Hari Ram," the voice intoned the name of a prominent Hindu god outside my bedroom window. *"Hari Ram, Hari Ram,"* it droned on and on, pausing for a moment and then intensifying. At first I felt annoyed. Who was this spoiling my Sabbath afternoon rest? *"Hari, Hari Ram!"* Since I could not turn off the sound, I lay listening to it. After a while I no longer heard the words but only the tone of voice. Neither impatiently rushing nor whining like a beggar, the chanted words continued. Suddenly the loving tone I detected in them struck me. This person loved her god.

I always enjoy hearing loving prayers. Have you heard that kind at your house? They don't beg God for things that one can buy with money. But they give thanks for the big things: life, health, home, and family. They ask for the lasting things: love, forgiveness, wisdom. But because God hears our prayers in *thoughts,* not *words,* we need not repeat the same words over and over again. As the little servant woman sat on her cot in the shade of her humble home, joyously beseeching her god I thought of my loving God. Though He lives in highest heaven, He is never far from us.

A few days after I heard the servant's prayer, people gathered in a nearby field for a nightlong religious festival. Astrologers had predicted that the close alignment of three planets heralded the end of the world. When the world did not end that night, the people returned to their homes and resumed their normal routines. And I never again heard the servant pray. Maybe she no longer felt threatened and did not need the help of her god. Had I known her language, perhaps I could have told her of our loving God in heaven who is interested in her everyday problems—not just end-of-the-world events.

KENTUCKY HILLBILLY

For this is what the high and lofty One says—he who lives forever, whose name is holy: "I live in a high and holy place, but also with him who is contrite and lowly in spirit." Isaiah 57:15, N.I.V.

Jason had waited with high expectations for the Sabbath of the combined meeting in Louisville. Stone Ridge had few juniors, and he looked forward to meeting some city kids.

But things went wrong almost from the start. They arrived late only to find that the architects had not provided a ramp for wheelchairs, and maneuvering up and down steps to the junior Sabbath school was out of the question. So Jason good-naturedly settled into place on the front row with the adults.

Between Sabbath school and church he saw many people his age. He wished he could meet some of them. But they were as shy as he was. Still Jason enjoyed the preaching and the special music. He wished someone could lure a preacher that good out to Stone Ridge.

After church some of the members from Stone Ridge stopped by his wheelchair to chat. The preacher of the morning came too.

"Hi, there!" he said. "How are you enjoying the meetings?" Jason admitted that he liked them. "What's keeping you in that chair?" the pastor asked with a look of concern in his eyes.

"I've got hemophilia. My blood doesn't clot properly."

"Did you know that the only son of the last czar of Russia had hemophilia?" the pastor asked.

No, Jason hadn't known hemophilia was a royal disease. In parting, the preacher asked about Jason's accent. "Oh, it's 100 percent Kentucky hillbilly," Jason answered humbly, wondering whether the preacher preferred midwestern.

When the speaker arrived home that evening, he told his wife, "I met a boy with hemophilia. His wonderful spirit warmed my heart and gave me a real lift." Truly our God lives " 'in a high and holy place, but also with him who is contrite and lowly in spirit' "—like Jason, from Stone Ridge.

WHICH ART

After this manner therefore pray ye: Our Father which art in heaven. Matthew 6:9.

Terry hardly knew his grandfather. He heard tales of him from Grandmother, how he had sailed in a Swedish windjammer around Cape Horn, and how as a young sailor he jumped ship in Australia and settled there. Grandfather's ability to locate Bible passages in a few moments was legendary. But he had died before Terry was old enough to appreciate his wry sense of humor or his love of God.

Fortunately God is not a grandfather—He has no grandchildren. Each of us may know Him as Father. And though the experiences of others in knowing God help us to find Him for ourselves, we do not experience His love secondhand. For while God proved to be a loving Father to our grandparents and perhaps also to their grandparents, He did not wear out as they did. He lives today, just as dynamic a God-person as ever He was.

We know this to be true because of the prayer Jesus taught us to pray: Our Father *which art* in heaven. Unlike humans who move from place to place and lose track of their own relatives, Jesus remains alive and active at His same address.

My earliest memories of my grandfather include dew on the early morning grass, the smell of woodchips, and the taste of rainwater and chicken feed. The latter smelled so good that I actually tasted it! I still remember the feel of dust between my toes as I walked down the road to the train station, and I hear yet the train roaring through the tunnel near the house. The old folks are long gone, and the house belongs to someone else. Every time I take the train up north and pass right by the old homestead I feel empty. But I am comforted to remember that nothing has changed with my heavenly Father. He is still by my side and will be there when at last I make my final journey home.

THRONES AND FOOTSTOOLS

Thus saith the Lord, The heaven is my throne, and the earth is my footstool. Isaiah 66:1.

Have you ever sat in a throne? Not many people have. If just anyone could sit in a throne, it would really be only a big chair. The thing that makes thrones special is that only kings or heads of government usually sit in them. The throne can become a symbol of a king's power.

Can you imagine the throne room in some fancy medieval European castle? A rich wool carpet covers the floor. But the main point of attraction is the high-backed throne. By today's standards it is an uncomfortable piece of furniture set on a raised platform.

The footstool is a low seat carved to match the throne. Beside the grand-looking throne, it seems humble indeed. Anybody sitting on the footstool would have a decided disadvantage trying to meet the gaze of the king.

When Nadir Shah, the last great Persian conqueror, invaded northern India 250 years ago, his soldiers stole great treasures from the palaces of Delhi. One famous object, the peacock throne, is still preserved in Iran. The back of this gold throne is shaped like the tails of two peacocks and is decorated with precious stones and pearls.

God's throne is the heavens. When you look into a bright blue summer sky and see the clouds scudding by, you feel its immenseness. Our earth seems enormous to us, but to God it is but a footstool by comparison. How big does that make a king or president on this earth? Each rules only a part of the earth. And how big does that make you and me? Smaller yet. But we may be like the 3-year-old who tells a 10-year-old, "I can walk farther than you." When asked how come, she says, "Because I hold my father's hand and he helps me." You and I may do great things today if we place our hands in the Father's mighty one.

I HAVE SEEN THE KING

"Woe to me!" I cried. "I am ruined! For I am a man of unclean lips, and I live among a people of unclean lips, and my eyes have seen the King, the Lord Almighty." Isaiah 6:5, N.I.V.

The year of King Uzziah's death Isaiah saw in vision "the Lord seated on a throne, high and exalted, and the train of his robe filled the temple. Above him were two seraphs . . . calling to one another:

"'Holy, holy, holy is the Lord Almighty;
The whole earth is full of his glory'" (verses 1-3).

When I try to imagine what Isaiah saw, I think of a great occasion at the White House. Visiting kings and queens from Europe enter in expensive silks and furs, their diamonds glittering in the brilliant light. And I know that those same brilliant people would look quite dull without the spotlights that shine on them.

But how must it be in heaven, where God *is* the light. He has no need of spotlights or of the sun to show up His glory. Unaided, it fills the whole earth. At the sound of the angels calling, "Holy, holy, holy," the temple shakes and fills with smoke.

"Woe is me!" Isaiah cries. "I am ruined! For I, a man of unclean lips, have seen the King, the Lord Almighty." In God's presence Isaiah thinks not of clothes or hair, but he worries instead about his sinful state. His lips feel dirty. Perhaps he remembers something unkind or untrue that he has said. An angel, noticing Isaiah's discomfort, takes some tongs and picks out a red-hot coal from the fire on the altar. With this he touches Isaiah's lips. "'See,'" the angel says, "'this has touched your lips; your guilt is taken away and your sin atoned for'" (verse 7).

Later, when God asks, "'Whom shall I send? And who will go for us?'" Isaiah humbly replies: "'Here am I. Send me!'" Our great God longs to send you too, though you feel like the worst garbage-mouth in your class. Humbly ask Him to cleanse and use you, and He will.

JACOB

" 'I will be with you, and I will protect you wherever you go . . . ; for I will not leave you until I have done all that I have promised.' " Genesis 28:15, N.E.B.

Jacob is tired. All day he has fled from his angry brother. At any moment he may be overtaken. He imagines an irate Esau catching up with him and, shuddering, he hurries on. Night begins to fall. Soon he can hardly find his way, and the odd-shaped rocks strewn about loom like shadowy apparitions. At least nobody can find him at night. But that thought provides little comfort. It only underscores his loneliness.

Tricking his blind old father into blessing him now seems like a hollow victory. All he has actually gained are a disappointed father, a grieving mother, an angry brother, and—well, he hardly dares think how God feels about it. For the first time Jacob realizes how sin separates one from God.

Overwhelmed by guilt and loneliness, he props his head on a rock and prepares to sleep. That night God reveals Himself to Jacob in a wonderful dream (verses 10-22). Dazzling angels hurry up and down a gigantic ladder of light that links earth with heaven. God reaches down to Jacob with the reassurance of His love and blessing.

" ' "I will be with you," ' " God says. Only a loving, forgiving God would have uttered a promise like that. Instead of making Jacob feel more guilty about the way he had lied to his father, instead of showing him how small his faith had been, God speaks to Jacob's immediate need—his loneliness.

" ' "I will be with you," ' " He says. Untruthful and tricky though you have been, I'm here to help. Next morning Jacob rises early and makes a solemn pledge: " 'If God will be with me . . . then the Lord shall be my God' " (verses 20, 21). God understands my good intentions, too. And though I fail Him, He promises to forgive and to be with me. But I must truly want Him as Jacob did.

A DAY TO LOVE

For this is the message which you have heard from the beginning, that we should love one another. 1 John 3:11, R.S.V.

Today is a special day in North America and some European countries—a day for celebrating the gift of love. Valentine's Day perhaps had its roots in ancient Rome, where young people put their names into clay pots. The name they drew out became their "beloved of the year." A similar custom prevailed in England during the 1700s, except that the young man pinned the name to his sleeve and wore it for four days. (Now you know what it means to "wear your heart on your sleeve"!) Tradition has it that the first valentine was a Christian bishop by that name. One tongue-in-cheek writer suggests that Bishop Valentine was the first (but by no means the last) to lose his head on that day. At least two bishops Valentine were beheaded in Rome, but the sentimental customs connected with the day have nothing to do with them.

Since this is the day to remember those you love, I checked out the dictionary meaning of *love*. I found six meanings: first, a deep and tender feeling; second, a strong, usually passionate, affection; third, a strong liking for something; fourth, a feeling of brotherhood; fifth, God's concern for us; and sixth, man's attachment to God.

The Bible is strewn with Valentine messages from God. Maybe you can find one just for you. If you sometimes wonder who would love you, read 1 John 4:10: "This is love: not that we loved God, but that he loved us" (N.I.V.). If you find someone hard to love, remember verse 11: "Since God so loved us, we also ought to love one another." If you are afraid to love, try verse 18: "There is no fear in love. But perfect love drives out fear." And what if you don't have a valentine? "Love comes from God. . . . God is love" (verses 7, 8, N.I.V.). Why not write a valentine message for God today, thanking Him that nothing can separate you from His love.

THE WAY

Jesus saith unto him, I am the way, the truth, and the life: no man cometh unto the Father, but by me. John 14:6.

Jesus' work was almost over. For three and one-half years He had worked with His disciples, teaching them and preparing them to spread the good news of God's love. Now on His final night with them He looked forward to a pleasant meal together.

But how could He relax, knowing how ill-prepared they were for what would happen that night? What could He say to help them later? " 'Do not let your hearts be troubled,' " He said. " 'Trust in God; trust also in me. . . . I am going. You know the way to the place where I am going' " (verses 1-4, N.I.V.). Jesus had tried to tell the disciples how He would return to heaven. Now He was assuring them that they would someday join Him there.

But Thomas, the doubter, shatters the calm. " 'Lord, we don't know where you're going,' " he protests. " 'How can we know the way?' " (verse 5, N.I.V.). I think I know how Thomas felt. I remember reading John Bunyan's story of the *Pilgrim's Progress*. He was trying to find the Celestial City, but he didn't know the way. Thus he made several wrong turns and met many weird people before he at last crossed the river to the city. I imagined myself on the bank watching him wade across. And I knew that if I ever found myself beside that river, I would plunge straight in and hurry across. But first to find the river!

Of course the way to follow Jesus does not necessarily take us through a river. And if Thomas had realized it, he *did* know the way. When you and I give our hearts to Jesus and promise to live the kind of life that pleases Him, we have taken our first step in following Him. And each step of walking with Him is like that first step. He is the Way to heaven; He will see that we make the final crossing when our life is done. Jesus leads the way—He *is* the Way home.

THE STRIKEOUT

"For everyone who exalts himself will be humbled, and he who humbles himself will be exalted." Luke 14:11, N.I.V.

"How was your day?" Mrs. Jennings asked as Jay stomped the snow from his boots. "That bad?" she sympathized, noticing his gloomy expression.

Mr. Peters had divided the Bible class into groups, the boy explained, for the purpose of planning a class presentation to be given the following week. Then Mr. Peters would grade the group as a whole and record the number of points for each member. "Our group chose Kelly as leader," the boy added. "And she chose Lori and me to do a science experiment while Randy makes the presentation. I'm sure I can earn us more points than Randy will."

Mrs. Jennings nodded sympathetically. She knew that Jay liked Randy but hated to miss even one point. But a perfect score in Mr. Peters' grade book wasn't everything. And anyway Jay needed to learn that he wouldn't get to call all his plays in the game of life.

"Jay, do you know what sin is?" she asked. He had always thought of it as the no-no's in his life. But his mother explained it differently. "It's selfishness—thinking of yourself first." Then she said that in life, as in a ball game, people sometimes have to sacrifice themselves for the good of the team.

That evening Jay's father told him about Jerry Koosman, then the number two starting pitcher for the New York Mets. He arrived at Shea Stadium ready for a game only to hear that the manager had assigned him to the bull pen. Shock and anger threatened to overcome him, but he figured that the manager was only doing his job. So Jerry determined to do his best for the good of the team. During the seventh inning the manager called him into the game, and Jerry not only played his best ball of the year but also regained his position as a starter.

"When our manager in the game of life sends us to the bull pen," Mr. Jennings concluded, "let's remember Jerry Koosman and do it for the good of the team."

A DAY IN THE CHAIR

When pride comes, then comes disgrace, but with humility comes wisdom! Proverbs 11:2, N.I.V.

Jon excelled at sports. He wished that his little church school gave grades on his report card for athletic ability. Surely he would earn an A for softball. The day Mr. Fitzgerald, the new teacher at Rockford, wheeled the chair into their upper-grades room Jon had no idea of the lesson it held for him. He was too healthy to need a wheelchair. "Sitting in a wheelchair for one whole day can teach you things," Mr. Fitzgerald explained. The mysterious twinkle in his eye teased Jon's curiosity, but the boy was too proud to admit it. I wouldn't be found dead in it, he thought. But after a while he thought it might be fun to manipulate the chair into tight corners and fly across the playground.

When his turn came, Jon at first enjoyed the experience. Mr. Fitzgerald must be a neat guy to plan a fun day like this for us, he thought, as he wheeled himself to the back of the room to get a drink. But by 11:00 A.M. it wasn't so much fun. When Jon wanted to get out and stretch his legs for five minutes, the class reminded him that they had each agreed to stay with the chair for a whole day. Jon hadn't realized how difficult such a small thing as fetching a dictionary from the bookcase across the room could be. Even sharpening a pencil was a chore.

The ultimate humility for Jon came when he had to sit on the sidelines and see his team lose the recess softball game. He couldn't do a thing to help but cheer them on.

The next day Jon's aching arms and blistered hands reminded him of the wheelchair. "My legs are something I've become tremendously thankful for," he wrote at the end of his story, "My Day in the Wheelchair." As he pinned the story to the bulletin board he wondered what he would do if for some reason his legs were crippled. Then he thanked God that the humble wheelchair had added to his store of wisdom.

THE GREAT IMPOSTOR

Be still, and know that I am God: I will be exalted among the heathen, I will be exalted in the earth. Psalm 46:10.

Ferdinand Demara liked to pass himself off as someone else. It all began when he stole a shoebox of personal belongings from a teenage friend. In the box were a birth certificate, diplomas, photographs of relatives, and personal information. Using his friend's name and papers, Demara began a new life. When his identity was blown, Demara moved to another town and assumed another name. Later he said that his most interesting identity was that of a surgeon. He knew nothing about medicine except what he read. Nevertheless he assisted with surgery until an alert nurse discovered that he was not a real doctor. Eventually he posed as a doctor of psychology, a college professor, a priest, a law student, and the warden of a prison. People called him "the great impostor."

Some people have said that Jesus was the greatest impostor of all time—that His claims to be the Son of God were false. They argue that there is no God; that religion is a lie. But people who don't believe the Bible have trouble explaining why they themselves exist, or what the meaning of life is and how they fit into the scheme of things. When Barbara Walters interviewed Brooke Shields for her CBS television show, she asked, "Who is the real Brooke Shields?"

"She's me," Brooke replied. But that wasn't what Ms. Walters wanted to hear. So she repeated the question. Do you know who *you* are? You'll learn the answer as you get to know God through the study of His Word. Don't be like Demara, trying to be someone else. When he died, his physician said, "He was the most miserable, unhappy man I have known." You see, Demara never did find out who he was. The psalmist said, "Be still, and know that I am God." That's the best way to find yourself.

DOUG FINDS GOD

The fool says in his heart, "There is no God." Psalm 14:1, N.I.V.

When I hear people say that there is no God, I wish I could introduce them to Doug Batchelor. When Doug was 13 he had life figured out—"It's for gathering as much happiness as possible before you die," he said. After that, he figured on becoming part of earth's natural fertilizer—but nothing more. People are just a higher form of monkey, Doug reasoned. "I'm going to get all the gusto I can," he vowed.

Doug began his quest for happiness by trying cigarettes. He supposed that they would provide a quick way to happiness. But they didn't. Then he tried alcohol. "You'll really feel good if you do drugs," someone said. And before Doug was 14 he used them regularly. To provide added excitement he began to steal. It brought him a lot of attention from his friends, but he felt miserable.

At 16 Doug had been jailed three times and was living by himself in Boston. Often he stole TVs from people's homes. "You shouldn't do that," one of his friends said. "God will catch up with you sooner or later. What you do comes back."

Sure enough, a couple of days later someone took Doug's own radio and TV while he slept. Maybe there is a God, he thought. The next day he stole $1.19 worth of pancake mix. When he arrived home, he found his kitchen broken into and $1.19 worth of orange juice missing. Doug felt that maybe God was trying to tell him something.

So he began searching for God. While living by himself in a cave near Palm Springs Doug found a Bible and began to read the New Testament. He discovered Jesus Christ, and after completing the book of Revelation, he knelt on his cave floor and gave himself to God.

Does Doug believe in God? Absolutely! How does he know for sure? First by reading the Bible. "Just reading it, I knew it was true," he says. "But the best reason for believing in God is the difference it made to me. I had no idea that anyone could feel this happy!"

THE ONLY TRUE GOD

And this is life eternal, that they might know thee the only true God, and Jesus Christ, whom thou hast sent. John 17:3.

For weeks the men of the village had climbed the hill each morning and filled the bush with sounds of chopping and laughter. The small boys often watched the men at work on the new canoe. During the early stages, while the adults removed the large limbs from the huge trunk, the boys had fashioned their own tiny craft, which they paddled around the lagoon, racing each other to the reef and back.

At last the day of launching had come. Every man and boy found his place beside the great canoe, ready to push it down to the water. Before the signal to start, the owner of the canoe turned to Johann, a gray-haired man of the village and the only Seventh-day Adventist among them, and asked him to offer prayer.

Reverently Johann asked God's blessing on the boat. But instead of pushing the canoe down the hill, some of the men stripped branches from nearby trees. "All the spirits in these branches, go inside this canoe and move it down to the sea," they sang as they danced around the boat, hitting it with the branches. Then they finally resumed their positions and began pushing. But the canoe did not budge.

When the men grew tired of trying to move the canoe, Johann stepped forward. "You have done wrong," he said. "You mixed the blessing of God with the worship of spirits. Had you pushed after my prayer, the boat would have slid easily. If God let it move now, you would say that the spirits did it." Realizing their mistake, the men humbly asked Johann to pray for forgiveness. And they easily pushed the canoe into the lagoon.

Ask God to help you not to mix worship of Him with the love of worldly pleasures, or the worship of sports and entertainment heroes today. For eternal life comes only with knowing and worshiping Him "the one true God."

IMPRINTED

I will put my law in their inward parts, and write it in their hearts; and will be their God, and they shall be my people. Jeremiah 31:33.

Imagine yourself a tiny unhatched chick about to crack your shell. You feel an urge for more space, a need to stretch your legs. But you are too busy breaking out to think about the big bad world out there or to wonder who will look after you. Suddenly you are aware of a presence much larger than you. You don't know it is your mother. By instinct—inborn instructions—you follow her anyway. A camera in your brain takes a picture of your mother. You *imprint* on that form so that when she moves, you follow. She leads you to your first food.

Scientists tell us that *imprinting* occurs only during the first day of a bird's life. After that another instinct takes over—fear. And fear makes the chick run from anything large it happens to meet. A duckling that hatches among hen's eggs will imprint on the hen. Even though you later put it with its real mother, it still considers the hen its mother.

When Tex, a female whooping crane, hatched at the San Antonio Zoo, she imprinted on a scientist. She thought he was her parent. When put with other cranes she did not behave as though she was one of them. You have possibly seen on television how the zookeepers use a pair of puppets that look like the head and neck of a grown condor to feed baby condors raised in captivity. They don't want the baby imprinting on them because they hope that someday it will live and mate with other condors.

People don't imprint like birds do. But in a sense Adam and Eve imprinted on God when He first created them. But sin spoiled that. Ever since, the imprint has been marred for all of us. If left to ourselves we follow sin. Fortunately God has not abandoned us to our instincts. The earth is still His and He has a way of reimprinting on us. He says, "I will put my law in your minds and write it on your hearts. I will be your God, and you will be my people." Won't you accept the imprint of the Creator today?

YOU, JESUS?

Thou shalt love the Lord thy God with all thy heart, and with all thy soul, and with all thy strength, and with all thy mind; and thy neighbour as thyself. Luke 10:27.

The worst part about being a pastor's daughter, Nancy says, is visiting new churches. "Sometimes when you don't know anybody, the other kids won't sit near you, and you feel awful."

Sandra agrees. "But it's much worse in a strange country where you don't speak the language too well," she adds. "At first you think that everyone is staring at you because you're different." But something happened once that changed her attitude.

"I was sitting close to my mom," she explains. "I suppose I was trying to block out my loneliness. Usually the village women act shy until somebody who knows some English introduces everyone. Then the shyness melts. But this day nobody understood English, and we didn't understand the village dialect.

"But, determined to make us feel at home, a shy little woman sat beside my mother and, pointing at her, asked, 'You, Jesus?' Then pointing to herself, she said, 'Me, Jesus.' We all laughed; we were friends. Now when I visit a church for the first time I try to remember that I am not a stranger. The love of Jesus makes friends of all believers."

I thought of Sandra's experience when I heard of a woman who fell ill while on a tour of Guatemala. In spite of her protests, her host brought in a local witch doctor renowned for her corn-magic cure. But the witch doctor hung back, not wanting to treat the patient. Then suddenly she noticed a Bible beside the bed.

Realizing that the American tourist was a Christian believer, the Indian woman smiled. She apologized for not using the magic. "Jesus is good," she said and offered to pray instead.

Isn't it amazing how our shared love for Jesus overshadows all our little differences? And remembering that has brought Sandra all kinds of interesting friends.

BE STILL AND KNOW

Be still, and know that I am God. Psalm 46:10.

You can do anything if you believe in yourself, Kenneth used to remind himself at examination time. And he believed it—hadn't he almost always pulled A's? When shy Sheri told him wistfully how she wished she could just make all C's, Kenneth tried to bolster her courage. "You can do anything you want," he said. "Just believe in yourself." Although Sheri genuinely tried, for all her believing, she still earned two D's. And for all her pretending she really didn't believe in herself.

Lester had been playing the piano since he turned 5. When his classmates were stumbling over "Peter, Peter, Pumpkin Eater," Lester was already into Bach minuets. And when they arrived at their first sonatina, he had memorized Chopin's *Minute Waltz*.

As much as Lester loved to play the piano, he hated to perform in public. Whenever his name was announced his hands went cold and clammy, and his fingers hit the wrong notes. People felt so sorry for him that they didn't enjoy his music.

Then Lester learned to believe in himself by believing in Someone much bigger. The more he came to know God, the more comfortable he felt with himself. Lester's stomach still turned flip-flops before he played in public, but today's text, "Be still and know that I am God," calmed his mind. Trusting God helped him relax and concentrate on the music.

"Believing in God helps you do your best," Lester says. "But because you don't turn out to be number one on the charts doesn't mean that you don't have enough faith in God. You may need to practice more. Or God may have another plan for you.

"Yes, it's important to believe in yourself," he concludes, "but it's far more important to believe in God. He doesn't promise to turn you into Superman or Wonder Woman. And He doesn't promise that you'll be a winner every time. But He helps you discover your talents and do your best. He helps you turn a defeat into success."

WHEN SILENCE IS GOLDEN

Verily thou art a God that hidest thyself, O God of Israel, the Saviour. Isaiah 45:15.

Have you ever wished that you could sit down and have a heart-to-heart talk with God? Don't you envy the children who sat on His knee and talked to Him face to face?

Jamie didn't want to mow the lawn. The grass had hardly grown since he last mowed it. "Give me one good reason why it should be mowed again," he demanded with an irritating whine.

Mother left the dishes in the sink and dried her hands. "Jamie," she said, "I have told you what needs to be done. Now, I will not discuss the matter further." And she walked to her room and locked the door. Although he started to follow her, it was no fun arguing with a locked door. So he decided to start the lawnmower.

As Jamie guided the noisy machine past the kitchen window he noticed that his mother was again washing dishes. She must have returned when he decided to obey. But why would she deliberately hide from him when he was talking to her? When his mother locked herself in the bedroom, she gave him a chance to recognize what he needed to do.

So it is with God. He would like to be here with us, but His absence is not all bad. It gives us a chance to think for ourselves and recognize what we need to do.

In his book *The Chosen,* Chaim Potok tells the story of Danny, whose father has not spoken to him since he was 6. Danny loves his father but remembers the days when they laughed and talked together. The boy doesn't understand the silence, but he never once doubts his father's love.

After Danny grows up, his father breaks the long silence and explains his unusual behavior. One day when he was 4 Danny had read a grown-up book, but though the story was sad, the child showed no sorrow. What good is a brilliant mind without an understanding heart? the father thought. And that is why he chose to raise his son in silence—to give him a sensitive heart. Maybe God has a purpose for us in His silence, too.

WHAT HAS HE PUT INTO YOU?

"Woe to him who quarrels with his Maker. . . . It is I who made the earth and created mankind upon it." Isaiah 45:9-12, N.I.V.

Josie had always hated spelling. "It's because you think you can't do well at it," her special education teacher explained. Then she drew the girl's attention to a bowl of roses. "See the beauty and detail in each flower," she said. "Well, if God could do that for flowers, think what He has put into you." Josie decided that maybe she was special after all. Maybe by hard work she would amount to something. So she and her teacher worked out a strategy for learning spelling words.

Some of Josie's classmates took time to help her, and after much time and effort she finally achieved 100 percent on a spelling test! The girl danced for joy, and the entire class gave her a standing ovation. But before she had time to enjoy her success, Lesley burst her bubble.

"Say, Josie," he called from across the room, "how long did it take you to study for that test?"

Josie added it up. An hour before supper each evening, twice on Sunday, ten minutes here and there every day. "Oh, maybe ten or eleven hours." The words froze on her lips. Everyone stared in disbelief. And instead of the recognition that her perseverance deserved, Josie sensed only failure. She was deficient, different, stupid—just because she couldn't spell.

But because a girl couldn't spell, why must she always get low grades? Josie knew she had what it took to write a good story. She would show them that God had put something special into her when she turned in the next assignment for English composition. Carefully she wrote out her story and with painstaking care checked the spelling of each word. She knew when she handed it in that it was a winner.

"It's no good fussing at God because it takes you longer to do some things," she says. "You have to ask yourself what special something He has put into you."

GOD AND SANTA CLAUS?

"I am the Lord, and there is no other; apart from me there is no God." Isaiah 45:5, N.I.V.

Nina Donnelly was a student chaplain when she visited Joe in the children's ward.* Joe sat on the edge of his bed, an IV tube stuck in his arm. Otherwise he looked like a fairly chipper 6-year-old. After introducing herself, Nina explained that she was the new chaplain on his floor. The boy wanted to know what a chaplain was. "It's like being a minister," Nina said. Joe brightened. He went to church every week and liked his minister. For quite some time he had been saving a question for his minister, but decided to try it out on Nina instead.

"Is it true what they say about God?" Joe asked.

"What do you mean by that?" She wanted to be sure she understood Joe's question.

"You know," Joe explained, "like He's there even though you can't see Him."

Solemnly Nina nodded and assured him that God was there even when He couldn't be seen. The little boy leaned back on his pillow and smiled contentedly. "That's good," he said. "Then I can believe in Santa Claus, too."

Many boys and girls much older than Joe want to believe in God *and* Santa Claus. Of course they know that family members bought and wrapped the presents under their tree, and they recognize their Aunt Bonnie in the Santa Claus suit at the Christmas party. But they think of God as being a generous old man with a flowing white beard who watches to see if they are "naughty or nice" before He loves them.

But in Isaiah 45 God says that, though we sometimes forget who He is, " '[He] will strengthen [us] . . . so that from the rising of the sun to the place of its setting men may know there is [no God] besides [Him]' " (verses 5, 6). The great God of the heavens wants to use you and me, imperfect though we are, to help people see His greatness. To assure kids like Joe that He really loves and cares for them. Doesn't that make you feel special?

---

* Nina Herrmann Donnelly, "When Children Suffer," *Leadership,* Spring, 1983, p. 45.

THROUGH THE LOOKING GLASS

For since the creation of the world God's invisible qualities—his eternal power and divine nature—have been clearly seen, being understood from what has been made. Romans 1:20, *N.I.V.*

"Dad, how come we can't see God?" Ronnie asked. "It would be so much more fun talking to God if you could see Him." Ronnie's dad had been snoozing while he and his sister, Rhonda, looked at nature books on the blanket beside him. But Ronnie's question popped his father's eyes wide open.

"How would you like to hunt for God?" Mr. McGee asked. Both children looked interested. "I want you to do three things while I finish my nap," he said. "Take a nature book and find the weirdest creature or the most fascinating. Next, mark off a small section of grass near you and observe it carefully. Write down what you see. Then lie back and look up through the trees at the sky. Wake me up when you are done."

Ronnie enjoyed looking through his underwater world book. He liked stingrays best, but the sea anemone was the weirdest. How could so many fascinating creatures have just happened? God must have enjoyed making each one different, Ronnie decided. After staring into the grass, he wrote, "A black ant almost stepped on a red ant. They have a pathway under the grass. I saw a beautiful beetle."

Just as he settled back to look into the trees and the skies, his dad woke up. "If I were an ant, the blades of grass would look as tall as trees," Ronnie said. "Wow! That makes God BIG!" After Ronnie had described the beautiful colored beetle he saw, his dad read him today's text: "Ever since God created the world, his invisible qualities—his eternal power and divine nature—have been clearly seen in the things that he made."

Nature can be a mirror in which you see the reflection of God. But you have to open your inner eyes and look for beauty.

MEASURING DAYS

"Show me, O Lord, my life's end and the number of my days; let me know how fleeting is my life." Psalm 39:4, N.I.V.

Do you remember when you learned to measure? Maybe in the third grade when you studied metrics you tried measuring the hallway at school by laying down the meterstick over and over again. I remember measuring the chalkboard by my handspan. Ten of those spans made about one meter and, as you know (but your mom may not), one meter is a little longer than one yard.

You have probably measured a freight train by counting the cars. The train takes a long time just to pass you at a crossing. If the train was one mile long and could travel as fast as the space shuttle (18,000 miles per hour), it would pass you so quickly that one blink at the wrong time and you might miss it! But it would take the space shuttle more than one year to reach earth's neighbor, Mars. That's a long way. How long would it take you to measure that far by the span of your hand?

When King David thought about the span of his life and how it measured against the whole expanse of time since the beginning, he realized that one lifetime is exceedingly short to God. "'You have made my days a mere handbreadth,'" he said in verse 5. "'The span of my years is as nothing before you. Each man's life is but a breath.'" Knowing that even a full life of seventy or eighty years passes quickly, David decided that he needed help in making good use of time. That's why he prayed for God to help us number our days. He didn't mean that we should sit around measuring time, but that we should value each day and make the most of it. And above all, we should live each day with our hand in the hand of God, the Lord of time.

A MAJESTIC NAME

O Lord, our Lord, how majestic is your name in all the earth! Psalm 8:1, N.I.V.

When I was a teenager almost every large city had a Ritz hotel. Neither I nor my friends had ever been inside one—we weren't "ritzy" enough. The Ritz was always the expensive and fashionable place in town. Years later, I returned to my hometown and passed by the Ritz. I couldn't believe how out-of-date and shabby it looked. Suddenly *Ritz* had a new meaning for me.

I'm glad that God is not ritzy. He has the real thing—an enduring quality called majesty. When Prince Charles becomes king, people will address him as "Your Majesty." But some kings in history have made a mockery of that word, also. When the leaders in the kingdom addressed King Richard, ruthless and lacking in moral consciousness, as "Your Majesty," I wonder what they were thinking. And King Henry VIII, who, on trumped-up charges, had some of his wives murdered, would not fit our idea of majestic.

A redwood tree towering above the forest is truly majestic. Two professional basketball players leaning against the trunk could hardly reach around it to join hands. And if they stood on each other's shoulders, twelve teams could barely reach the top of the tallest redwood tree. You would feel small beside Kareem Abdul-Jabbar, but positively insignificant looking up into that majestic redwood.

God's name is majestic. When you look up at the stars and realize that they are suns spinning around in space, you get an idea of how large the universe is. If the earth were the size of a blueberry, the sun would be like a weather balloon by comparison. And our sun is only a tiny, dull star. Some stars are even hundreds of times bigger. Does that help you sense the majesty of a God who created the universe—who holds the worlds in His hand? Imagine yourself moving about a hill of ants. Think how you would crush some. But nothing is too big or too small for our majestic God. Doesn't it make you feel good to know that He wants you for a friend?

'ELOHIM

And God said, "Let us make man in our image, in our likeness." Genesis 1:26, N.I.V.

One of the words used for God in the Old Testament (more than 2,500 times) was *'Elohim.* Genesis 1:1 first employs it to describe God as the great Creator of our world. In verse 26 *'Elohim* says, " 'Let us make man in *our* image, in *our* likeness.' " I feel a little shiver run up my spine when I stop and think that I have been made in the likeness of the Great One who revealed Himself in creation.

Ever since I was very small I have enjoyed playing the piano. For some reason I particularly like the music of Bach and Handel. After a lot of playing and listening you sort of get to know the composers. You can recognize them in their music. If you listen to Handel's *Messiah* many times you will notice, for instance, that there is something very straightforward about how he ends each song. Both Bach and Handel like to take melodies and mix them. It sounds as though the music runs along, now high, then low. Melody overlaps melody, and a new melody may run along at the same time. Later composers used rich chords to support a melody. When we drive along the freeway, we like to listen to music on the radio and guess who wrote it. For no matter who performs the music, you can detect something of the composer, though you may not remember hearing that selection before.

And that is how it is with you and your Creator. When you love Him and follow Him, people see little flashes of God in you. When you give Him the place of honor in your life—when you put Him first—you honor His name. That is what Jesus meant when He prayed, "Hallowed be Thy name"—or may Your name be honored.

The interesting thing about *'Elohim* is that God once told Moses that Aaron " 'will speak to the people for you, and it will be as if he were your mouth and as if you were *'Elohim* to him' " (Ex. 4:16). In another place He says that Moses would be like *'Elohim* to Pharaoh. So as you and I live close to Jesus others may see *'Elohim* in us.

THE GREAT *I AM*

"Suppose I go to the Israelites and say to them, 'The God of your fathers has sent me to you,' and they ask me, 'What is his name?' Then what shall I tell them?" God said to Moses, "I am who I am." Exodus 3:13, 14, N.I.V.

Even as the burning bush crackles away without so much as singeing a leaf, Moses listens skeptically while God outlines His plan to rescue the Israelites from Egypt. " 'Who am I, that I should go to Pharaoh and bring the Israelites out of Egypt?' " Moses wonders (verse 11).

The former self-appointed savior of his people now mistrusts his own leadership ability. Realizing that he is no match for the ultimate big mouth, Pharaoh, Moses shrinks from the task. But God reassures him saying, " 'I will be with you' " (verse 12).

Immediately Moses recognizes that herein lies the reason for his failure forty years before—he had tried to save Israel on his own. How will Moses convince the Israelites that God sent him? What should he say when they ask for proof? He will give God's name.

Saying that I AM sent him sounds strange to us, but the Israelites understood. They never needed to compare their great God to any other, nor did they ask where He came from. But they liked to be reminded of His faithfulness. So God instructed Moses to say, " ' "The Lord, the God of your fathers—the God of Abraham, the God of Isaac and the God of Jacob—has sent me to you." This is my name forever' " (verse 15).

Do you sometimes wonder whether the God of your parents is the God for you? Are you tempted to think that you can win a place for yourself in the world without His help? Not that you reject Him—you simply don't include Him in your plans.

God says to you today, "I am who I am—the God of your fathers." He is still there. The One who made Moses a great leader wants to help you reach your goals and more if you will let Him on the team. You can't help winning with a coach like Him.

THE ALL-POWERFUL GOD

When Abram was ninety-nine years old, the Lord appeared to him and said, "I am God Almighty; walk before me and be blameless." Genesis 17:1, N.I.V.

Don't you envy Abraham talking to God! I wonder what His voice sounded like. Did Abraham even notice? When Jehovah, the one true God, said, "I am *'El-Shaddai,"* Abraham must have trembled. *'El* meant a God of power and authority. So when the all-powerful God says, " 'Walk before me and be blameless,' " we could feel afraid.

Our Pathfinder unit once participated in a parade through town. All kinds of youth groups and bands formed up and marched off before the Advent Brass Band finally struck up a stirring march and led the Pathfinder contingent down the parade route. The crowds of people lining both sides of the street amazed us. People all seemed to turn our way, smiling and pointing as we approached. We must have presented a fine sight, but I doubted that we merited so much interest. "What's with all these people?" I whispered to Myra, who marched beside me. "Why are we attracting so much attention?"

"Look what's following us," she replied with a laugh. I almost missed a step, craning my neck to look. Only a step or two behind was a beautiful contingent of mounted police bringing up the rear of the parade. One false step—one trip over a shoelace—and I could have all the power and might of the police horses on my back. I couldn't get the thought out of my head.

God did not mean to unnerve Abraham when He introduced Himself. For, while *'El* lent strength to His promise that Abraham would become the father of nations (verses 2, 3), *Shaddai* meant the God of inexhaustible gifts. The same God promises you the power to live victoriously and a share in the riches of His love. So when you walk with Him, you know that He doesn't just wait for you to miss a step. He helps you walk with confidence and makes the trip pleasant and worthwhile. So why not ask Him to walk beside you today and always!

WELCOME TO THE CLUB

"I am the Lord your God, who brought you out of Egypt, out of the land of slavery." Exodus 20:2, N.I.V.

Most people enjoy belonging to a club. When you were smaller, you may have joined a neighborhood club like Josh's. He and several friends on Meadowside Lane formed the Meadowside Athletic Club. They met after school in Josh's carport and did push-ups, worked out on the trampoline, and shot baskets. To keep the club together they chose some simple rules: keep a record of warm-ups, try to increase your endurance some every day, and take care of equipment. Sticking to the rules gave them pride in the club.

In a way, the Ten Commandments are a code of rules for Christians. You join the club by accepting Jesus as your Saviour from sin and keeping the rules that He set down for members. Have you already memorized the commandments? When you repeat them, do you begin, "Thou shalt not"? Most people do. But actually God's code begins with His name: "I am the Lord thy God" (verse 2, K.J.V.). One could translate it, "I am Jehovah"—the One who always existed, the Eternal God, the Living One, the great I Am.

Then follow the ten rules. The first two remind us that we may join only one spiritual club—worship only one God. The third commandment warns members to honor and respect the Leader. Nobody wants to join a club where members bad-mouth their leader. Keeping the third commandment helps you to enjoy membership as a Christian.

Russ used to think that taking God's name in vain meant swearing. And Russ would never swear. His heart sank the day Miss Thompson asked him to give the mission story in Sabbath school. He couldn't say No, but neither could he risk looking pious in front of his friends. So he decided to give the story *his* way—in his own inimitable smart-talk style. At first his presentation met with some stifled giggles, but by the second page he knew he had blown it. He had made fun of worship and belittled God. Russ discovered a truth that day: When we honor God, we feel better about ourselves.

GOD WITH US

Behold, a virgin shall be with child, and shall bring forth a son, and they shall call his name Emmanuel, which being interpreted is, God with us. Matthew 1:23.

Hanukkah, the Jewish Festival of Lights, usually falls in December. It commemorates something that happened in ancient Jewish history after the Jews had driven the Syrians out of Jerusalem. The Jews removed the Syrian gods from their beloved Temple and then tried to relight the holy lamps with only one tiny cruse of oil.

Remembering how those lamps were never allowed to go out, the people anxiously prayed that the oil would last. And according to Jewish tradition, the oil kept the lamps burning for eight days until the priests could bring in more. Even today Jewish families light one candle for each of the eight days of Hanukkah.

One Hanukkah eve Rebecca lay in bed, recovering from scarlet fever. Reports of Jewish families disappearing, never to be seen again, disturbed her thoughts. She felt a special pride for her people and the God who had chosen them long ago. But for all the happy traditions, for all that they *knew* about God, her strict Jewish family hardly *knew* Him. Yet, surely He cared for them. Peace flooded her heart as three words rang over and over in her mind—"God with us." Her family could find strength for whatever lay ahead if only they remembered those three words.

Rebecca chose to present her special discovery to the family by lettering "God With Us" in brilliant colors on a poster that she taped to the wall beside her bed. "We do not know the future," she told them as they gathered around her bed to light the first candle on the Hanukkah menorah, "but there *can* be comfort if we take the Master of the universe at His word." And that day she opened her heart to God and never let Him go.

The prophet Isaiah called Jesus "Emmanuel . . . God with us"—the One who cares for us enough to stay by our side when we're lonely or worried. Maybe, like Rebecca, we need to letter those three words not only on a poster but on our innermost heart as well.

THE LORD, HE IS GOD

The prophet came near, and said, Lord God of Abraham, Isaac, and of Israel, let it be known this day that thou art God in Israel. 1 Kings 18:36.

He differed in many ways from the other children. His dress was more simple and he spent little time fooling around with the gang after school. He knew where he was going in life. Most of his friends came from families who once professed the same religion as he, but they did not take it seriously. And they differed in one basic point—their understanding of who God is.

They must often have teased him. "You can't see your God; we can see ours." But when he replied, "I cannot see God, but He sees me; I talk to Him, He hears me," they made no reply.

God laid a dangerous mission on him one day, and he strode away from his home in the hills with never a backward glance. The testimony he bore to the king was bold. But his daring saved him. Escaping the angry king, he hid by a brook.

During the three years of the drought, what might those former playmates of his have said? They had surely heard of Elijah's long-term weather forecast (chap. 17:1), and they blamed him for its fulfillment. And they must have remembered his claims about God—how He saw and heard His followers.

I hope some of them witnessed that flash of fire on Mount Carmel when God answered Elijah's prayer. And I like to believe that some from the hills of Gilead joined in shouting, "The Lord, he is the God; the Lord, he is the God," and resolved to serve Him always—all because of Elijah's boyhood example.

Some of my friends know about God; they call themselves His, but don't get excited about who He is. How can I live so that people know that I serve the living God—that I really care about Him? If your answer to that question has to do with cheerful obedience, praying, and loving, you might be close to letting it be known today that the Lord is God in your life.

WHAT'S IN A NAME?

And his name shall be called Wonderful, Counsellor, The mighty God, The everlasting Father, The Prince of Peace. Isaiah 9:6.

"Come home with me after school," Debbie invited the girls at her new school. "You must come meet my beautiful mother." Every girl in school rushed home and begged permission to visit Debbie's house. And learning of Debbie's reference to her "beautiful mother," other mothers became jealous.

When at last Janice was allowed her long-awaited visit to Debbie's house, she wondered what to expect. Mrs. Saunders welcomed her at the door with hugs and smiles. "Janice, this is my beautiful mother," Debbie glowed. Her mother's eyes shone at the compliment. But the truth was that Mrs. Saunders looked plump and tired. However, when her eyes lit up you forgot her weight problem and her plainness. "Now don't listen to Debbie," Mrs. Saunders joked. "Come try this batch of cookies I baked."

Janice found her own attractive mother in the kitchen when she returned. "Well, how was Debbie's beautiful mother?" she asked with a hint of sarcasm. "Is she really beautiful?" Pictures of Mrs. Saunders' plain clothes and tired face flashed through Janice's mind. But she also saw again that lively smile and the warm glow. She remembered the welcoming hug and the cookies. "Yes," she answered. "Debbie's mother really is beautiful."

What's in a name? For Debbie's mother there was love and appreciation. Calling her beautiful transformed her. But with God it is a little different. He *is* those names Isaiah used in our text today. Notice that they were the names of Jesus. He too is our everlasting Father. We may never fully understand God—who He really is—but we understand His names: Wonderful (first-rate), Counsellor (He listens, has good ideas), the mighty God (power you can count on), the everlasting Father (love you never outgrow), and the Conqueror who brings it all together, the Prince of Peace.

JESUS AND THE MEDICINE MEN

When he had thus spoken, he spat on the ground, and made clay of the spittle, and he anointed the eyes of the blind man with the clay. John 9:6.

For thirteen years Marilyn Laszlo has worked with a Sepik Iwam village, of Papua New Guinea, helping them to write down their own language. To them, writing on paper is "carving on a banana leaf." Thinking that only the missionary's words could be carved, they were thrilled to learn how to "carve" their own language.

The medicine men of the village at first refused to participate in Marilyn's language classes. When they did attend, they helped enrich her understanding of their language. Marilyn learned, for instance, that the word for doctor means "he who spits." To treat malaria they cut the patient and spit the powerful juices of chewed-up plants into the wound. When the class translated John 9:6, the witch doctors could hardly believe their ears. Not only was Jesus a spitter, but He was the most powerful spitter of all. He healed a blind man, and none of the Iwam spitters could do that. Suddenly those big men identified with Jesus. They went out into the village and spread the story that Jesus spits! He heals the blind! From that day the medicine men began attending church. They wanted to know more about Jesus.

Today more than half the people in that village are Christians. I have often wondered about the strange remedy Jesus used for healing that blind man. Could He have known it would help the Iwam Sepik people identify with Him almost two thousand years later?

As Jesus prepared the clay for anointing the blind man's eyes He told the people, "As long as I am in the world, I am the light of the world." And as the Sepik River people accepted Him, their village became a light shining across the swamp and jungles to other villages. Today let's ask Jesus to open our eyes and to let His love shine through in words of encouragement to others.

GOD'S HOLY HILL

Who may ascend the hill of the Lord? Who may stand in his holy place? He who has clean hands and a pure heart, who does not . . . swear by what is false. Psalm 24:3, 4, N.I.V.

"What a marvelous view!" I exclaimed as I gazed out the dormitory window at the Adventist college in Collonges-sous-Saleve, France. One enormous cliff face dominated the scene.

A mellow golden glow from the late afternoon sun bathed the sheer wall of rock. And then I saw them. Tiny colored specks clung to the mountain and crept upward in some cases and down in others. The longer I looked, the more dots I counted. "People practice on the Saleve in preparation for climbing Mont Blanc at Chamonoix," my husband explained. It looked like fun.

Next morning the mountain stood in shadow. Mist hid the top from view. And as I watched, the mist slowly floated upward and melted in the sunshine above. The sun must have been shining brilliantly on the eastern side of the Saleve because the mists in our valley rode the updrafts and melted away in the warmth that bathed the summit. I wished I could climb to the sunshine myself.

The more we watched the early evening climbers and the morning mists, the more we longed to climb the Saleve. So one afternoon we set out to walk by the roadway. Although we discovered some shortcuts along the way, we missed the thrill of mountaineering. But we did enjoy the summit. There we discovered fields of early summer flowers and cows with tinkling bells. We looked out over the valley and felt close to God.

Wouldn't you like to climb His holy hill? You won't find pain or sickness up there; neither hatred, loneliness, nor injustice. And who may climb that holy hill and stand in the presence of a holy God? Those with "clean hands and a pure heart, who [do] not lift up [their] soul to an idol or swear by what is false." Are your heart and hands clean?

HOLY UNTO THE LORD

Preserve my soul; for I am holy: O thou my God, save thy servant that trusteth in thee. Psalm 86:2.

"I wish I were good like Mother," Kelly sighed. "Why do I get myself into scrapes because I act first and think later?"

"Yeah," Tammy sighed. "Look at Angie! She never gets into trouble like we do. But how come I don't like her?"

"Oh, don't let Angie get you down," Kelly sympathized, forgetting her own problems. "Angie's always been a goody-goody as long as I've known her."

"I envy good people," Tammy sighed. "It's me I don't like."

Kelly laughed. "Don't be hard on yourself," she said. "Nobody's perfect—except Mr. Watson, maybe. And he's 'holier than thou!' "

Have you noticed that when you work real hard at being good, sometimes you aren't sympathetic to others who do the dumb things you used to do? When you act like that, people say you are "holier than thou." They mean that you think you are better than they are—and that you are the last person that they would ask to help them with a problem.

The *SDA Bible Dictionary* says that Scripture uses the word *holy* not only for God, who is perfectly sinless, but also for something that is set aside for a sacred use. Thus the Sabbath is a holy day, the sanctuary a holy place. By saying that he was holy, David did not mean that he was perfect, or that he was as good as God. He meant that his life was devoted to serving the Lord. In that respect you and I may also be holy.

At the age of 16 George gave his heart to Jesus. He vowed to begin every day with Bible reading and prayer. "I won't read anything else before I read the Bible," George promised. And he meant it. People come to George when they have problems. They know he loves people, and just talking to him helps them feel better. People know that George walks with Jesus. But nobody could say that he is "holier than thou" because George doesn't try to act good. He lets God make him a better person day by day. Why don't you try that kind of holiness? You'll really like yourself.

EYE OF THE STORM

Those who know your name will trust in you, for you, Lord, have never forsaken those who seek you. Psalm 9:10, N.I.V.

As the small plane taxied to the runway 14-year-old Kelly checked her seat belt and closed her eyes while her mother offered prayer. Kelly had no idea how thankful she would be for that prayer before the day was over. Mr. Curtiss gunned the engines and soon had the plane airborne over Sarasota Bay. The girl could see the Gulf Coast stretching northward. They would follow its westward curve all the way to Texas.

"What was the weather forecast?" Mrs. Curtiss asked. Her husband replied that it called for only scattered clouds. The teenager sighed with relief. Perfect flying conditions.

They met the first of the scattered clouds just out of Mobile, Alabama. Kelly was used to the roller coaster effect of the updrafts. But over Lafayette, Louisiana, they encountered a thin cloud cover and then a dense wall of thunderheads.

Suddenly the plane jerked violently as gale force winds struck. Kelly felt the bottom fall out from under her as the plane plunged downward. Just as unexpectedly it bounced upward again. The Curtisses had flown into a monster storm that blocked their view of the ground. The girl couldn't even see the wingtips. In fact she couldn't tell if they were flying right side up, or in which direction they were headed. She hoped her father could.

Kelly began to cry softly, all the while praying frantically. Every lurch of the plane seemed like it would be the last.

"Look down there!" Mrs. Curtiss' voice snapped Kelly's eyes open. The plane had flown into the eye of the storm. For two miles all around everything appeared calm and clear. Mr. Curtiss found a rice field and carefully landed the plane. Happy to be alive, the three waded across the muddy field to a dike, where they found help.

"I can't believe you walked across that field. It's full of water moccasins," the farmer said. But Kelly knew that the Lord had cared for them. She was glad she trusted Him.

THE IN THING

But let all who take refuge in you be glad; let them ever sing for joy. Spread your protection over them, that those who love your name may rejoice in you. Psalm 5:11, N.I.V.

An unemployed writer a few years ago decided that his life was too ordinary. So, with a stolen credit card and posing as a wealthy lawyer, he lived it up for three weeks in Dallas, Texas. By the time the police caught up with him he had charged more than $5,000 worth of merchandise at Dallas' more expensive stores. He figured that to be successful he needed fame, and to be famous he needed wealth.

Before we judge the man's warped ideas of success, maybe we should take one long look at ourselves. Take that shirt, for instance. Why do I wear it? Because of a designer logo stitched on the left pocket? And my shoes, did I choose them for comfort and durability? Or because of the brand name? And how about my jeans? Why do I always want a more expensive brand?

When I dress to look like everyone else, maybe I have something in common with that phony lawyer. Unsure if he could be a successful person in his own right, he thought he needed things—the right brand of clothes and make of car—to prop up his reputation. And unable to relax and be himself for worrying about what other people might think, he didn't even notice how unhappy he felt.

Today's text brings good news for those of us who have to wear hand-me-downs and last year's styles, as well as for those who are fighting to keep up with everybody else. True happiness doesn't come from wearing the right things, knowing the Top Forty, or telling the latest jokes. Happiness results from knowing God, from looking to Him when we aren't sure how well our friends like us. When we "take refuge" in God like that, we will sing for joy. The happiest people of all love God's name. The in thing for them is not the latest names in clothes or on the charts—it's God Himself.

THE RAZOR'S EDGE

Whoever does not love does not know God, because God is love. 1 John 4:8, N.I.V.

An old Australian ballad tells of "the man from Ironbark," a place far from civilization without the convenience of a barber. On one of his occasional visits to Sydney the man went to a barbershop for a shave. Thinking to give his other customers a laugh, the barber lathered the man's face and then, dipping his razor in boiling water, ran the back of the blade across the man's throat from ear to ear. Assuming his throat had been cut, the man from Ironbark almost went berserk—to the great amusement of all.

A razor can do fearful damage if wrongly used, but one man made it a symbol of trust and love. A prison warden once learned that a certain prisoner was planning to "bump him off." Rather than live in fear of the prisoner, the warden decided to meet the problem head on. He knew that the convict had once been a barber, so he sent for the man and handed him a razor. "I want you to shave me," he said.

The inmate looked in alarm at the razor in his hand and then at the warden, the only other person in the room. Perspiration broke out on the man's face, and his hand shook. Seeing that the man could not do it, the warden spoke up. "Some of the fellows say that you want to kill me," he said. "They think we are enemies. But I thought we could prove to them that we are friends. I trust you to shave me well." Not only did the prisoner give the warden a first-class shave, but they became good friends. The man's hate turned into love—all because a Christian warden showed his faith and trust.

"This is how God showed his love among us: He sent his one and only Son into the world that we might live through him. This is love: not that we loved God, but that he loved us and sent his Son as . . . sacrifice for our sins. . . . Since God so loved us, we also ought to love one another" (verses 9-11).

LOVE THAT NAME!

Then the Lord . . . proclaimed his name. . . . "The Lord, the Lord, the compassionate and gracious God, slow to anger, abounding in love and faithfulness." Exodus 34:5, 6, N.I.V.

When you were small, did you ever wonder why you couldn't see God? You talked to Him every night. How come you couldn't see Him? The idea of seeing God fascinated Moses, too, even though he was a grown man. In fact, the older he became, the more he longed to see God. So one day the Lord passed before Moses on Mount Sinai and proclaimed His name: "'The Lord, the Lord, the compassionate and gracious God, slow to anger, abounding in love and faithfulness, maintaining love to thousands, and forgiving wickedness, rebellion and sin.'"

That's rather a long name! In fact, it isn't merely a name; it's a description of His character.

Think for a minute of one name you would not give a child of yours. Everyone can come up with some name that produces in them a bad reaction. Why? Because you once knew somebody by that name whom you disliked. So the name came to represent that character. That's why you would never call a child Judas or Barabbas. On the other hand, you smile at the Burmese names Laughing Water or Clever Queen. They tell you something pleasant about the person.

When God told Moses His name, He was describing Himself. He wanted Moses (and all of us) to know more about who He is and how He feels about us. First of all He is compassionate—He knows how we feel. He hurts when we hurt, and laughs when we laugh. God is gracious—He treats us as if we are important to Him. He has plenty of patience—doesn't get angry easily. The funny little things you do when you aren't thinking don't make Him mad. Also He never has a bad night, never wakes up grouchy. And as if that isn't enough, He is full of love and faithfulness—you can count on Him, He won't grow tired of you when He finds another friend. As a Christian, you take God's name. And He helps you to become all of these wonderful things. Don't you love that name!

THE RANSOM

Thou, Lord, art our father; thy name is our Ransomer from old. Isaiah 63:16, N.E.B.

In the Middle Ages the son of a prince would leave home at the age of 11 or 12 to serve in the court of another prince who had agreed to teach the boy all the skills and manners of a knight. William of Orange was 11 when he inherited his title to the principality of Orange, a tiny independent hamlet completely surrounded by France. The same year his father took him to the court of Emperor Charles V in Brussels, where his education began in earnest.

Later, when Prince William had a son of his own, he sent him to the court of Philip II the son of King Charles. And while the boy was busily learning the art of jousting and court politics his father took up the cause of the Dutch Protestants. Considering Prince William to be at war with Spain, Philip immediately treated the son as a hostage. Whenever he could, the lonely and frightened boy wrote to his father, begging that he not be forgotten and that he be saved.

When the Netherlands soldiers captured the Spanish Count Bossu, the Dutch began to talk of exchanging him for one of their own prisoners of war—Sainte Aldegonde. But the Prince of Orange would hear none of it. He would ransom his own son first.

Ransom is a sweet word to a prisoner or a slave. It is the price of freedom. When a slave was placed on the auctioneer's block and men bid for him, the slave usually had little interest in the process. When the money exchanged hands, he was still a slave. He was not free to choose the type of work he enjoyed. Nor could he decide where he would live, and often he was separated from his wife and children. But occasionally we hear of slaves whom someone bought for a good price and then told them that they might go free. More than one slave chose to work for the man who freed him—out of gratitude.

When Jesus died on the cross, He paid the ransom that freed us from the slavery and guilt of sin. I'm so happy to be free I want to serve Jesus always. How about you?

WONDERFUL NAME

"Why do you ask my name, seeing it is wonderful?" Judges 13:18, R.S.V.

Ever since she had married Manoah she had dreamed of having children—a son to carry on the family name and a daughter for companionship. But over the years the couple had remained childless. Then one morning, as she weeded the garden and prayed earnestly for a child, an angel appeared with the good news of a promised son. After giving instructions about the training of the child, the angel disappeared, and Mrs. Manoah rushed home to share the glad news with her husband.

Overwhelmed by the responsibility of training a special child for the Lord, Manoah prayed for the angel's return so that he might inquire further about its upbringing. The angel reappeared and repeated his instructions to Manoah. Then Manoah begged the angel to stay and eat with them. "'If you detain me, I will not eat of your food,'" the angel said. "'But if you make ready a burnt offering, then offer it to the Lord'" (verse 16). Before preparing the sacrifice Manoah asked, "'What is your name?'" (verse 17). To which the angel replied, "'Why do you ask my name, seeing it is wonderful?'"

"So Manoah took the kid . . . , and offered it upon the rock to the Lord, to him who works wonders. And when the flame went up toward heaven from the altar, the angel of the Lord ascended in the flame of the altar while Manoah and his wife looked on; and they fell on their faces to the ground. . . . And Manoah said to his wife, 'We shall surely die, for we have seen God'" (verses 19-22).

The sight of an angel awed Samson's parents, particularly after they discovered that His name was Wonderful. As you kneel in prayer this morning and pray to your wonderful God, imagine yourself in His presence, speaking to a real Being—because He is.

CHANGE YOUR NAME

The disciples were first called Christians at Antioch. Acts 11:26, N.I.V.

Alexander the Great, the great Greek leader who conquered the world in three years, was greatly honored and admired by his people. One day his officers brought before him a soldier charged with disorderly conduct. "What is your name?" the great commander asked.

"Alexander," the man replied.

"Young man," Alexander the Great demanded again. "What is your name?"

"Alexander," came the reply.

"Young man," the commander thundered. "Either change your ways or change your name."

Do you call yourself a Christian? Do you need to change your ways so as not to dishonor His wonderful name?

What is a Christian? The disciples and early believers did not call themselves Christians. In their reverence for the Master's name they felt undeserving to use His name.

After the death of Stephen, the Jews in Jerusalem persecuted the followers of Jesus so that they fled as far as Phoenicia and Cyprus. Wherever they went they witnessed to Jews of the saving power of their Lord. Some of the believers moved from Cyprus to Antioch "and began to speak to Greeks also, telling them the good news about the Lord Jesus" (verse 20). And God blessed their witness.

Barnabas and Paul converted many people there in the course of one year. "The disciples were first called Christians at Antioch." The Greeks noticed how the hard-working followers of Jesus were honest and took care of the poor. What makes them different? they wondered. Soon they realized that the believers were living what Jesus had taught them. So they called them Christians. Jesus can help you change your ways and bring honor to that name, too.

PROUD OF THAT NAME

However, if you suffer as a Christian, do not be ashamed, but praise God that you bear that name. 1 Peter 4:16, N.I.V.

Most Americans believe in God, according to a 1981 Gallup poll. Seven people out of ten belong to a church or synagogue, and most say that they pray. Half of the people attend church every week, and nearly every American home has at least one Bible.

But underneath, things don't look all that great. Only half the adults polled could name four or more of the Ten Commandments, and one fourth of the teenagers had never opened a Bible. Most people prayed only when they wanted to ask God for something—as if God was a heavenly Santa Claus. While it may be easy to call yourself a Christian in the United States, being a Christian—living like Jesus would if He were in your shoes—is not always easy.

When his dad transferred to a small town in the South, Gary had to finish the eighth grade in public school. "It's only for a little while," he moaned. "Next year I will be in academy." Gary could tell that some of the fellows in his class were Christians. They didn't use bad language and, well, Gary felt that he could trust them.

"Which church do you attend?" Shawn asked as the two boys walked home together after school the second day. What would you have said? "Oh, a little church you never heard of." Not Gary. He liked his church. "I'm a Seventh-day Adventist," he answered. Shawn didn't ask any more questions, but Gary wished he would. He would have liked to explain what the name meant. Wisely he decided to live his beliefs so Shawn could see what a Seventh-day Adventist was.

Unfortunately for Gary, Shawn was a good friend when he and Gary were alone. But at school he often made fun of Gary, calling him a "peanut." Gary didn't like having his classmates laugh at him, but he decided to praise God that he bore His name. He laughed good-naturedly when teased and tried to befriend someone else who was the butt of everyone's jokes. What would you have done had you been in Gary's shoes?

AWESOME NAME

Holy and awesome is his name. The fear of the Lord is the beginning of wisdom. Psalm 111:9, 10, N.I.V.

When you pray, "Hallowed be Thy name," you are saying that the name of our great God is special, and you will remember to use it reverently. Jesus came to earth to bring the good news that God loves us and is on our side. We need not be afraid of Him, but we should fear to dishonor His name.

Pete couldn't remember how he lost his driver's license, but it had been gone for more than a year and he had not bothered to replace it. "Shouldn't you have it replaced?" his friend Bob asked. "I mean, you could be in trouble if a policeman stopped you." But Pete wasn't afraid—he could talk his way out of anything.

Pete and Bob were driving the college van the morning they were stopped. When the officer asked to see his license Pete put on a great performance. He explained how he had rushed out of the house without it and how it was his first day on the job. His story was probably all the more convincing because Pete looks like a Christian—the kind of person you could trust.

I'm worried about Pete's story. And I'm worried about Pete. He probably feels great about not getting caught that day. But I'm afraid for God's name. What might happen when Pete doesn't produce his license within the time the police officer gave him? What if the officer discovers what really happened? Will he ever again trust someone who looks like a Christian? And suppose he noticed the name of the college on the side of the van—what will he think of Adventists? Or someone with a convincing story that is true and who deserves to be trusted? Might he or she suffer because Pete misrepresented the truth?

"The fear of the Lord is the beginning of wisdom." Caring about living like we know Him shows that we hallow His name. Ask Him to help you hallow that name today.

"I HAVE LONGINGS"

I will be glad and rejoice in you; I will sing praise to your name, O Most High. Psalm 9:2, N.I.V.

Opal Whiteley, a sensitive child born at the turn of the century, began to keep a diary while only 5 or 6 years old. A 5-year-old who could print on scraps of paper the deepest thoughts of her heart is rare indeed. One entry in Opal's diary begins:

"Today I went not to school.
The mama did have me cut potatoes into pieces.
Tonight and tomorrow night the grownups
will plant the pieces of potatoes.
After, the ones with eyes on them
will have baby potatoes under the ground.
Up above the ground
they will be growing leaves and flowers.
One must leave an eye
on every piece of potato one plants.
It won't grow if you don't.
It can't see how to grow
without its eye. . . .
I did have meditations about what things
the eyes of potatoes do see there in the ground.
I have thinks they do have seeing
of black velvet moles
and large earthworms.
I have longing for more eyes.
There is much to see in this world all about." *

Of all the Bible writers, King David is probably the most loved. Like Opal he had "longing for more eyes" to see the glories of God. The mighty works of Creation filled him with praise and adoration for the Creator and for His mighty name. Let's open our eyes today and look for evidences of God's love and might. Maybe we'll sense something new and special in that name.

---

* Opal Whiteley, *Opal,* arranged and adapted by Jane Boulton (New York: Macmillan, 1976), pp. 110, 111.

WHY LIE?

I speak the truth in Christ—I am not lying, my conscience confirms it in the Holy Spirit. Romans 9:1, N.I.V.

Your favorite aunt has waited years for a baby. At last she announces the news of the glad arrival. You can hardly wait to see your new cousin. When your uncle stops by the house he bubbles over with a description of his son and heir. "I have to see that baby!" you declare and demand to be taken to see him. With much fuss your aunt produces little Eustace for you to admire. Standing on tiptoes to get a good look, you are horrified by the striking resemblance to E.T. He's positively ugly, you think.

"How do you like your cousin?" your aunt asks. Can you tell the truth and risk hurting her feelings? Or is it OK to lie and say that he is beautiful.

Suppose you were Corrie ten Boom's sister, Nollie, hiding Jews in the house during World War II. Soldiers burst in and ask you if the young blonde woman seated at the table is a Jew. She doesn't look like one. If you tell the truth they will send her to the gas chamber. Is it OK to lie? Nollie thought it wasn't. She told the truth and the occupation forces imprisoned both her and the Jew. Corrie ten Boom admitted that she would never have told the truth under those special circumstances. What would you have done?

According to the experts, people in America don't trust each other to tell the truth anymore. Most people don't believe that government officials tell the truth, and nearly half don't even believe their doctor. I think it's time to stand up with the apostle Paul on the side of telling the truth, don't you? Then people can depend on us to mean what we say.

That doesn't mean that we should go around hurting people's feelings. But let's find truthful compliments. Instead of saying, "I like your new dress," when we don't at all, let's say, "That color (or whatever) looks good on you," knowing that we have told the truth.

HE AIN'T GOT NO NAME

"One will say, 'I belong to the Lord'; another will call himself by the name of Jacob; still another will write on his hand, 'The Lord's,' and will take the name Israel." Isaiah 44:5, N.I.V.

"Can you remember something that your son did to make you especially happy?" someone asked Pastor Max Church. The pastor scratched his head thoughtfully before replying. "Once when Max Junior was trying to entertain some house guests he told them proudly: 'I have my father's name.' That made me proud."

People often go through a stage when they hate their name—especially the middle one. But later they come to treasure it—not necessarily because it sounds good after all, but because it is their own. Married people express their attachment for each other by sharing the same name.

I didn't think I particularly liked my name until the time I heard Chip call it. I had moved to a new school where I knew nobody. Seldom did anyone but the teacher call me by name. But when Chip called me clear across the parking lot just to say Hi, I knew I belonged.

Elder Tom Ashlock tells of a little boy sitting in the gravel path in front of a row house in the city. Tom felt the little boy's gaze riveted on the car as he parked. "Hello, Tiger," he called, trying to spark some interest. "What's your name?" The little fellow shifted his vacant stare to Tom's face. "He ain't got no name," a 6-year-old girl called from the porch.

"Well, what do you call him?" Pastor Ashlock persisted.

"Nothin'! His gramps brings him here, and we just keeps him."

Who could blame a person for staring vacantly into space when nobody recognizes him as a person—no one calls him by name! Whatever you think of your name at this stage of your life, rejoice that God knows you by name. And by showing your love and respect for Him you are stamping His name on your life.

CHEAP TALK

"You shall not misuse the name of the Lord your God, for the Lord will not hold anyone guiltless who misuses his name." Exodus 20:7, N.I.V.

A visiting Canadian priest was a guest on the local TV talk show. Many different people called in to say Hello. Then a woman, flying high possibly from drinking something a lot stronger than water, called in and began to berate the priest with a string of bad language. The priest remained calm and friendly until the woman used the name of God in an offensive way. "Excuse me, ma'am," the host interrupted. "I do not appreciate your speaking about God in that way." And he hung up.

"Gee!" the next caller said, "that was disgusting. I don't believe in taking the Lord's name in vain."

"I'm glad to hear you say that," the priest chuckled good-naturedly. "By the way, did you know that the first word you used just now was a cheap corruption of the name Jesus?" The woman sounded embarrassed. But she got the point. No matter how politely used, we dishonor God when we speak His name carelessly. In fact, the commandment clearly shows that it is sin.

God must not let anyone cheapen His name or image. He's listening every time someone says, "Oh, Lord!" "My God!" "god-awful," or "for God's sake." In fact, before you say "Praise the Lord" or "God bless you," make sure that you are sincere and not just saying empty words. God pays attention when you use His name.

When you are tempted to use one of those expressions, think of yourself in that TV commercial. You are one of two people talking in the midst of a bustling scene—beside the pool, or on a busy street. You say, "Well, my broker is E. F. Hutton. And E. F. Hutton says . . . " Suddenly everyone has turned to listen. When you say God's name you have His instant attention. Don't disappoint Him with cheap talk or empty words.

IS THAT REALLY YOU?

"But I tell you that men will have to give account on the day of judgment for every careless word they have spoken." Matthew 12:36, N.I.V.

Yesterday I was walking through crowded streets after a rained-out parade in honor of our town's victorious Super Bowl football heroes. As we left the excitement and turned toward the Metro station a teenager crossing our path uttered a string of bad words that made me feel dirty just hearing them. I wondered whether he realized what he was telling everyone about himself.

What makes some people foul-mouthed, I wondered. I thought of Gene who developed into quite a garbage mouth in the seventh grade, to get attention. And Trudy, who used bad language to shock people. And Tom, who tried a bad word or two just because it was forbidden. But mostly, I decided, people use bad language to vent anger.

Bill attended an exclusive American school in a small south Indian resort town. One day he rode his American ten-speed bicycle to the only service station in order to inflate the tires. But he misjudged the pressure and his front tire blew up like a bomb. Instantly he filled the air with loud, angry cusswords. The few townspeople within hearing looked shocked. I felt embarrassed, because Bill represented a Christian school.

Gene, Trudy, Tom, Bill, you, and I " 'will have to give account on the day of judgment for every careless word [we] have spoken.' " Does that mean that some place God has a rule book of words not to use? If He does, He would need one book for every language with a list of exceptions for various places. For example, some words innocently used in America disgust people in England. If you are in England and you cut your thumb, you should not describe it as "bloody." But you may in North America. Does God keep up with the finer distinctions of such words? And should we?

Maybe a better question would be: Do I represent well the hallowed name of my Father when I speak?

WHAT KIND OF GOD?

Who, being in very nature God, did not consider equality with God something to be grasped, but made himself nothing, taking the very nature of a servant. Philippians 2:6, 7, N.I.V.

Hearing excited squeals of merriment from up the street, I wandered along to see what was generating the fun. Kathy stood in the middle of their lawn laughing hysterically as Potts, her enormous part-Dalmatian-part-boxer, leaped into the air trying to catch a balloon. But each time it bounced off his nose and sailed out of reach. Finally the old mutt speared it with a tooth and barked angrily when it popped.

"You know," Kathy panted, "Potts is so funny. I wish I could be him for a while. What fun it would be!" As a lover of poodles I had never particularly admired Potts. As the lord of our mission compound, he often made enemies of us who owned lesser breeds. Once he almost swallowed my dog in one bite.

"I don't know, Kathy," I responded unenthusiastically. "Are you sure you want to be Potts? I mean, do you want to sleep in the doghouse and drink your water without ice cubes? Not to mention scratching for fleas and eating dog chow!"

She grew thoughtful. "I guess not," she admitted when she faced it, the difference between her life and Potts's was too great.

The God of heaven once stopped to consider the difference between His life and ours. And though His was light-years removed from ours, He stooped to our level. He became a babe in a smelly stable. At a time when life was none too comfortable, He chose to join a humble carpenter's family. He ate their plain food and wore their scratchy clothes. He lived like them, laughed like them, sweated like them. What kind of God would do that? One who loved so much that He set aside His kingly power and name. Aren't you glad He did? Giving up an hour or two on a Sabbath afternoon to cheer up someone who is sick seems like a very small sacrifice by comparison, doesn't it?

THE SHEPHERD

I am the good shepherd, and know my sheep, and am known of mine. John 10:14.

"Just look who He hangs around with!" the scribes and Pharisees muttered. But Jesus was proud of His friends. "If any of you had a hundred sheep and lost one, you'd go look for it," He reminded them. "You'd get excited when you found it. Well, I get excited about finding lost people." That's why people call Him the Good Shepherd.

One minute we had been standing together beside the Christmas card display of a large department store, and the next he was gone. Panic gripped my heart.

Remembering how it felt to be lost in a crowd, I worried about how alone and scared he must feel. After looking up and down the nearest aisles, I rushed over to the toy section where my other two brothers were secretively selecting their gifts.

"I can't find Bernard," I blurted. "What shall I do?"

After a quick search of the area we headed toward the store manager's office, near the office where Mother paid on the monthly account. And there we found the missing boy chatting to a security man as if nothing had happened. Though our rescue would not make headlines, the joy and relief we felt would have done justice to any dramatic rescue. And ever since, I have taken special delight in stories of rescued people.

One story I particularly enjoyed involved a young man who jumped in front of an oncoming subway train to rescue a little girl who had fallen onto the tracks. With the deafening noise of the onrushing train in their ears, most of the commuters waiting on the platform thought that the child was beyond help.

But a young man left the safety of the crowd and, jumping onto the tracks, scooped up the child and threw her to waiting arms on the platform. Helping hands drew him to safety seconds before the train crashed by.

People slapped his back and shook his hand. But their relief and excitement were nothing compared with the celebration in heaven over the rescue of a lost sheep. To the Good Shepherd each one of them is dear—including you and me.

SAVIOUR

For the Son of man is come to seek and to save that which was lost. Luke 19:10.

Have you noticed how often we call Jesus, Saviour? What does that particular name mean? Dwight Nelson was not yet 4 years old when he discovered the meaning. When he wandered away from his parents at a corn roast and fell from the dock into a fog-enshrouded lake, nobody might ever have known what happened to him. But an army chaplain and his wife, returning from a boat trip, saw Dwight's still form lying face down on the water. They jumped into the deep water and rescued him.

Dwight tells of how he grew up listening to the often-repeated story of how someone had saved him from drowning. And as he grew older he sometimes wondered who his savior was. He had graduated from college when, at a potluck, the various people seated around the circle introduced themselves. The last couple in the circle, Chaplain and Mrs. Bowen, asked him if he had ever heard the story of how he was rescued from drowning.

"Oh, yes," Dwight exclaimed. "Many times. And I always wondered who saved me so I could thank them. I owe my life to that couple."

"Shall we tell him?" Chaplain Bowen teased. And then he revealed the fact that he and his wife were the ones to whom Dwight owed his life. Dwight jumped to his feet and hugged the Bowens tight. With misty eyes and choked voice he thanked them for what they had done for him.

"I have found my savior—that is, my small 's' savior," he says. But Dwight knows he will feel even happier when he meets his "big 'S' Saviour"—the One who gave up all heaven to plunge into the muddied waters of human existence to save us all from sin. Meeting his "small 's' savior" helped Dwight to want to know his "big 'S' Saviour" better. To Dwight the name Saviour means love. What does it mean to you?

PEACE CHILD

But now, this is what the Lord says . . . "Fear not, for I have redeemed you; I have called you by name; you are mine." Isaiah 43:1, N.I.V.

When the Richardsons went to work among one of the tribes of New Guinea they could hardly wait to tell them of Jesus. But first the couple had to learn the language. Gradually they began to compile a list of words with the help of villagers. And the more they learned of the language the more they discovered about the people.

Don Richardson gathered the men of the tribe about him one day and began to tell them the story of Jesus. They listened in silence, trying to understand the strange events. When they came to the crucifixion they applauded Judas. They thought he was the hero of the story. Admiring his treachery and deceit, they could not identify with someone who would willingly die for any reason, much less for love.

Then one day all the men of the tribe prepared to battle their nearest neighbors. The two groups had been friends until recently. And they knew that Don Richardson had been trying to teach them a better way to settle differences. They genuinely wanted to please him. So the chief of the village called for someone to bring a baby boy. The people all approved, but nobody wanted to part with a child. Then, with tears streaming down his face, one father took his baby boy and carried him across the lines of fighting and presented him to a man from the other tribe.

With proper solemnity the other man accepted the child. He would bring up the boy as his own son. The whole tribe would carefully guard the child's life. Because bound up in this child was the peace and happiness of them all.

That night, as the men explained to Don Richardson what had happened, he knew that he had found the perfect way to explain Jesus the Redeemer. He came to earth as a Peace Child. He took our name and became part of our tribe so that someday we might forever bear His name and live with Him. Jesus became our Redeemer.

THE PEACEFUL SCENE

The Lord is my shepherd; I shall not want. He maketh me to lie down in green pastures: he leadeth me beside the still waters. Psalm 23:1, 2.

Why is it that when the bustle and care of everyday life gets you down, green pastures and still waters sound good? Is it because you think of yourself one-on-one with Jesus? When you put yourself into that psalm, do you think of the Good Shepherd and choice grazing land where water fills safe, quiet pools? Do you see yourself resting with Him and talking alone—not in the midst of a noisy flock of sheep. Most of the time you don't relish such an inactive scene. It's when the challenges pile too close for comfort and threaten to get you down that you wistfully remember the Shepherd.

I once read of a young sailor who liked to read the Shepherd's Psalm when he felt the first tinges of loneliness coming on. As a young American sailor during World War II he sometimes didn't glimpse land for weeks on end, and time hung heavy on his hands. Sometimes he wondered whether he would ever see home again, and when familiar faces sprang to life in his imagination, he longed to feel them close.

One night as he sat alone in the radio shack, Grayce read the Psalm again. The words brought such comfort that he wondered if his friends had discovered its beauty and peace. Taking his position at the wireless he began to tap out the words: "The Lord is my shepherd; I shall not want. He maketh me to lie down in green pastures." (The feel of dry ground would cheer any sailor's heart right then.) "He leadeth me beside the still waters." (A rest from the rolling, swaying motion would be rest indeed!) "He restoreth my soul." (How many of the men needed peace of mind? Grayce knew that he did.) Busily he tapped away his message of cheer. "Surely goodness and mercy shall follow me all the days of my life: and I will dwell in the house of the Lord for ever" (verses 1-3, 6). Had anyone heard his message? More than a dozen operators signaled back, "Amen."

WHEN WORDS DON'T COUNT

Dear children, let us not love with words or tongue but with actions and in truth. 1 John 3:18, N.I.V.

When Jesus told His disciples about His newly established kingdom, He surprised them. They expected a wonderful domain established by power and force. But instead Jesus set up a kingdom of love in men's hearts. Loving people—even enemies—was to be at the heart of it.

"You can't love *everyone,*" Richie fussed. "Those small boys need a lesson in respect. I'm tired of you telling me I mustn't fight."

"You remind me of a girl I read about once," his mother said. "Her family had moved to an inner-city neighborhood, and older girls bothered Addie on her way home from school. She wanted to fight them, but couldn't because of how her mother had said to love her enemies."

"Out of love for them she should have taught them respect," Richie interrupted. "That's why you sometimes spanked us when we were little."

Mrs. Anderson laughed. "That was exactly what the girl said: 'I love them, but I want to teach them a lesson.' But her mother had a better idea. She said that loving with words didn't count. You have to love with actions, too."

Richie looked doubtful. "That's hard," he said.

And it is, too. It's easy to say "I love you, Mother," and run out to play and leave her with all the work to do. It's just as easy to pray, "Thy kingdom come," and not do anything to make life nicer on this earth.

But when we accept Jesus into our hearts, we belong to His kingdom of love. That means we live by the rules of that kingdom now. And love for Jesus makes us want to treat other people with kindness. When Jesus says, "Love your enemies," He knows that Richie can't do it on his own, and neither can you or I. But we can do it through Him.

When Richie decided to take that promise and put it into action, he didn't need to fight for self-respect. God gave him that, too. It's a wonderful thing, God's kingdom of love!

HEIRS

Now if we are children, then we are heirs—heirs of God and coheirs with Christ, if indeed we share in his sufferings in order that we may also share in his glory. Romans 8:17, N.I.V.

The exciting thing about God is that we don't have to wait until the "sweet by and by" to be His children. If we accept Jesus we are God's children *now,* and that means we are also His heirs.

Our pastor recently told us the story of Wilma, who, since her teens had known that she was an heir to her grandfather's fortune. Her portion was kept in trust, earning interest, until Wilma's twenty-first birthday. More than once she dreamed about the things she'd like to buy with that money. But on her twenty-first birthday she was glad she had not received it sooner, because she would have wasted it.

Wilma went to her grandmother's home to receive her inheritance. "You know that you are one of fifty grandchildren," her grandmother said. "And I can assure you that, had your grandfather known which of you would have used this money for the best good of humanity, that person alone would have received it all. But since he had no way of knowing, he divided it equally among all of you."

For the first time Wilma realized that an inheritance brought not only wealth, but also responsibility. She wondered if that was why her grandfather had always seemed so serious. He had been generous with his love and praise and never missed a birthday, but nobody could accuse him of spending lavishly.

Now Wilma resolved to show the family that she was a worthy heir to her grandfather's sense of responsibility. She would neither waste her money nor horde it selfishly. As heirs to God's fabulous blessings and to everlasting life, I wonder how we could show that we accept our responsibilities? Maybe we could begin by setting aside part of our allowance for offerings. What do you think?

EASTER AND EGGS

By faith we understand that the universe was formed at God's command, so that what is seen was not made out of what was visible. Hebrews 11:3, N.I.V.

In some lands people associate Easter with decorating eggs. To many people, eggs symbolize resurrection and life, for the fertilized egg contains the life of a tiny chick. So people paint on the eggs intricate designs representing different aspects of the gospel.

The famous nursery rhyme about an egg is supposed to have originally been a riddle that asked, "What, when broken, can never be repaired—not even by the strongest or the wisest man?" And, of course, the answer is an egg. For, just as "all the king's horses and all the king's men" couldn't repair the smashed Humpty-Dumpty, so nobody can rebuild broken eggshells. You have to live with the mess.

Our world is not quite the same shape as an ordinary egg, but in a sense you could say that an egg represents the circle of the earth. Can you imagine its beauty when it first came from the hand of the Creator? Imagine the exquisite trees and flowers that adorned its shell. Adam and Eve were the crowning decoration on an earth that He meant to be one joyful kingdom of His love.

But that was before the first tragic Humpty-Dumpty story. Adam and Eve's disobedience shattered the fragile shell of the egg. And we've been living with the mess ever since. Sin, suffering, and dying entered our world, and not one of us may escape their fearful consequences. But in the *real* Humpty-Dumpty story the King Himself comes down to clean up the mess. And He promises that one day the egg will be made new—the perfect kingdom of love will be put back together. And that isn't all. He promises to restore the original perfection of our own Humpty-Dumpty hearts if we believe. And we don't have to wait. He's making people over, all the time. Isn't that worth painting an egg in celebration?

A NEW THING

"Forget the former things; do not dwell on the past. See, I am doing a new thing!" Isaiah 43:18, 19, N.I.V.

I noticed her on the playground the first day of school. "Who's the new girl with glasses?" I asked the teacher on duty.

Leonie was new and needed friends, the teacher said. Though she was in a lower grade, I could help her feel at home. "By the way," she added, "Leonie has Down's syndrome."

I knew that Jesus wanted me to make friends with Leonie, but I couldn't. Whenever I saw her in the hall I said Hello, but that was all. One day she asked me to help her read a storybook. I could understand why she required assistance to read it. But I wished that she hadn't picked on me. What would my friends think?

One day that winter I had to stay in at recess for talking back to the teacher. I wished I hadn't done it. Now he was out on the playground catching the softball with my friends, and I couldn't join in.

Overcome with misery, I hadn't noticed her come in until she slipped her arm around my neck and patted my back. She wasn't ashamed of me, I thought as I looked into her eyes, so why had I been ashamed of her?

"Leonie, you're a great friend," I whispered. "You bring any book you want, and I'll be glad to help you read it." I truly meant it.

I changed schools soon after that, but I never forgot the new thing that she sparked in my heart.

Some friends of mine have four children, one of whom has Down's syndrome, as Leonie has. Every time I see them with Danny I marvel at the new thing Jesus has done for them. I know of no eighth-grade boy who likes to baby-sit a 2-year-old, but Lauren good-naturedly cares for little Danny, making him feel special. And that makes others want to accept Danny too.

Why not let God do something new for your heart as you make somebody feel special today.

LIGHTHOUSES

"Let your light shine before men, that they may see your good deeds and praise your Father in heaven." Matthew 5:16, N.I.V.

The story is told of a captain of a great ship who noticed a flashing light in its path one dark night. Immediately he signaled ahead to warn the captain of the other vessel. "Alter your course 10 degrees south." Back came the reply, "Alter your course 10 degrees north." Again the captain transmitted the message, this time adding, "I am the captain." Back came the same reply, with the addition "I am seaman third class Jones."

Deciding to put fear into Seaman Jones, the captain commanded, "Alter your course 10 degrees south—I am a battleship."

"Alter your course 10 degrees north," Jones persisted. "I am a lighthouse." Of course you know who veered—the captain. He knew better than to argue with a lighthouse.

Jesus is the Light of the world—the Lighthouse of truth. But He needs each one of us to also act as warnings of danger and beacons of truth. That's why He said, "'You are the light of the world. A city on a hill cannot be hidden. Neither do people light a lamp and put it under a bowl. Instead they put it on its stand, and it gives light to everyone. In the same way, let your light shine before men, that they may see your good deeds and praise your Father in heaven'" (verses 14-16).

Simon felt bad about some of the things he had been doing. When he could stand the guilt no longer he told his mother about it. "Everyone does it," he said. "They won't listen to me when I tell them not to do it."

"But Si," his mother said, "one person can make a difference. If you stand for the truth you might help someone else do what is right. Even if you help only one person, it's worth a try." The boy agreed. The next morning in the math test when the others copied each other's answers, he refused to be a part of it. Some of the fellows teased him, but by the end of the week Randy and Jon had admitted he was right and promised to change their ways. When you love Jesus and obey His commandments, you too may be a lighthouse.

LIKE BREAD DOUGH

"The kingdom of heaven is like yeast that a woman took and mixed into a large amount of flour until it worked all through the dough." Matthew 13:33, N.I.V.

"Wow! Do you make bread?" Billie Henderson asked as he sniffed the tantalizing aroma from the Taylors' place. "Would you teach me to make it?"

Mrs. Taylor agreed to, and the next afternoon she helped him put on a big blue apron and scrub his hands. He measured out the flour and watched as she shook some little tan-colored granules into a small bowl. "Yeast," she said. "You stir it into this warm water and add a tablespoon of sugar." When the yeast was stirred well he left it to stand for a while. Mrs. Taylor said that the yeast would grow. Billie waited for it to sprout and grow leaves. But it just produced a lot of foam and air bubbles.

He stirred the flour while Mrs. Taylor poured in the yeast mixture and some salt and oil. When the dough became stiff she took over the mixing until the dough was just right for kneading. Billie couldn't quite get used to kneading. Taking the outside edges of the dough, he pulled them up on top and then pushed them down into the middle of the dough. Sometimes he felt like he was pummeling a floppy ball.

"What are we doing this for?" he asked.

She explained how that kneading made the dough smooth and elastic and spread the yeast thoroughly throughout the mass. After they left the dough to rise in a covered Tupperware bowl for an hour, Billie was surprised to see how the dough had doubled in size.

"That little packet of yeast did that?" he asked. Mrs. Taylor nodded.

Whenever Billie reads that the kingdom of heaven is like making bread, he thinks he knows what it means. He gets excited to think that God's love can grow in him like yeast in the dough. And his own good influence can quietly work for the good of a whole neighborhood.

NEW HEARTS AND MINDS

A new heart also will I give you, and a new spirit will I put within you: and I will take away the stony heart out of your flesh, and I will give you an heart of flesh. Ezekiel 36:26.

I once read a parable of a wolf who used to hang around with a flock of sheep. At first the sheep would run away from the wolf because they feared him. But a kindly sheep helped the wolf dress himself in a sheepskin. Now the sheep accepted the wolf. But he knew he was not one of them for, no matter how hard he tried, he could not get used to eating grass. "Your problem is that you are still a wolf at heart," a wise old sheep told him.

You and I are like that wolf. We want to belong to God's kingdom of grace. And we have promised to serve Him always. But we keep doing things that hurt God. Sometimes we sin before we realize what we are doing. At other times we know, yet do it anyway. But afterward we feel bad and ask for forgiveness. And Jesus not only forgives and loves us, but He offers us a solution to our problem—a new heart.

While a handful of people have actually had a heart transplant, and though the second heart has extended the lives of some, the results were not quite as exciting as expected. Doctors recently invented a machine that would act as a heart for Barney Clark. But had he ever regained good health he still could not have moved away from that life-giving device.

Jesus offers not a heart transplant, but a *new* heart—a brand new way of looking at things. In the Old Testament a "pure heart" meant a mind tuned to God. A "heavy heart" referred to a sad feeling. So a "new heart" is a changed attitude—a feeling of love for God that makes one want to do right. I'd like a new heart, wouldn't you? "Create in me a clean heart, O God; and renew a right spirit within me" (Ps. 51:10). Is that your prayer today? If so, remember that God never despises a "broken spirit," a repentant or a "wounded heart." They are the only hearts He can renew.

A KINGDOM FOR YOU

"And I confer on you a kingdom, just as my Father conferred one on me, so that you may eat and drink at my table in my kingdom." Luke 22:29, N.I.V.

On His last day with His disciples, Jesus plans a pleasant meal in an upstairs room, where He will share good news about the coming kingdom with His twelve friends.

Everyone is tired when they gather for the Last Supper. They can't bring themselves to eat a meal with dusty feet, so they wait for someone to wash their feet. When nobody offers, Jesus brings water and towels and does it Himself. Peter hates to see Jesus doing a servant's work. He wonders why someone else didn't offer to help and protests that he is willing to eat with dirty feet.

The other disciples feel vaguely troubled over the matter. Someone should have taken care of washing the feet. They look about for someone to blame—the person who is least among them. And who was that?

"Don't look at *me,*" Peter says. "You heard Him say that I could have no part with Him unless He washed my feet." John knows *he* is not the least important disciple—he's the one Jesus loves. And so they argue until Jesus intervenes by explaining that earthly kings tell other people to do their dirty work. But in the heavenly kingdom only the person who puts on an apron and serves everyone else has a place there.

"'The greatest among you should be like the youngest,'" Jesus says, "'and the one who rules like the one who serves. . . . I confer on you a kingdom'" (verses 26-29).

Just as the King of the universe stooped to humbly serve His disciples, I, as an heir to that kingdom, must serve others. The truly great people in the world today are not the movie stars who have someone to dress them and fix their hair, not the rich and pompous, but people who, forgetting themselves, roll up their sleeves and get to work.

So what am I waiting for? I have work to do.

THE MUSTARD SEED

"The kingdom of heaven is like a mustard seed, which a man took and planted in his field." Matthew 13:31, N.I.V.

"This *dahl* doesn't taste quite right," I told Lally, an Indian friend who had come to stay with us so she could attend a Christian school. "I know," she replied. "It needs mustard seed." So, before my next lesson in cooking Indian food I purchased some. But Lally shook her head. It wasn't the right thing. So Lally bought some mustard seed from a little Indian store.

"Those can't be seeds," I said. "They're too small." But next time we cooked red lentils Lally threw a spoonful of mustard seeds into some hot oil. The seeds popped like popcorn. And though each seed doubled its size, it was still tinier than a pin head. But how they flavored that *dahl!*

Now, apparently those same seeds will sprout when planted and develop into a large bush that branches out like a small tree. It is strong enough to support the weight of a bird on its branches. How can the mustard seed tell us something about God's kingdom of grace? First of all, it shows that the kingdom of God begins small, within us. And as it grows it makes a good deal of difference in our lives.

When Andy accepted Jesus he didn't know about the mustard seed. But he did know that things needed to change in his life. And the more he came to know Jesus the more he loved. And the more he loved, the more he wanted to change. Andy hated the way he felt angry when people disagreed with him.

Before he accepted Jesus he would clench his fists and start swinging before he had time to think. But one of the first signs of the kingdom of heaven in his life was his growing self-restraint. Now Andy is a hero to the younger boys at school. They see that he isn't ashamed of being a Christian on the ball field and in the locker room. Without realizing it, Andy influences them to do the right thing, too.

Maybe you can't see the mustard bush flourishing in the garden of your life. But don't give up. Someday others will.

ZAPPING KIDS FOR GOD

Suffer the little children to come unto me, and forbid them not: for of such is the kingdom of God. Mark 10:14.

"Sometimes God talks to you and you just don't listen," Pastor Dwight Wymer, of Grand Rapids, Michigan, told the boys and girls of his church. "But sometimes God can shock you into listening." To demonstrate his point Pastor Wymer used a specially wired "hot seat" to send an electric shock into the buttocks of children who were not listening.

"The shock hurt me until I went home and got into the tub," one 8-year-old told reporters. Seven-year-old Pat volunteered for the "hot seat." He wouldn't do it again, though, he says. "It hurt. I wanted to cry but all my friends were watching." Pastor Wymer stopped using the hot seat and apologized for offending anyone after newspapers carried a story about it.

How would you feel if God zapped you every time you dozed off in church? Do you think Jesus might ever have fallen asleep in church when He was small? Does He understand how hard it is to sit on a hard, sticky pew when your feet feel like dancing? I'm sure He does. He notices how long you sit quietly to show your love and respect for Him.

But just supposing someone zapped you to make you wake up and listen. How would you feel? Surprised? Angry? Would you get a sudden impression that God loved you? Or would you feel more like a failure that nobody loved?

Once when a village refused entry to Jesus and His disciples, two of His disciples wanted Jesus to zap that village. "Why don't you bring fire down from heaven?" they suggested. But that is not God's way. Even when you turn Him away, He goes on loving you. "Let the children come to Me," He says. And He does nothing to frighten them away. He waits until you are quite ready to come by yourself.

You are no longer a little child—you're tough and grown up. But Jesus says to you, "The kingdom of heaven is made up of people who love and trust as they did when they were little."

EVERYONE FOR HIMSELF

"At that time the kingdom of heaven will be like ten virgins who took their lamps and went out to meet the bridegroom." Matthew 25:1, N.I.V.

One of our family's valued possessions is a tiny clay lamp from the time of Christ. You could easily hide it in your closed hand. While I haven't tried to fill it with oil, I suspect that it would hold little more than one tablespoonful. I can just imagine the ten bridesmaids standing in readiness for the wedding procession. Their lamps, like glowing dots, will mark the way for the bridal party. But when the bridegroom does not come at the appointed time they adjust their plans and decide to rest until he arrives.

Supposing that such a tiny flame burns oil slowly, five of the girls place their lamps in a safe place and lie down to sleep. But the other five think ahead and snuff out their lamps to conserve fuel. By the time the bridegroom arrives the first five girls realize that they are almost out of oil and ask to borrow some from the others. But each has brought only enough for her own lamp and has none to spare.

At this point I usually have difficulty with this story. I wonder why the girls don't share the oil around so that at least each has enough to get to the reception. But the maidens with the lamps have a special purpose in the wedding procession. The shared oil will soon run out. To march without a light would embarrass them. Like a flower girl with no flowers or a Bible boy with no Bible. What point would there be in sharing the oil for a while and then leaving the wedding party in darkness later on? Each girl was on her own when it came to keeping her lamp alight. This is especially true of membership in God's kingdom. Because my parents belong to Jesus and are saved does not guarantee my salvation. I must take care of my own "oil" during this time of delay, knowing that when the Bridegroom appears, it is only my choice that counts.

HOW TO BE SAVED

Believe on the Lord Jesus Christ, and thou shalt be saved. Acts 16:31.

Doug did not like himself. For that matter, he didn't like anybody. So he found himself a nice little cave 3,500 feet up on a mountain near Palm Springs. Inside the cave he found a Bible. Having lots of time and nothing much else to do, Doug began reading the New Testament. And that's how he met Jesus Christ. He felt drawn to this Man who could look any person squarely in the eye and say, "Him that cometh to me I will in no wise cast out" (John 6:37). Gladly he gave his heart to the Lord.

Knowing that he could not live in an isolated cave the rest of his life, Doug began planning for the future. At the top of his list of things to do he wrote, "Search for the true church." As a result he went down to the city and visited the various churches, asking the pastors what he must do to join them. "You only need to believe," they would say.

Now Doug believed in Jesus, but he knew that wasn't enough. Why even the devil believes. He thought of the time he sailed around the Mediterranean. When the yacht ran into a storm all the passengers began to pray and promise God things if He would save them. But when the storm blew by, so did their promises.

Then Doug discovered James 1:22: "Be ye doers of the word, and not hearers only." Believing on Jesus means *hearing* and *doing,* he decided. Doug wondered what God wanted him to do. "God, show me the truth," he prayed one night sitting under the stars. The next day someone walked by his isolated cave and gave him a copy of the book *The Great Controversy,* by Ellen White. It helped him understand the Bible better.

Doug learned how to live what he believed. Also, God helped him change some of his bad habits. And that kind of believing brought Doug the happiness that he had been searching for all his life. At last he was part of God's kingdom of grace.

MOONBOWS

Now faith is being sure of what we hope for and certain of what we do not see. Hebrews 11:1, N.I.V.

Ever since I saw my first rainbow I have associated them with hope and wonder. Nothing in nature quite matches the brilliance of a complete bow arching across the heavens. It seems to raise the ceiling of my mind until it merges with the vaulted dome of the sky. Ordinary things of earth seem to shrink into insignificance. The only sight more magnificent is a double rainbow. But the most mysterious type of rainbow is called a moonbow, or lunar rainbow.

You have probably not heard of a moonbow before. That is because they are extremely rare. In fact, people have sighted them in only two places: Victoria Falls on the Zambezi River in Africa, and the Cumberland Falls in Kentucky. Scientists believe that moonbows occur in other places, too, but people have not been able to see them because they cannot stand in just the right places to view them.

Moonbows form when the light of a full moon shines on tiny drops of moisture formed by rain or mist. In order to see the moonbow, the moon must be behind you and low in the sky, with no rocks or trees blocking the moonlight or preventing you from standing where you could see the moonbow.

If you are fortunate enough to see one, it will appear as a ghostly white path of light. But if you photograph it, don't be surprised if it comes out on film looking like a rainbow. The film in your camera can pick up the colors because during a long exposure it is more sensitive to light than your eyes are.

That's how it is with faith—that inner eye by which Christians accept the promise of God's kingdom in their hearts. They can't see it. But bright moonbows of His love flash into their lives from time to time. Like when Tony felt desperately lonely in a new school. God opened his eyes to see someone else who was lonely. Ask Jesus to help you see the moonbow of His kingdom today.

YOU CHOOSE

Choose you this day whom ye will serve; . . . but as for me and my house, we will serve the Lord. Joshua 24:15.

Animals are born with inner promptings that urge them to do certain things without training from their parents. We call that *instinct*. Squirrels bury nuts, not because they know winter is coming, but because of instinct. Baby squirrels raised in warm, comfortable cages will try to bury nuts in the bare floor of the cage. They can't dig a hole, of course, but they paw the floor and drop the nut. They make motions in the air as if covering the nut even though it is in plain view. The squirrel seems satisfied with having gone through the motions.

You were born with the instinct to cry and suck. But they are almost your only instincts. You *learn* all the other skills you need in life. Already you have been learning for many years and you still have years of it ahead.

Long before you knew you were learning anything you felt the warmth of your parents' love. Learning to obey came more easily because you loved them. Then you discovered something that animals do not have—the power of choice. You could choose whether or not to come when someone called you. Because your safety at times depends upon your obedience, your parents used more than love to convince you to comply. Sometimes you felt a little persuasion warming your seat. Still, you learned your lessons well—how else would you have survived so long?

But nevertheless, every day you find yourself some place where nobody is looking. And you decide whether or not to do the right thing. Like Billy. He knows why it is best not to smoke. But no one can stop him from hiding someplace and trying it out. Joshua knew that when he spoke to the children of Israel. He couldn't make their choices for them. "You choose whom you will serve," he said. "I will choose the Lord."

The experts say that man has an inborn need to worship someone. Today, why not exercise your choice to join God's kingdom and worship God in love. Don't be like the squirrel and just make the motions.

GOD'S HAPPINESS CLUB

Now when he saw the crowds, he went up on a mountainside and sat down. His disciples came to him, and he began to teach them. Matthew 5:1, 2, N.I.V.

When you were in the fourth grade did you ever start a club? If you did, you probably sat down with your charter members and decided on some rules—when you would meet and who could join. Jesus came to earth to form an exclusive club—a brotherhood, if you like. He called it the kingdom of heaven.

Every club has a purpose. Some meet to practice a particular sport. So you might have a road runners' club, or a tennis club. Or the club may form to promote learning—as in a stargazers' club, a Civil War club, or a stamp club. Some clubs organize to help people have fun. People pay hundreds of dollars to join a country club where they go to play golf or swim. They may also eat at the club and stay to watch movies or play cards.

The purpose of the kingdom of grace, the special club that Jesus started, is for learning and for practicing skills. But above all it is a club for pleasure. When Jesus gave the opening address that introduced His club and started the membership drive, He spoke first about the happiness that it would provide. In the introductory remarks He used the Greek word *makarioi* (which means "happy" or "fortunate") nine times. It was His way of saying that it's OK to want to feel happy. The Creator made us with the capacity to laugh and rejoice. We were meant to *enjoy* life as we live in harmony with God.

But somewhere along the way men lost the secret of happiness. And the more they search for it, the harder it is to find. Doug found that out when at 12 he started to smoke and drink. He thought it might bring him happiness. But it made him more miserable than ever. "It is so simple. How come it took me so long to figure it out?" he tells people now. "Happiness comes from obedience." That is why God set up His kingdom of grace in men's hearts.

Have you joined the club? Ask Jesus to show you true happiness as He helps you learn to obey.

HAPPILY POOR

Blessed are the poor in spirit: for theirs is the kingdom of heaven. Matthew 5:3.

Who may join God's exclusive club—the kingdom of heaven? The first point Jesus made when kicking off His membership drive was that the poor in spirit were the most welcome members. In fact, before applying for membership, you should check yourself to see if you qualify as poor in spirit.

Once two teenagers received invitations to take part in Sabbath school. The first had been rebellious lately, giving his teachers a rough time. He often preferred to stand around outside instead of going inside. When he did go and sit down he made jokes that cracked up those around him. But one day he took a second look at himself and realized that he didn't know God. If God came for me today I wouldn't be ready, he thought. And suddenly he wished that he knew how to be saved. He decided to listen in class and began reading his lesson quarterly again. The leader, noticing a change in the boy, asked him to give the prayer in Sabbath school.

The second boy had always been interested in spiritual things. The Sabbath school leaders could always count on him to take whatever part in the program that they asked. He had almost uninterrupted daily study as long as anyone could remember. When he heard who was to offer the prayer that morning it appalled him. Why did they ask *him* to pray? the second boy wondered. He will just make a mockery of prayer. They should have asked him to announce the song.

"Dear God," the first boy began. "Thank You for—er—that we can come here and learn about—er—You. And help us to listen to our—er—teachers." And then with a little catch in his voice like he might cry, he added, "Please forgive our sins and help us—er—to—do better. Amen." It shocked the second boy that the first one finished his prayer so soon, without any mention of the missionaries or the Bible. One of those two boys went home a member of God's kingdom. Which one do you think it was?

HAPPY FOR TEARS

Blessed are ye that weep now: for ye shall laugh. Luke 6:21.

The first thing you did when you came into the world was to cry. That cry cleared your lungs and enabled you to breathe. If you didn't cry by yourself the doctor slapped you until you did. But that cry produced no tears. It takes several days—sometimes weeks—for tears to form.

You soon learned that tears attracted attention, so you cried when you felt hungry or uncomfortable. Later you cried when you were angry or frustrated, or when someone hurt your feelings. Do you remember a time when you felt ashamed to have others see you crying? Perhaps they accused you of being a crybaby, and you wished you wouldn't cry so easily. Boys soon learn that society does not consider crying manly, and they feel more pressure to hold back their tears.

Solomon, the wisest man who lived, says in Ecclesiastes 3:4 that there is "a time to weep." The shortest verse in the Bible tells us that "Jesus wept" (John 11:35). In fact Jesus said, "Blessed [happy] are ye that weep now" (Luke 6:21). So tears are not all bad.

And what's in a tear? Mostly salt water plus some sugar, proteins, and an effective germ killer called lysozyme. As one writer put it, "Without tears, the eyes would be sitting ducts for infection." Maybe that is why tears are not considered dirty—unlike the other body excretions.

Specialists believe that when you continually fight the urge to cry you are asking for trouble. They suspect that suppressed tears may have links with bed-wetting, hives, and other problems. A recent experiment suggests that crying helps to rid the body of chemicals produced by stress.

So maybe we all should cry a little more. But be sure you cry for the right reasons. Crying to get your own way is childish. But crying because you hurt helps you bounce back quicker. Remember, God did not make or plan the evil that causes you to cry, but He did give you a way to release the tension you feel. And when you belong to God's kingdom on earth, you know that though you may cry today, He will bring you happiness.

A MAN'S MAN

Blessed are the meek: for they shall inherit the earth. Matthew 5:5.

Are you wondering what kind of people you will find in God's kingdom? The poor in spirit, the mournful, and the meek—what kind of person fits those three descriptions? It doesn't sound like your all-American hero, does it? Did you ever see Superman cry? Can you think of a meek star of the National Football League? Society looks up to people with power, wealth, and popularity. But the members of God's kingdom model themselves after Jesus.

What kind of man was Jesus? He was an outdoor person. His hair was often windblown, His skin tanned from walking by the sea. He knew who He was—He didn't copy the fashions of the day. Instead, He set His own pace. And because He understood Himself, He walked with an air of confidence. When the religious leaders confronted Him, He was not afraid to tell them that they were like their "father the devil." And it was no sissy that drove the money changers from the Temple.

Jesus would not have fit the macho image of today's male. Consider that tough, good-looking, hairy-chested type that you see in beer commercials. He demands respect because he has made it on his own. Can you imagine him admitting that he needs advice about anything? Yet Jesus spent hours talking with His Father. He prayed all night once. Jesus was not ashamed to admit that "'the Son can do nothing of his own accord, but only what he sees the Father doing; for whatever he does, that the Son does likewise'" (John 5:19, R.S.V.).

Can you picture the meekness of Jesus? Anger could flash from His eyes—so could comfort. And yet He could take time for little children. Although He spoke with the authority of a king, He wasn't too proud to do the work of a servant. At the Last Supper He washed the feet of His disciples—the lowliest of tasks. He cared about the needs of the poor and the maimed and accepted women without trying to prove His superiority. Mixing with sinners, He made friends with them. It takes real courage to develop that brand of meekness!

A HAPPY HUNGER

"Blessed are those who hunger and thirst for righteousness, for they will be filled." Matthew 5:6, R.S.V.

Did you know that 12 percent of the world's population is starving, and another 12 percent goes to bed hungry night after night? Knowing how starvation can seriously retard small children, Teresa and her friends wore T-shirts last summer that showed the head of a lion and the caption "Let 'em growl!" Her Bible class had pledged themselves to go without food for one day and let their tummies rumble, to highlight the plight of the world's hungry.

When Jesus said that those who hunger are fortunate or even happy, He was not talking about that kind of hunger. He referred to a deep longing of the soul for God.

Andreas had accompanied one of his father's farm laborers on a trek deep into a tropical rain forest. Twice he rescued the drunken man from drowning after the man fell into a canal. As the two were drying themselves by a fire at their journey's end an epileptic fit seized the laborer and almost threw him into the fire. When the spasm passed, Andreas sat shaking with fear.

Beginning to think about God, he wondered if such a person really existed. For two or three hours he sat staring into the star-filled night. He longed to know God for himself. Twice he knelt and prayed every prayer that he had ever memorized. Suddenly a whirlwind swept through the forest, violently shaking the treetops above Andreas. When it was gone, Andreas heard a beautiful melody and a warmth filled his heart. From outside himself had come a message from God. Later, the boy heard an Adventist neighbor singing the same melody that he heard that night. When the neighbor invited Andreas to attend Bible studies, the boy went along, and his wish was fulfilled. He found Jesus.

Those who belong to God's kingdom long to know Him better and become more like Him. And just as you cannot feed someone who is not hungry, so God cannot help you build a strong character unless you long for it. You must hunger and thirst, not for an exciting experience, but to know God.

"THE GLAD SONG EVER"

"I tell you the truth, unless you change and become like little children, you will never enter the kingdom of heaven." Matthew 18:3, N.I.V.

Opal Whiteley lost both of her parents at a tender age and went to live with foster parents. She remembered little of the past except that her parents had taught her to love nature. "There were five words my mother said to me over and over," Opal later said. "These words were: What, Where, When, How, Why."[1] As Opal walked in the woods she listened carefully and investigated all that she saw and heard. Sometimes her conclusions were wrong—like the time she thought that Elsie couldn't keep her new baby because Opal concluded that it was the one she had asked the angels to give to another friend.

Opal might easily have decided that she lived in a cruel world, as people so often mistreated her. But in her 5-year-old way she wrote about her world in glowing terms. One lonely day, longing for her biological parents, she wrote:

"The glad song in my heart is not bright today.
I have thinks as how I can bring happiness to folks about.
That is such a help when lonesome feels do come."[2]

Then she remembered how her mother used to say, "Make earth glad, little one—that is the way to keep the glad song ever in your heart." And so she looked around to see what she could do to be helpful. She picked watercress for her foster mother and saved her pennies (she had nineteen of them) so that one day she could buy "Mamma" singing lessons—"a whole rain barrel" full of them. Opal's blind friend once said of her: "Here is come the kingdom of heaven."

But Opal says: "I have feels she has mistakes about that because the kingdom of heaven, being up in the sky, is there beyond the stars."[3]

But I think they are both right. Don't you?

---

[1] Opal Whiteley, *Opal,* arranged and adapted by Jane Boulton (New York: Macmillan, 1976), p. 172.
[2] *Ibid.,* pp. 84-86.
[3] *Ibid.,* p. 172.

THE PURE IN HEART

"Blessed are the pure in heart, for they will see God." Matthew 5:8, N.I.V.

" 'The kingdom of heaven is like a king who prepared a wedding banquet for his son' " (chap. 22:1). Can you imagine the excitement a royal wedding causes? Everyone wants an invitation. When Prince Charles wed Lady Diana Spencer many Americans flew to England for the big occasion. Mrs. Nancy Reagan had an invitation, of course, but many people who did not, went anyway. They joined the happy throngs waving flags and hoping for a glimpse of the bridal coach.

Can you imagine Jesus coming out to greet His guests only to find that just a few have arrived. Since the great and the wealthy failed to come, He sends His servants to invite people off the streets. Half the fun at a royal wedding is looking at the clothes the guests wear. But as they arrive at this wedding they receive special wedding clothes—not a shawl to decorate their own clothes, but a robe that completely covers them. Maybe this explains why so many didn't want to come at first. The robes offended them.

" 'But when the king came in to see the guests, he noticed a man there who was not wearing wedding clothes. "Friend," he asked, "how did you get in here without wedding clothes?" The man was speechless. Then the king told the attendants, "Tie him hand and foot, and throw him outside" ' " (verses 11-13).

In Revelation 3:18 an angel brings a special message to members of the church. He offers them white robes to wear. In chapter 19 we find that those robes represent righteous lives (verse 8). So the wedding clothes represent Christ's goodness and right doing that covers our sins. He makes us pure and clean within—not the kind of clean that comes from washing with soap, but the clean that comes of wanting to live a good life in obedience to Jesus.

Happy are those who want to do what is right, " 'for they will see God' "—they will know Him now and see Him face to face when His heavenly kingdom comes.

THE BUTTERFLY GIRL

Therefore, if anyone is in Christ, he is a new creation; the old has gone, the new has come! 2 Corinthians 5:7, N.I.V.

Suppose that you had been born an animal instead of a human being. Which creature would you like to have been? Thom Schultz would probably say that he wanted to be a butterfly. You see, one day a paper butterfly soared past the shelves of potato chips and cookies in the store and came to rest on his arm. Surprised, he looked down and discovered that the butterfly belonged to a little girl. Her happy face caught Thom's imagination. Trying to match her enthusiasm, he called, "Hi!" The girl replied, "I love you."

You probably remember some little person in your life like the butterfly girl who loves you. In fact, you probably once used those three magic words a lot yourself. You knew that certain people loved you and told you so. So loving them back came naturally. But after a while you discovered that your expression of love sometimes met with scorn and ridicule. So you became more cautious. And now you don't often tell even the people you love most how much they mean to you. As Thom would say, Your paper butterfly is crumpled and now, scared to soar with the butterflies, you hold back.

But the good news of the gospel says that when you accept Jesus, when you walk with Him day by day, you become a new creature. It doesn't happen all at once. But every morning as you read a little more from His Word, as you store away those memory verses, as you give yourself to Jesus and ask Him to guide your life, you change. The butterfly in you leaves its cocoon and stretches its wings—not the delicate paper butterfly, but the real thing. And it challenges you to "live dangerously." So what if it's risky doing nice things for people, showing that you care. It's also courageous and right. Jesus invites you to experience a metamorphosis—to become a new creature. He dares you to join the butterflies of His kingdom today.

OUT OF THE COCOON

Let us have no imitation Christian love. Let us have a genuine hatred for evil and a real devotion to good. Romans 12:9, Philips.

Larry loved God and wanted to be in His kingdom. As he read his Bible one morning he noticed the verse in Luke 6 about loving one's enemies. He felt smug—he didn't have any enemies. But the idea kept tugging for attention until he had to admit that he needed to be more friendly. The next day he noticed Jeanie sitting alone at lunch. If Larry sat with her some of the others might also act friendly toward her. But he couldn't break out of his cocoon and he left her sitting alone.

"I'm not getting anywhere," he told God the fourth day. "I promised to be friendly but nothing has changed. Sure, I say Hi and smile, but friendliness involves more than that."

If Larry could have heard God's answer to his prayer, it would have sounded like this: "Larry, relax. You made a good start by recognizing that you need to be friendly. Keep trying. And rely on Me. I want to help you. When you make a move to be friendly, don't be scared. I'll be there to back you up."

Do you need to break out of your cocoon? Here's a quiz to get you started toward being more friendly. Rate yourself from 1 to 10 on the following questions according to how comfortable you feel in each situation. A 10 means you feel most comfortable. One is least comfortable. How do you feel about

____ inviting the new boy next door to play ball?
____ asking the visitor in Sabbath school to sit by you?
____ going by yourself to a new school the first day?
____ introducing yourself to a complete stranger?
____ chatting with grown-ups while they wait to see your mom?
____ telling someone why you can't play team sports on Sabbath?
____ saying the prayer up front in Sabbath school?
____ Total

If you scored 7-27, you need to break out of your cocoon; 28-60, you've begun, but keep at it; 61-70, you've made it! Maybe you can help someone else break out of his cocoon—but do it gently.

THE MERCHANT AND THE PEARL

The kingdom of heaven is like unto a merchant man, seeking goodly pearls: who, when he had found one pearl of great price, went and sold all that he had, and bought it. Matthew 13:45, 46.

Pearls are valuable gems. But they differ from the mineral gems that we find in the earth's crust. Pearls form within oyster shells. When an irritating grain of sand enters its shell the oyster forms a thin pearly layer around it in order to stop the irritation. Only the oysters found in tropical seas produce a beautifully colored pearly layer highly valued by gem merchants.

In Jesus' day when people considered something in life as valuable, they called it a pearl. A mother might croon to her little one, "Oh, my little pearl!" Or a learned teacher might tell his class, "Here is a pearl to remember"—meaning a wise saying.

Jesus said that the kingdom of heaven is like a merchant who finds a most expensive pearl. The man wants to buy it. Why? To wear it on his collar? Or is it not really a pearl but something else that Jesus is talking about? What could possibly be so valuable about the kingdom of heaven that you would hold a giant garage sale and sell off your TV and all your video games, your bike, your skates, and all your toys—everything—just to get it?

Jon can think of something more important than toys. When his family received word that they must leave everything in their home and race toward higher ground before the river flooded their town, Jon realized that he valued *his life* more than the things in his room. And think of all the people you have read about who risked their lives to read the Bible. They valued God's Word more than life. Why would people value the Bible so highly? Because the Bible tells about Jesus and eternal life. Knowing that you will live forever with Him makes life worth living. Without Jesus, life loses its zing. Jesus puts joy into living. After you know Him and feel His love, you never want to be without Him. You know that He is the Pearl of great price. Because of Him, you want to belong to His kingdom.

LIKE GROWING WHEAT

Jesus told them another parable: "The kingdom of heaven is like a man who sowed good seed in his field." Matthew 13:24, N.I.V.

As Jesus talked to His disciples about His kingdom, they couldn't understand Him. They thought that the Messiah would raise up a strong army and drive the Romans from their land. Thus they wondered why Jesus didn't get started on His conquest, and set up His government on earth.

So Jesus told them about the farmer who plowed up his land and sowed it with wheat. " 'But while everyone was sleeping, his enemy came and sowed weeds among the wheat, and went away. When the wheat sprouted and formed heads, then the weeds also appeared' " (verses 25, 26).

The farmhands were disturbed. Hadn't their master planted good seed? Then why all the terrible weeds? It looked as if they had not prepared the ground properly, so they wanted to pull the weeds. But the farmer knew it wasn't their fault. An enemy had done it. If they pulled the weeds they would also uproot some of the wheat, for the young weeds looked like the wheat. So he told his workers to wait until the wheat was ready for harvest. Then they could easily separate the weeds and burn them.

So how is God's kingdom like growing wheat? Some people in the church do not truly love Jesus. But He doesn't want us to root them out and send them away. Why? Because we might make a mistake. We might send away the wrong people.

You see, we are the plants in Jesus' story. And just as plants don't harvest each other, neither do we. Our job is to grow in usefulness as the wheat did. And when we keep close to Jesus, He helps us grow. Then in the great harvest He will not throw us away, but will gather us into the happiness of His everlasting kingdom. Why don't you ask Him to help you grow like the wheat today!

LIKE HIDDEN TREASURE

Again, the kingdom of heaven is like unto treasure hid in a field; the which when a man hath found, he hideth, and for joy thereof goeth and selleth all that he hath, and buyeth that field. Matthew 13:44.

I once read of a Spanish farmer who struggled to raise enough food to feed his family. Thinking that he could grow more if he had more land, the farmer rented a field from an elderly neighbor. As the farmer and his son began to clear an overgrown section, they came upon a box of treasure long hidden there. Hurriedly burying the box, the farmer swore his son to secrecy. "Don't mention a word to your mother," he said.

The next day, instead of setting out early for the field, the farmer advertised his house and farm for sale. But the price he received was not quite enough. So he auctioned off every one of the family's possessions and bought the field. All the while the farmer's wife fussed at him for his foolishness.

During their last night in the house, the farmer woke his family and ordered them to follow him. By cover of darkness they returned to the field, dug up the box, and began their journey to a far city, where they sold the treasure and bought a lovely new estate large enough to support them even through bad years.

The kingdom of heaven is like treasure to the Christian. But, like the Spanish farmer, we must give up everything in our lives in order to receive God's gift. We cannot have the kingdom *and* fill our minds with worldly fashions, worldly heroes, worldly books. People sometimes pride themselves that they have the best of both worlds. That might be true if you are talking about mixing the world of learning with the world of business, or the world of travel with a good steady job. But nobody can live for himself and enter the kingdom of God, or live a life of pleasure while seeking salvation. If you want to be part of the kingdom you have to give it all you have—your time, your money, your energy, and your full attention.

CAUGHT IN A NET

Again, the kindom of heaven is like unto a net, that was cast into the sea, and gathered of every kind. Matthew 13:47.

"Why don't we put on our own evangelistic meetings?" Dan's youth group said. So they rented a hall, advertised, and planned. On the opening night the hall was full.

"Wow!" Dan enthused. "See how many people came out!"

"Yes, but did you notice what kind?" Marybeth replied. When Dan peeked through the stage curtains he saw a group of town punks sitting to one side. "Oh, no!" he moaned. "What should we have done to attract the right kind of people?"

"What kind of people did you have in mind?" the youth pastor asked. Dan thought for a moment. Hadn't he planned this effort for the Lord? So if the Lord sent people, who was Dan to be choosy? The pastor explained it this way. The kingdom of heaven is like fishing with a net. And the gospel net draws in all kinds of people. But not everybody recognizes the true value of every fish.

Years ago while vacationing on a little deserted beach in Goa, India, our family sat around in the shade of coconut palms on Sabbath morning having our own Sabbath school. We noticed dozens of fishing craft moving out to sea. Soon they turned and slowly sailed toward the shore. A string of bobbing corks alerted us to the fact that the villagers were dragging in an enormous fishing net. As they approached the shore dozens of screaming gulls circled and swooped in anticipation. When at last the net was dragged up onto the beach we walked down to investigate. Hundreds of silver-bellied fish lay squirming in the net. But here and there we noticed a squid or jellyfish. The villagers busily worked to sort the fish. The inedible varieties they tossed back into the sea while the good ones they prepared for market. So " 'it will be at the end of the age' " (verse 49, N.I.V.). By loving people and sharing the gospel, you and I help spread the net and drag it to shore, but the angels do the sorting.

WINNERS

"Zacchaeus, come down immediately. I must stay at your house today." So he came down at once and welcomed him gladly. Luke 19:5, 6, N.I.V.

When Jimmy agreed in Sabbath school to participate in the quiz, he had no idea that the teacher would put Wally and Andrea on the same team. No way could they match Buzz, Lela, and Luke. Jimmy held up his end pretty well, but they still lost, seven points to three. It wouldn't have been so bad except that all his friends backed the other team.

Simon Peter thought he had joined a winning team right from the time his brother, Andrew, breathlessly reported, "'We have found the Messiah'" (John 1:41). But after the arrest of Jesus, Peter felt like a loser and wasn't anxious to talk about it. So when the maid asked if he was not one of Jesus' team, he denied it.

Fortunately, Jesus does not choose the people for His kingdom on the basis of whether they are winners or losers, popular or unpopular. He accepts anyone on His winning team who wants to join. That's why He stopped under the sycamore tree and invited Himself home with Zacchaeus.

Zacchaeus had made himself rich at the expense of other people. Everyone in his community despised him for this. But Jesus didn't worry about what the crowd thought. He saw only a man who desperately wanted to make it into the kingdom. When the crowd saw the two of them walking away together they criticized Jesus for picking a loser. But Jesus' rules were simple. "Whoever declares publicly that he belongs to me, I will do the same for him before my Father in heaven. But whoever denies publicly that he belongs to me, then I will deny him before my Father in heaven." Jesus was trying to say that when you decide to join His team you should act like a winner—proud of the team.

Next time you are invited to a cookout on Friday night don't be afraid to say why you can't go. Remember, you belong to the winning team in the biggest "play-off" this world has known.

A HARD SAYING

"Whoever eats my flesh and drinks my blood has eternal life, and I will raise him up at the last day." John 6:54, N.I.V.

How would you have reacted when Jesus said, " 'I tell you the truth, unless you eat the flesh of the Son of Man and drink his blood, you have no life in you' " (verse 53)? Would you have found it a "hard" saying? The idea of drinking blood especially revolted Jews. They were taught not to eat blood because the " ' "life of a creature is in the blood" ' " (Lev. 17:11). So does Jesus really want us to eat His blood?

What is blood, anyway? To a blood brother it is something held in common with another. To an actor, blood is tomato sauce spread around for effect. It represents danger and the possibility of death. But to a surgeon blood is a life-giving "soup" made up of microscopic cells.

If you dotted this letter *i* with a speck of blood, that speck would contain 5 million red cells, 300,000 platelets, and 7,000 white cells. So blood literally teems with life. The red cells—which really aren't cells at all—give blood its color. They lost their nuclei when they left the bone marrow that made them. Without the nuclei they can carry more oxygen to the body. If you laid out all your red cells side by side they would carpet fifteen rooms.*

For every 700 red cells, your blood contains one larger white cell. Under the microscope white cells look like fried eggs with spots of pepper on them. The spots contain powerful chemicals that fight germs. Platelets, flower-shaped cells, roam around your blood vessels ready to plug up any leaks that might appear. They collect together to form something like a net that traps red cells. Like cars blocking a freeway, they stop your precious life-giving fluid from leaking away.

When Jesus says one must drink His blood, He means that you must rely on Him for spiritual life. When you put Him first in your life, and begin each day with Bible study and prayer, you take hold on eternal life now. Isn't that wonderful!

---

* Paul Brand with Philip Yancey, "Blood, the Miracle of Cleansing," *Christianity Today*, March 4, 1983, pp. 40, 41.

WILLING WORKERS

"Father, if you are willing, take this cup from me; yet not my will, but yours be done." Luke 22:42, N.I.V.

As the time of Jesus' death drew near He felt lonely and sad, just as any human being would. In agony He pleaded with His Father to save Him from the awful death that awaited Him. But, knowing that you and I would not get to live with Him in the eternal kingdom unless He died for our sins, He calmly said, " 'Not my will, but yours be done.' "

What a wonderful example for us! Sometimes others ask us to do something unpleasant. If we stopped to think about it, we would have to admit that we ought to do it. God would want us to. It is His will.

Like when Ben had to clean the bathtub. "I don't want to do this women's work," he grumbled under his breath. And though he scrubbed until the tub sparkled, the air around it was blue from his complaining. I hardly think he had the sense of having done God's will. Ben had forgotten about Jesus. Had he taken a few minutes to think about walking with Him, he would have cleaned the tub out of love. You see, you don't have to love every job you are asked to do, but it helps to love the person for whom you are doing it.

"Come, Lyndell," Mother called one Friday morning. "Let's run over to Grandma's and clean her house for Sabbath."

"Oh, no!" Lyndell groaned. "I just got through helping you clean our house." But she hurried to get her coat. At least she could talk to Grandma while Mother cleaned.

By the time they left Grandma's, they had just enough time to rush home and fix supper for the family. Lyndell felt a little guilty as she noticed how tired her mother looked. "Why did you clean Grandma's house?" she asked, sincerely wanting to know.

"Well," Mother said with a smile, "I love Grandma. I remember how she always scrubbed the house for Sabbath. I loved to smell the fresh polish when I came in from school. She can't do it anymore. So it's not too much to go help her after all she did for me." When you work as if you are doing it for Jesus, you are truly doing His will.

WHEN BAD PEOPLE PROSPER

"Your heavenly Father . . . makes his sun rise on good and bad alike, and sends the rain on the honest and the dishonest." Matthew 5:45, N.E.B.

When Andrea set out on a ski trip to the Rockies, she felt like she was set up for one giant blind date. She had never met any of the people in her tour group. As she began to get to know the group she realized that she had been thrown in with a bunch of wealthy but worldly people. Her mismatched pieces of luggage and equipment looked cheap beside the expensive gear that the others had brought along.

Maybe you know how Andrea felt. Do you ever wonder why others seem so much better dressed than you do? Why does God bless them with all the goodies even though they are no more deserving than you? The boy who already has enough money in the bank to buy a brand new Trans Am but isn't old enough to get a driver's license—why would God single him out for such blessings? And the girl with the flawless beauty who loves to show it off—the one who asks you why you wear shorts when they make your legs look so fat—why does God waste beauty on someone like her?

And that superathlete Nick. He makes the dazzling plays that electrify the cheering section. Yet he hasn't the strength to help with your class car-wash project because he was out late Saturday night. Did God make a colossal mistake when He gave Nick all that athletic ability?

According to the Bible, God does not hand out His blessings like Santa Claus—because you're naughty or nice. Rather, God " 'makes his sun rise on good and bad alike, and sends the rain on the honest and the dishonest.' " He practices what He preaches: " 'Love your enemies' " (verse 44).

When she looked closer, Andrea discovered that what she had envied in others—popularity, wealth, and good looks—wasn't of lasting value. She had to admit that she was richer than she thought. After all, she had peace and treasures galore stored in heaven.

STAR PERFORMANCE

"Whoever can be trusted with very little can also be trusted with much." Luke 16:10, N.I.V.

The teacher passes out the parts for the Christmas play right after Thanksgiving. You hope for the starring role, but Jessica gets it. But you have to admit that she does speak better than you. So you try not to mind when you receive only a minor part.

But Jessica gets sick one week later. "Chicken pox," your teacher announces. "Jessica could be out for the rest of the year." So you gladly agree to learn her part. You work hard on it, too. After all, you don't want people saying, "What a pity Jessica couldn't do it."

The big day arrives, and you are all ready for the dress rehearsal. In fact, you have memorized not only your speaking part but every entry, every gesture. Just as the rehearsal begins, Jessica walks in and taps you on the shoulder. "Thanks for filling in," she says. "I'll take it from here."

Todd knows he is good at football. He has exactly the right build and mind for a quarterback and had lots of experience in his little one-room school where he was the leader in sports. But he can't sign up for football intramurals in academy because he needs to spend all his time settling in to his studies. After the first big tests, however, Todd discovers that his grades are better than expected. So he talks to the coach about joining intramurals.

"B team is a man short since last week," the coach says. So Todd joins their team. The first day he suits up and comes out expecting to play first-string quarterback.

But things don't work for either Jessica or Todd. Jessica can't join the play at the last minute because she missed all the detailed practice. She doesn't know her cues and would mess up the play. And the coach sends Todd to the sidelines. "You haven't learned the plays," the man reminds him. "You get into shape and show us how you can follow instructions on the easy stuff. Then we'll consider you for quarterback." It's the same way with following God's will. If you learn to walk with Him every day by reading the Bible and praying, then He will show you what to do with the big decisions of life.

WALKING IN THE LIGHT

God is light; in him there is no darkness at all. . . . But if we walk in the light, as he is in the light, we have fellowship with one another. 1 John 1:5-7, N.I.V.

The students at Vincent Hill School, an academy perched 6,500 feet up in the Himalayan Mountains of India, liked to carry flashlights with them when they walked about at night. In the winter leopards sometimes wandered onto the hillside, and once one of them snatched the principal's dog from beside his back door.

One Friday night after vespers Dennis, Johnny, and Larry left the chapel and headed down to the boys' dormitory. They had not gone far down the path when they realized that not a single light shone on their path—not even starlight. They missed the first turn past the woodpile, and Larry walked right off the path. Fortunately he fell only two or three feet and was not hurt. But the three boys determined to walk slowly and carefully the rest of the way. Just before the last turn in the path, Bill, one of the older students joined them with a flashlight.

"You boys go first," Bill directed. "I will light up your path from behind."

And he motioned for the boys to go down the steep short-cut—a glorified goat track winding around thorn trees and over boulders embedded in the hillside. Trusting Bill to shine the light, Larry started down the shortcut, Johnny and Dennis close behind. And true to his word, Bill followed them with the light.

"It's amazing how effective that light is, shining from behind," Larry said more than once. "When I can't see the track, Billy comes up and shines the light just where I need it. I soon know it if I am not walking with him."

It's the same way when you walk with Jesus. You want to do the things that please Him. And you spread friendliness and kindness to those you meet and feel an inner happiness that lights up your day. Soon you know it when you stray from His side because you get into trouble and your laughter doesn't bubble up from inside. So don't forget to ask Jesus to shine His light for you today.

WALKING IN HIS SHOES

Whoever claims to live in him must walk as Jesus did. 1 John 2:6, N.I.V.

One way you know if you are doing God's will is by asking yourself, "Am I walking as Jesus did?" Wouldn't it be great to go over to Palestine and travel along the same dusty paths that He did and wander up to the Garden of Gethsemane and sit in the shade of one of those old twisted olive trees! Anyone could do that if he had the money for the air ticket. But you really don't need to go to Palestine to walk as He did. You don't even need to wear leather sandals.

Let's suppose that you decide to walk like Jesus. You don't wake up as early as He did, but you climb out of bed and get down on your knees to talk to God. You tell Him all about your plans for the day and ask Him to help you make good decisions. Then you listen while He talks to you through the Bible. As you read a chapter or two you learn a little more about how Jesus would live if He went to school in *your* shoes. Would He fool around during the Bible lesson? Would He push and shove in line? Would He compliment Cheri on her new dress? Or lend His new calculator to Tom? It's good to stop and think about it. You get to know what He would do as you read the Bible more.

As you rush into the shower and get dressed, you hum to yourself. You feel good walking in Jesus' shoes. While enjoying your breakfast you spill the milk. Did Jesus ever spill the milk? Does it matter? Apologizing to your mother, soon you have it cleaned up and determine to be more careful in the future.

It goes like that most of the day. You enjoy what you are doing. Some things you mess up on, but you don't let it get you down. Instead you apologize quickly and whisper a little prayer asking Jesus to help you do better next time. At bedtime you know for sure that you grew up a little today. Walking in Jesus' shoes is fun.

As you walk with Jesus day by day you are "in him," as the apostle John put it. You keep close to Him as you walk.

OFF TO A GOOD START

In the morning, O Lord, thou wilt hear my voice; In the morning I will order my prayer to thee. Psalm 5:3, N.A.S.B.

Have you ever awakened in the morning and had the feeling that you dreamed one long dream for most of the night? Men who have studied dreams tell us that some dreams last only a few seconds. One man began a dream as his clock was beginning to chime. He thought he had experienced a long dream, but he woke up just as the clock finished striking. We know that some dreams last a long time. Sometimes if we wake up and then go back to sleep, we pick up the dream where we left off. Occasionally dreams leave you feeling out of sorts when you get up in the morning. Your whole day gets off to a bad start.

King David was onto a good thing when he discovered the value of seeking God in the morning. He said, "In the morning, Lord, You will hear my voice." You can't get off to a bad start when you begin the day with God. He gives you a good outlook.

Jenny planned her day the night before. After putting out her new dress and shoes, she went to sleep still planning how she would impress Judy and Donna and how the three of them would sit together at lunch. But things went wrong from the start. So concerned about keeping her dress unwrinkled, she started fighting with her brother in the car when he sat too close. And Judy and Donna hardly noticed her dress, anyway. Jenny's day was ruined. Now she smiles when she looks back on it, realizing that the way to plan a good day is to begin with Jesus. She keeps her Bible beside her bed and reads a chapter first thing after she wakes up. Then she asks Jesus to walk with her through the day. He helps her to think of His way of doing things.

"Sometimes I find myself mad at someone or, worse yet, a lot of people mad at me," Jenny says. "And it always turns out that I forgot to start that day with God. It really pays to walk with Jesus."

A BIRTHDAY TREAT

"First go and be reconciled to your brother; then come and offer your gift." Matthew 5:24, N.I.V.

It is your mother's birthday. You get up early with your brother and sister and tiptoe out to the kitchen. "Let's give her a birthday she'll never forget," you whisper as you organize everyone. Little sister knows how to fix a white cake mix, and she insists on preparing this for breakfast. But you would feel mortified carrying in a white cake with chocolate icing for breakfast.

"No! Let's prepare hashbrowns and pancakes," you say. "Mother loves them, remember?" But sister won't give in—neither will you. It's time somebody taught her a lesson, you decide, and you use the wooden spoon on sister's behind instead of the mixing bowl. The howls that follow bring Mother running from the bedroom, spoiling the whole surprise.

Eventually little sister climbs into bed with Mother, and you begin fixing hashbrowns with your brother. He doesn't say much. You know his heart isn't in it anymore. For that matter, yours isn't either.

Suppose you go through with your plan and fix the neatest breakfast. Any mother would be tempted to forget her diet with a meal like yours! But your mother forces a smile and just picks at it. The rift between you and little sister ruins your whole labor of love.

Fortunately you realize the problem. You wouldn't enjoy the food yourself with little sister still sobbing under the pillow.

So you tickle her feet until she has to raise her head. Then you quickly say you are sorry and assure her that after breakfast you will help her bake her cake. Everyone smiles, and the meal is saved.

It's the same way with God. He can't enjoy our expressions of love when we hold bad feelings against a brother. Even if you don't know what you did wrong but you feel that someone is mad at you, first go set things right if you would walk in step with Jesus today.

TO DO YOUR WILL

Teach me to do your will, for you are my God. Psalm 143:10, N.I.V.

Alfred's parents had never taken him to church. But he knew that some people went there to worship God. He wasn't sure who God was, except that Millie, the girl next door, said that you could pray to Him if you wanted something and He'd take care of it. Oh, goodie! Alfred thought. Now I know I'll get that new bicycle I've been wanting.

But he never did get the bike. The next Christmas it came to his brother instead. And from that day to the end of his life Alfred refused to put any faith in prayer.

Alfred was a middle-aged businessman when I met him. Knowing that I was a Christian, he sometimes teased me about prayer. "God never gave me anything I asked for," he used to say. One time he heard that I wanted a new sofa for my family's empty family room. "Why don't you pray for one?" He smiled. "Tell God the color and make you want and sit back and wait. And wait. And wait."

But I don't think prayer is just for getting things. What Al didn't understand was that prayer is for trusting—for giving up fears and doubts. Prayer is depending on God's wisdom even if you can't figure out His game plan. Praying means you know that God hears and answers—and that He may say No.

I once read of a sick woman who fussed at God because she wasn't getting well quickly, even though she had prayed for healing. One day her nurse built a roaring fire in the grate and then placed the skillet on the logs. That old grease-encrusted frying pan gradually turned red and then white hot. And the built-up crust popped off into the fire. When the fire died down it left the pan gleaming black.

Maybe like Al you wonder why God didn't send you something you asked for. Or like the woman you wonder why you don't heal more quickly. Just remember that sometimes people go through the fire too. And if they trust God they too come out gleaming and new.

NO MEANS NO

"I tell you the truth, until heaven and earth disappear, not the smallest letter, not the least stroke of a pen, will by any means disappear from the Law until everything is accomplished." Matthew 5:18, N.I.V.

Corey stamped his feet as he walked to his room. How come his parents were so strict? The parents of the other boys allowed them to drive cars before they had a driver's license. He sighed as he sat on the end of his bed. Then he remembered an earlier scrape with authority. He had been only 4 at the time.

Living on a college campus, he and his friend Michael often visited the cafeteria before supper. "Mom, we're going to the cafeteria. OK?" Michael called one day as they left the house. "No, Michael. Please stay in the yard," his mother replied. But the boys kept on walking.

"Where are we going?" Corey asked. Michael pointed toward the cafeteria. "Won't you get a spanking if you disobey?" Corey persisted. The other boy shook his head.

"It doesn't matter," he explained confidently. "No means Yes, and Yes means No! Didn't you know that?"

Corey was afraid to believe Michael, but the idea was too tempting to forget. Mother soon burst the bubble when he asked her about it. She refused to even *pretend* that it was right.

God knew how important it is for people to know what are the boundaries. That's why He gave the Ten Commandments. To violate any one not only breaks confidence with God, but it invites disaster. A recent survey in the United States shows that of every ten Americans, nine believe that most of the Ten Commandments apply today. But only seven accept the commandment against taking God's name in vain. And only six consider the Sabbath commandment still binding.

Like Michael, many refuse to accept a rule when they see no reason for it. So they say that No means No for eight commandments, but it means Yes or Maybe for the other two. But Jesus, knowing how important obedience is for happiness, left no room for doubt. He promises never to so much as change the dotting of an *i* or the crossing of a *t* in His law of love.

RULES

I delight to do thy will, O my God: yea, thy law is within my heart. Psalm 40:8.

Can you believe David liked rules that much? Could you sincerely say, "I delight to keep your rules"? True, you don't mind observing most of the rules at school, but do you enjoy them enough to write a song or a poem about them?

Billy had a warm feeling for rules—so warm he almost burned up just thinking about them. He disliked his family's rules about cleaning his room and coming straight home after school. "You can't make me," he would mumble under his breath when his mother asked him to stay in the yard until supper. That was his attitude at school when his teacher told him to keep his eyes moving to the right as he read. "You can't make me," Billy would mutter and then go on reading any way he pleased.

And he felt the same way about some other rules. Why shouldn't he put his elbows on the table? Billy wanted to be free of rules. And he thought he was for a year or two. But in the fifth grade the school kept him back a year in school because he couldn't read. However, Billy's real moment of truth came later when his family received an invitation to eat with the president of his dad's company. "Are you coming with us?" his dad asked. Billy shook his head. He knew that he would feel uncomfortable about his lack of table manners. "I never realized how rules could give you freedom," he admitted. "Maybe if I let Mom tell me about her rules, I will feel comfortable enough to go with you next time."

You see, knowing the rules of etiquette will give Billy the freedom to enjoy himself in company. And knowing and keeping God's rules provides you and me with the freedom to enjoy life. Yes, sometimes you are tempted to think them inconvenient and restricting. But as you come to live by them you will realize that they prevent you from messing up your life. In the end you may say, "God, it is a pleasure to do Your will. I've made Your rules my own."

IN ALL THINGS GOD WORKS

And we know that in all things God works for the good of those who love him, who have been called according to his purpose. Romans 8:28, N.I.V.

"That doesn't even look like my mother," Shelley whispered at the funeral home as she stood by the heavy wooden casket. "Mother was always so full of fun. She knew just how to help people feel better. Why did God let her die? Was it His will?"

Shelley's Aunt Marie wrapped her arms around her niece and whispered, "God thought it best for her, Shelley."

Aunt Marie did not know the answer to Shelley's question. But the answer she gave made sense to Aunt Marie, because she believed that nobody should question God's decision. But how did Shelley feel about it? Did she wonder why God would choose death for a mother more than to let her stay with her 10- and 12-year-old children? And anyway, couldn't Mother help more by working for Him on earth?

One day God will explain the whole thing to Shelley. I don't know exactly what He will say, but it may sound like this. "Shelley, when children and young adults are struck down before their time, you can be sure that sin is to blame—not Me. When Eve first took that apple, she knew that I had said it would bring death. But it didn't—not right away, so Adam ate some, too. And ever since, death has stalked this planet. It came early for Abel, though he was a good man. And still it strikes—sometimes soon and sometimes late. Only Elijah and Enoch escaped it; I took them to heaven. Even My Son Jesus, the best Man who ever lived, was killed while still young. In this imperfect world death strikes everyone sooner or later."

Today's text tells us not to let the tragedies of life get us down. God will work them out for the good of those who love Him. So Shelley, God is there beside you when you cry. He has lost a dear friend and helper, too. And if you let Him, He will help you grow into a wonderful person. What better surprise for Mother when you are all reunited again!

DOING GOOD IN SECRET

"Be careful not to do your 'acts of righteousness' before men, to be seen by them. If you do, you will have no reward from your Father in heaven." Matthew 6:1, N.I.V.

"I'll bet you couldn't get Lisa to think she was your girlfriend," Mike teased Jeff.

"I'll bet I couldn't, too," Jeff retorted. "But I double dare *you* to try!" Then, turning to the others in the gym, Jeff said, "Hey fellahs! What will we give Mike if he gets Lisa to go out with him?" After some haggling back and forth they struck a deal. Each one separately would throw a party for the whole gang if Mike proved successful before school was out.

Mike didn't exactly dislike Lisa, but you might say that she was not a favorite with any of the boys. If Mike just walked up and asked her out, she would probably suspect a trick and refuse. So Mike planned his strategy carefully. If he would win Lisa's confidence and get her to go with him to the eighth-grade banquet, then all summer long he could look forward to a constant round of parties at no expense to himself.

Next morning when Mike approached Lisa's locker, he noticed everyone watching. Just as he was about to turn and walk away Lisa dropped her math book. But before Mike could pick it up she retrieved it herself. "You shouldn't do that," he said so that his friends would be sure to hear. "How can a fellow pick up your books if you do it yourself?" Fortunately the bell for class drowned out the laughter.

No matter how hard he tried, Mike could not get near Lisa. Why? Because he was putting on an act. People can tell when we do things for show. And showing off doesn't impress others, even though they laugh. If Mike wanted to impress Lisa, he should try to get to know her when nobody else is watching. He should be interested in her for herself and not to make himself look good.

It's the same way with God. Showoff Christians can't fool Him. He knows whether or not their heart is in it. And it is *why* you do things that matter with Him. Ask Him to help you to be yourself as you please Him today.

GOD'S DELIGHT

"If you turn back your foot from the sabbath, from doing your pleasure on my holy day, and call the sabbath a delight and the holy day of the Lord honorable; . . . I will make you ride upon the heights of the earth; I will feed you with the heritage of Jacob your father." Isaiah 58:13, 14, R.S.V.

Have you ever sat and watched people walk by on the street and tried to guess what each one was doing and thinking? One Friday I sat at a busy intersection waiting for the lights to change. The golden rays of the afternoon sun lit up the buildings on one side of the street. On the other side a young Jewish man wearing a little black skullcap stepped from a florist shop, carrying a bunch of fresh flowers wrapped in green. He looked worriedly about him before walking up the street.

"He's noticing how long he has until the sun sets," I thought, sensing a bond between our two faiths. Before the sun set at five-ten I needed to buy some fresh bagels. All the way to the store I wondered about the other people in Washington who would welcome the Sabbath hours that evening. What special food would they enjoy tonight? Potato soup and bagels with cream cheese? Sweet rolls and fruit salad? Or some delectable dish with a foreign name that I have not yet discovered?

I wondered about other families. Did they scrub the house already? Do they enjoy the feeling of being ready, the smell of furniture oil and shoe polish? Have they noticed how Sabbath is just not the same when you don't prepare for it or when you are still rushing frantically around after the sun has set?

I thought of God. How does He feel when you and I disregard the edges of the Sabbath? Memories of Friday night candlelight suppers, and crackling logs in the grate flooded my mind. "Thank You, God," I whispered, thinking of the loved ones with whom I enjoyed those special hours. And I resolved not to lose a minute of the Sabbath blessing. God has an appointment with you and me at sunset Friday night. Let's not keep Him waiting.

BRAIN SURGERY

Do not conform any longer to the pattern of this world, but be transformed by the renewing of your mind. Romans 12:2, N.I.V.

Did you know that brain surgeons can operate with their feet? The brain is the most precious organ, and brain surgery the most delicate. One slip of the knife, be it only an eighth of an inch, could result in permanent damage to sight or hearing. That's why neurosurgeons are using their feet.

Of course they need their hands in preparing the patient. First, a three-dimensional X-ray, called a CAT scan, locates the brain tumor. When the patient is fully anesthetized, the surgeon opens and elevates the skull. Then the doctor uses a microscope with a laser attached to it. He employs a "joy stick" to move a red dot over his target. Then, removing his hands from the controls, he triggers the pre-aimed beam of light onto the tumor by a foot pedal. His hands aren't needed and they don't get in the way when the surgeon must see what he is doing.

Carbon dioxide lasers can burn out a tumor without injuring the healthy tissue beside it. With laser surgery the physician does not need to touch the tumor or pull or cut it—either of which could damage nearby nerves. And laser surgery produces less chance of bleeding.

Without Jesus the deadly tumor called sin fills our minds. Just as brain tumors may cause personality changes—a normally cheery person may become mournful; an energetic person, slow and listless—so sin alters people. It makes us miserable and prevents us from fully enjoying life. But when we give our lives to Jesus, He promises to renew our minds. His type of surgery is painless and sure. Jesus promises to give you a new mind—to make you a new person—when you allow Him to control your life. His type of brain surgery helps you to understand God's will and how to live so that you will please Him. Don't forget to ask Jesus to give you the victory over sin and to renew your mind today.

TURNING THE OTHER CHEEK

"If someone strikes you on the right cheek, turn to him the other also. And if someone wants to sue you and take your tunic, let him have your cloak as well." Matthew 5:39, 40, N.I.V.

Today's text goes against everything that comes naturally. When someone slaps you, you instinctively raise your arm to protect yourself. If you do not strike back, you look and feel like a coward. So you soon learn to raise your dukes first.

When the angry mob came to the garden to take Jesus, Peter instantly reached for his sword. Remember, this happened quite a while after Jesus gave the advice in today's text. So why was Peter still carrying a sword? He probably reasoned that he just didn't feel dressed without it. And not wishing to stand by looking like a coward, he slashed off the ear of the high priest's servant.

Quietly, and without a lot of fuss, Jesus told Peter to put up his weapon. "Those who kill with the sword shall die by the sword," He added. Peter felt foolish. But he got the point.

If Peter had listened to Jesus' advice in the first place, he would have stopped carrying a sword—after all there is no point in carrying a weapon if you don't intend to use it. To fake is a low form of cowardice. But Jesus' idea of offering the other cheek gives you a way to show bravery instead of cowardice.

Many years ago a man known as Mahatma Gandhi helped his fellow countrymen understand Jesus' words. He organized his people to march across India to the sea, where they began to make their own salt and sell it. In this way they protested an unjust tax on salt. When soldiers attacked Gandhi's followers, they took their blows without flinching. But they would not give in. Another time Gandhi discovered that many Indians were hurt because of a law that forced them to buy their cloth from England. "If they want to keep us poor by taking away our right to spin yarn, then let us give them back our clothes," he said. So people began to dress simply in homespun khadi cloth. They made the cloth a symbol of national pride. Maybe it's time you and I took a new look at the idea of not fighting back.

LOVING ENEMIES

"But I tell you: Love your enemies and pray for those who persecute you, that you may be sons of your Father in heaven." Matthew 5:44, 45, N.I.V.

The exciting thing about belonging to God's kingdom is figuring out how to live according to His will. It's like you love Him so much that you hate to displease Him.

Marty found that loving Allen was hopeless. It was easier just to hate him and let it go at that. But, knowing that hatred takes the joy out of living, Jesus says, Love your enemies.

Suppose you read today's text and decide to put it into action at once. You take a few minutes to jot down the names of all your enemies. Immediately you think of the boy down the street with the red hair and glasses. Every time you ride your bike down there, he tries to scare you by ramming his bike against yours so that you have to ride on the grass. And there is the bully a couple of grades ahead of you who likes to push you around at recess. Don't forget that girl who thinks she is so smart at math. And the captain of the other summer baseball team—the one with the loud mouth. You may think of one or two more.

Now that you have your list, you need to decide how to love them. You could begin by writing out fifty times, "I love the bully with the red hair." When you are done, will you like him any better? Whenever Billy fought with other boys, his dad made them look into each other's face and shake hands for five minutes. That usually cracked him up so that it took only two minutes for them to be friends again. But would it work with an enemy? Jake took his list of enemies to school and tried to do something nice for each one. He would look at his list and say, "Hmmm. Let me see. It's Bill's turn. What can I do nice for Billy?"

Somehow I wonder if it would work. It might. But I can't imagine a loving person doing that. You see, he doesn't have to. Because he *is* loving. So instead of trying to *do* loving things, why not ask Jesus to help you to *be* loving. That way you won't overlook anybody, and the kind things you do will be genuine. Best of all, after a while you won't be able to think of a single enemy.

THROUGH SACRIFICE

And by that will, we have been made holy through the sacrifice of the body of Jesus Christ once for all. Hebrews 10:10, N.I.V.

In his book *In His Image,* Paul Brand tells of a mission doctor who needed to remove a 12-year-old's lung. "We can perform this surgery, and there is a good chance that Ranjit will recover nicely," the doctor told the girl's relatives. After huddling together to discuss the news, they sadly nodded their heads. It was a bad thing for her to lose a lung. But it must be done.

"I'm glad that we agree on that." Doctor Betts smiled with relief. "But this type of surgery requires three pints of blood," he explained. "We have one pint of Ranjit's type. The family must give the other two."

The relatives frowned as they huddled together again. As the doctor prepared the syringes and the bottle he looked over to the girl's relatives. Her father and three uncles appeared healthy enough to give the blood. "We have talked it over," the oldest uncle said. "Ranjit must have the blood. We will pay for it."

"But no blood is available," the doctor explained. "Your family must donate it." Again the family withdrew to discuss the problem. When they returned, the uncles pushed forward the frail little grandmother. "She will give her blood," they said.

Furious that the men would endanger the life of their frail mother, the doctor rolled up his own sleeve. Calling another doctor, he asked him to begin drawing the blood. As the red liquid spurted into a bottle the relatives watched with alarm. "See, the great doctor is willing to give his own blood!" they said. Quickly an uncle stepped forward and offered his, assuring Ranjit's surgery.

When the uncle gave his blood to help Ranjit, his body produced new blood cells to take the place of what was lost. But when Jesus gave His blood, He gave His life, as well. As you walk in the will of God today, sacrifice your own comfort in order to help your brother or sister. After all, it took a much greater sacrifice to save us from sin.

FREE TO BE A HERO

It is by this that we know what love is: that Christ laid down his life for us. And we in our turn are bound to lay down our lives for our brothers. 1 John 3:16, N.E.B.

That wintry Wednesday in January, 1982, when a Boeing 737 struck Washington, D.C.'s 14th Street bridge and plunged into the icy Potomac River the whole city was numbed with shock. Snow and ice hampered rescue efforts. With a growing sense of helplessness, rush-hour commuters delayed by the weather and now by the accident stood by watching.

Six of the seventy-four passengers soon bobbed to the surface and clung desperately to debris. Within minutes a rescue helicopter hovered overhead to pluck survivors from the water. As the six clung to the plane's blue-and-white tail, the chopper repeatedly dropped a life-preserver ring to them. Each time it lowered the lifeline, an unidentified man caught it and passed it to one of the others. But when at last the pilot returned to pick him up, the man had disappeared beneath the ice.

When that man deliberately passed the lifeline to the others he must have known that he could not survive the icy fingers of the river much longer. And yet he repeatedly offered total strangers the freedom that could have been his. He gave away his last chance to live.

The man did not know how his unselfish actions passed a different kind of lifeline to those who watched on TV and who remember him. What he reminds us all is that within each lies a little of the heroic, of the supremely unselfish. For although none of us lay claim to greatness, we do have moments when we make courageous choices. Perhaps you deliberately decide to ignore the gossip of classmates and to plunge through the icy chill of unfriendliness to rescue someone who gets left out. Or perhaps on a class trip you think of the comfort of others before making yourself comfortable. Won't you let God use the hero in you to do His will today?

SANTA CLAUS IN MAY?

Delight yourself in the Lord and he will give you the desires of your heart. Psalm 37:4, N.I.V.

Nancy often noticed the Scripture verse that hung above her grandmother's desk. "Delight yourself in the Lord and he will give you the desires of your heart." To Nancy it sounded like an open checkbook—like her father signing every check in his book and saying, "Here, you may fill them out and use them any way you wish." It would be like Santa Claus coming in May.

Nancy could have read the text this way: "Seek happiness with the Lord, and He will give you the desires of your heart." Seeking happiness with the Lord is like discovering a new friend. You want to talk to him or her on the phone after school. If he or she likes to listen to a certain musical group, you also enjoy them. Or if he or she does long distance running or tumbling, you get into it, too. The more you come to like that friend, the more you appreciate the same things. It is the same way when you love Jesus.

Paul Weston was the wildest boy on the street. Adults shook their heads in despair when anyone mentioned his name. That was before Gail moved to town. Everyone liked Gail, but she especially liked Paul. She would help him with his English and ask him to explain her math. Before long Paul tried harder to make good grades. He wanted to show her that he could do it. The girl did not like his rock music, and soon he lost interest in his records. He learned to like French fries without catsup and onions on his pizza. For the first time since anyone could remember, Paul wore a tie to church and arrived in time for Sabbath school. In fact, he graduated from eighth grade as pastor of the class.

Gail gave Paul the things that he craved most: friendship, recognition for his success in school, and the approval of his friends. Paul discovered that "the best things in life are free." And those best things are what Jesus offers with His open checkbook—the things you value when you walk with Him.

WHATEVER YOU WISH

"If you remain in me and my words remain in you, ask whatever you wish, and it will be given you." John 15:7, N.I.V.

Doesn't that sound like the open checkbook again? "Ask whatever you wish, and it will be given you." Have you ever had an experience like that of the little boy who wrote to Santa Claus: "How come you didn't bring me the Pac Man that I asked for last year? You gave one to Doug Hilliard, and he already had Space Invaders!"

Of course you know that Jesus does not answer every prayer with a Yes any more than "Santa Claus" did for the little boy. That's why you always remember to add *"if it be Your will"* to the requests that you make. So why does Jesus say, "Ask *whatever* you wish, and it will be given you"?

It isn't difficult to understand if we back up to the beginning of the verse, where Jesus said, "If you remain in me and my words remain in you," then you may ask. You see, if you are walking with Jesus, reading His Word every day, you begin requesting the things He wants you to have. You want to do the things He wants you to do.

Like Stu. His father was not a Christian. Stu often found cigarettes and half-empty beer cans in the house. He first tried using them when he was only ten. By the time he was fourteen Stu couldn't get along without them. When Pastor Miller became the youth pastor he made friends with Stu. Never once did he mentioned the evils of smoking or drinking, but he told Stu about his wonderful Friend, Jesus. Gradually Stu came to like Jesus, and he began reading the Bible.

One Saturday night Stu told the pastor, "Guess what I did last night! I flushed all my cigarettes down the toilet. I'm through with them." The pastor was stunned. "Why did you do it?" he asked. Of course, he knew, but he wanted to hear Stu say it.

"I always knew it was bad for me," Stu explained. "Last night I asked Jesus to give me the victory." Pastor Miller grinned. "Keep on walking with Jesus, Stu, and He will make *His* desires *your* desires."

GOD WORKS IN YOU

For it is God who works in you to will and to act according to his good purpose. Philippians 2:13, N.I.V.

As you learn to delight in doing God's will a wonderful thing happens. Not only do you feel like doing the right things, but He puts *His desires* in your heart.

Sergio was traveling home from a long trip. In thirty minutes the bus would reach Santos, and, after a brief stopover, would take another thirty minutes to reach his hometown. Just before the bus pulled into Santos he heard a voice whisper, "You must go and visit your aunt in Santos." But he put aside the thought—home was too inviting. "Go and visit your aunt," the voice insisted again.

"I surely will visit my uncle and aunt sometime soon, but not today," he told himself. "I wish I could help them know Jesus as I do, but they never want to listen to me."

When the other passengers left the bus at Santos Sergio remained in his seat. But just after everyone had reboarded and the driver had started the motor, the inner voice insisted, "Go see your aunt." Quickly Sergio grabbed his bag and hurried to the door.

"Don't get off now," the driver urged. "We are leaving." Sergio thanked him but explained that he would take the next bus home. When he arrived at his aunt's home he found her ill in bed. Quickly he gathered his unbelieving uncle and cousins around her bed and instructed them to kneel and close their eyes while he prayed. Next, Sergio knew, he must get his aunt to the hospital. He ran to the marketplace to find a taxi, a truck—anything with wheels. Finding none, he sadly returned to the house. To his surprise his aunt was sitting up in bed. "God answered your prayers," his aunt said. "I want to study those Bible lessons you once showed me so I can follow Him, too."

What if Sergio had not walked with Jesus? He would not have known to leave the bus that day.

MAY 22

TANK-UP TIME

Being confident of this very thing, that he which hath begun a good work in you will perform it until the day of Jesus Christ. Philippians 1:6.

"Why would you set aside a week of prayer?" Ronda, the new girl, queried. "We already have worships and chapel periods."

Kay chuckled to herself. "It does sound awesome—a *Week* of Prayer!" she said. "But you'll like it. During that week teachers won't assign homework, and class periods will be shorter to allow time for a chapel period every day. Special speakers will present really interesting talks. Then we'll divide into prayer bands and pray for about five minutes each day."

"I thought this school had a reputation for making kids study hard," Ronda persisted. "Can you afford to take all that time from study?"

"Keeping right with God helps me study better," Kay explained. "I'm usually a better person after a Week of Prayer. I remember one time when my little brother asked me some real meaningful questions three nights in a row. I wondered what was going on. He seemed so pleasant and helpful, too. Then on Friday night when he came to supper the first time he was called, I got suspicious. And wouldn't you know it! He'd had Week of Prayer at his school all week. That's when I first realized that Weeks of Prayer do make a difference. I don't know why, but they do!"

If you have given your heart to Jesus, do you still need Weeks of Prayer? Won't He just go on performing His "good work" in you whether you have a special week for Him or not?

When you go on a long trip in a good reliable car, you can't just keeping driving. You need to stop once in a while and tank up with gas and check your oil. In a way, that's why you need Weeks of Prayer. They provide an opportunity to consider how far you have come with the Lord and where you are going. It's also a time to fill up on love and faith. Then you may continue on confidently, knowing that "he which hath begun a good work in you" will keep you chugging toward the kingdom.

DOES CHEATING PAY?

Be not deceived; God is not mocked: for whatsoever a man soweth, that shall he also reap. Galatians 6:7.

"When you are done with chapter 35, correct your own papers using the key at the front table. Then I'll show you how to fix your errors," Miss Miller instructed her sixth-graders.

Becky finished first. As she corrected her work she noticed that problem 17 was wrong. Quickly glancing over the problem, she found her mistake, and since nobody was looking, she quietly erased the problem and reworked it. She took the red marker Miss Miller kept on the table and gave herself a big fat 100 percent. "I found the error," she told herself. "It's the same as getting it correct the first time."

Later as the rest of the class began to line up to correct their work, Miss Miller asked Becky to use her paper as the key for marking those of some of her classmates. When Becky came to Brian's paper she discovered a whole row of wrong answers. "Why don't you just change that 2 into a 7?" she whispered. "Then it will be correct. And make this 4 into a 9." But he refused.

"Why do I want to do that?" he asked. "It won't help me find out what I'm doing wrong. Is that what you did to your own test?"

Becky felt her face flush. She realized that Brian was much smarter than she thought. Thinking ahead to the consequences of cheating, he realized that it would show up in the final test—unless he cheated on that, too. For "whatsoever a man [or boy or girl] soweth, that shall he also reap."

Brian knew that happiness is not ever having to say, I'm sorry I cheated. Becky tried to tell herself that what she had done was not really cheating, but she couldn't fool herself. Somehow she knew that she was not walking with Jesus while she had that sin nagging on her conscience. One morning at recess time she made things right with Miss Miller. Now Becky tries to sow only good seed, and already she's reaping happiness.

I LOVE YOU

Dear friends, let us love one another, for love comes from God. Everyone who loves has been born of God and knows God. 1 John 4:7, N.I.V.

Bonnie's mom and dad were arguing again. She could hear them shouting around the breakfast table about who had left the butter out overnight.

Running late for school, Bonnie dashed through the kitchen, pausing only to say, "I love you, Mom." After giving her father a bear hug, she added, "I love you, Dad. See you both tonight." On the way out the back door she grabbed an apple.

Speechless, her parents watched her leave. They didn't budge as she disappeared around the corner. Finally they slowly turned to each and blurted, "What did she say?"

Three simple words—"I love you"—had made a powerful impact on Bonnie's parents.

It sounds easy to do what Bonnie did. But if you haven't told your parents in a long time that you love them, you might find it hard to say. But I promise you it will be easier next time.

"I love you, Dad," 12-year-old Mike said as he sat on the arm of his father's easy chair. His dad's eyes did not leave the TV screen. "Yeah?" he drawled in his deep voice. "What do you want this time?" Mike felt offended, but suddenly his dad wrestled him to the floor and tickled him. They both laughed at the fun.

Love is something you give without asking anything back. So don't misuse those three words. But think how you would feel if nobody wished you Happy Birthday—if everyone decided that you already knew they loved you a lot. Saying "I love you" tells Mom and Dad that you have found a new reason to love them. So they like hearing it from you again. And what if they ignore your love? Love like Jesus. He loves even the most unlovely and unresponsive people. Loving people is a sign that you are growing in His will.

WHAT IF YOU AREN'T PERFECT?

Be ye therefore perfect, even as your Father which is in heaven is perfect. Matthew 5:48.

Danny's motto in the eighth grade might well have been "Don't let your studies interfere with your life"—because he didn't. Science class best illustrated his style. He began the year by choosing a seat at the back so he wouldn't be tempted to listen. The teacher moved him to the front. Whenever the class split up for lab experiments, Danny deliberately put the wrong chemicals into his test tube, hoping that he could cause an explosion. But his efforts failed to produce more than an irritating odor.

Once, after one of his escapades, Miss Nash asked Danny and Bob, his lab partner, to leave the room. Later she scolded them. "I don't understand why you behave so badly," she said. "Don't you have any sense of responsibility for your behavior? Aren't you both baptized?" Bob hung his head and admitted that he was.

"That was the first time that I thought about the difference baptism might make to a person," Danny said. "How come Bob behaved the same as me—and he was baptized? Wasn't his baptism any good?" Danny also wondered about himself. Would he automatically be good after his baptism? Or should he wait until he was good enough?

Pastor Miller answered his question at worship one morning. "The difference between a Christian and a non-Christian is that the Christian believes in the saving power of Jesus Christ," he said. It does not necessarily mean that you are better behaved. But knowing that you love a forgiving God makes you try harder. And though you feel like a fourth grader trying to dunk baskets you can't possibly reach, don't give up! Some day you *will* if you keep at it. God wants to help you in your reaching today.

GROWING UP

Don't let anyone look down on you because you are young. 1 Timothy 4:12, N.I.V.

"I wish my parents would talk to me about growing up," 12-year-old Megan said. "I mean, they have been through it all. I wish they would tell me what it's like."

Megan wonders when she will grow up. She possibly charts her height and can see that kind of development. But she wonders about maturing—about leaving childhood behind. And just as her 6-year-old brother thinks he isn't growing because he can't see much difference from one day to the next, so Megan wonders when she will ever reach the magic state called *grown-up*.

But there are ways to measure your growing up. Answer these questions about yourself—maybe you are more grown-up than you realize.

Are you still afraid to eat new foods? If you add new foods to your diet from time to time, you are growing up. Can you smile or at least say nothing when someone makes a comment about you that is not complimentary? If you don't have to "get back at him," you are growing up. Do you do the right thing because you want to and not because you'll get it if you don't? That's also a good sign.

Are you making friends with your parents? Do you have special things you like to discuss with your mom or dad? And how do you react to criticism? Do you learn from it?

Nobody can give a definite age for grown-up. Children may act grown-up on a class outing or in church. Some people may be grown-up in many respects but act childish about one or two things. And occasionally you meet an adult who never grew up when it came to accepting responsibility.

One day you will know in your heart that you are grown-up, yet you will also know that you still have lots of growing to do. You may even think longingly about when you were little. So don't be in too big a hurry! And remember: Growing up is fun when you are growing with Jesus.

If you feel an itch to grow up, why not keep your Bible near your bed and read it every morning? Don't forget to pray. Jesus will help you grow—and grow and grow.

THE CONQUERORS

We are more than conquerors through him that loved us. Romans 8:37.

The Conquerors at Mesa High School in Arizona all have one thing in common—they know what it's like to face painful treatments and the possibility of an early death. Every Wednesday they skip their fourth-period class in order to support one another as they face the pain together.

Shawn Cheves was a charter member of the Conquerors group. He suggested the name. Doctors diagnosed Shawn's leukemia when he was 7. He did not realize its seriousness until he was 12. But he continued his gymnastics into high school. Shawn's mother was not at first in favor of the Conquerors club. She thought it would be a pity party where Shawn would mope around with others. But she needn't have worried.

The Conquerors sympathize with and support one another through the tiredness and sickness that follow chemotherapy injections. They know how it feels. Some of their classmates don't understand the club. They wonder why Shawn and his friends would form a group if the people in it are just going to die. But the Conquerors say that they don't sit around talking about death. They struggle to help each other live with the pain and fear.

What can you and I do to help kids like Shawn who have cancer? "Don't pity them," counselors say. "And don't act as if the cancer will spread to you." That means treating them as if they are normal, not dwelling on their illness, but looking for every opportunity to help them feel part of our larger group.

We belong to a conquerors' club, only we call ourselves a church. We get together every Sabbath morning to encourage one another as we wage our individual battles with the cancer of sin. Occasionally some of our members die. But we don't sit around talking about death either. We draw strength from the victorious life of Jesus, who helps us cope with life here and now, and promises a bright new painless future. We are more than conquerors through Him.

CANCER AND GOD'S WILL

"Father, if you are willing, take this cup from me; yet not my will, but yours be done." Luke 22:42, N.I.V.

When Krissie discovered that she had cancer she felt angry. Cancer was for old people, not kids, she thought. "God has a plan for your life," Krissie's dad told her. Together the two began to explore the problems of suffering.

Did God create cancer? they asked. Definitely not! they soon decided. Satan is the source of all evil, including cancer. But God can help His children handle the disappointments and pain. The more Krissie thought about pain as she suffered through the radiation and chemotherapy treatments, the more she thought of Jesus. When Jesus faced death He begged His Father to remove the cup of horror. But in the next breath He trusted the Father to know what was best, and He added, "'Yet not my will, but yours be done.'"

How does Krissie trust God to care for her future? "When other kids heard that I had cancer, they expected me to lie down and die," she said. "But I hardly think about dying." Each new morning Krissie thanks God for life and does the best she can. She doesn't plan far into the future, because she doesn't know how she will be feeling a month down the road. "But," she says, "I really enjoy today."

When cancer first struck, Krissie pled with God to take it away. And at first it was hard to add "but Thy will be done."

"God has a wonderful plan for your life," her father often reminded her. "God can turn your misfortune into a blessing."

"And it isn't all bad," Krissie adds. "I didn't take time with God before. I may have grown away from Him had this not happened." But she doesn't think that God gave her cancer to turn her life around. She knows that God doesn't need evil to glorify His name. But she's glad He helped her learn to face death. Saying "Thy will be done" takes special courage. God helped Krissie find it.

SISTER—AND BROTHER

"For whoever does the will of my Father in heaven is my brother and sister and mother." Matthew 12:50, N.I.V.

Janee yawns as she reaches over and flicks off the alarm. Well, up and at 'em! She slides her feet down to the carpet and feels the cold smooth leather of her Bible. A good way to start the day! Turning to Matthew 12:48, she reads how Jesus' mother and brothers come to see Him. " 'Who is my mother, and who are my brothers?' " Jesus asks (N.I.V.). The girl smiles. She remembers the youth pastor saying that those who love Jesus are His brothers and sisters. Wow! She always wanted a big, grown-up brother.

Janee reads on. "Whoever does the will of my Father . . . is my brother and sister." She doesn't remember noticing that before. She mustn't merely call herself a Christian but must *do* God's will to be His sister. "You know how I notice little things that I should do to help people, but I don't do them? Well, help me to do them today," she prays before charging into the shower.

The day goes well. Janee doesn't do anything notable, but she stays cheerful all day. That's something! she thinks. That evening she notices her mother folding clothes on the porch and chatting with the new neighbor and her two little girls. The 5-year-old flits around like a joyous curly-headed butterfly. How could one child get all the good looks? No little sister can compete with her, Janee thinks. Then she notices the 2-year-old. A terrible skin disease has badly disfigured her.

Mother catches Janee's eye and beckons her over. "I'd like you to meet—." Janee's not listening. She's thinking how she needs to hug that tiny child. But she freezes. She can't even look at her. At that moment the little one places her dirty shoe on top of Mother's pile of clean clothes.

Janee kneels down beside her. "That's the clean pile," she says softly as she removes the offending shoe. "I'll bet you could be a real helper and line up your shoes by the door." The little face smiles as tiny hands reach for the shoes. Janee glows. She has found a little sister—thanks to her Big Brother in heaven.

PAM'S WITNESS

"I have made you known to them, and will continue to make you known in order that the love you have for me may be in them." John 17:26, N.I.V.

Pam and I had looked forward to the start of school with great anticipation. After attending public school for six years, we at last were allowed to ride the bus across town to the Adventist school. We had dreamed all summer about our new school. "Won't it be great not to be left out of all the special events because of Sabbath?" Pam had said. And I had sighed about how great it would be to study the Bible in school.

The first week of school we discovered that children our own age weren't all that different in a church school. At least *we* didn't stand out as being different. But sometimes I felt let down. "Don't they know how lucky they are?" I asked Pam one night. "They complain about the food and fool around in worship."

"Well, some of them do," Pam said, giving me a funny look. "But maybe we looked pious to them."

One morning when Miss Buckley had to leave the room during Bible class, she asked us to go on reading the chapter in our books. We had plenty to do. But some kids started talking back and forth across the room. I could hardly concentrate. "Sssssh," I said, glaring at the worst offenders. One or two others hissed about keeping it quiet. But Kay and Keith would not settle down. They just got mad at everyone for trying to hush them up.

Pam noticed the anger on Kay's face and quietly said to her, "Come over here, Kay. I'll read the assignment to you." The look of love in her eyes defused the situation. Seeing that Pam was not mad at her, Kay went over to her.

I couldn't forget how Pam's love and patience contrasted to the anger in my heart. As a result I decided to remember that if you love someone and don't yell at them, they might cooperate and make things pleasant all around. It was certainly an idea worth trying. And I silently thanked Pam for witnessing to me that day.

THE FIRE FIGHTER

"'Well done, my good and trusty servant!' said the master. 'You have proved trustworthy in a small way; I will now put you in charge of something big. Come and share your master's delight.'" Matthew 25:23, N.E.B.

"Why should we have to clean out the chicken coop?" 12-year-old Harvey muttered as he helped his older brother shovel the smelly floor. "When we get done he'll only say we didn't do it right."

"Well, let's do it right," Doug suggested. "If we open our eyes and then clean all the things that we see need it, maybe he'll be satisfied."

Harvey wished he hadn't brought up the matter when Doug insisted he redo one section because it didn't look clean enough. But after they spread fresh straw around and called their dad to check their work, Harvey felt proud of his effort.

Have you ever wondered why some people stick at unglamorous jobs? Why does your mom get down on her knees to scrub the bathroom floor? You'd "die" if she asked you to do it every week. And why do men risk their lives fighting fires or cleaning windows on skyscrapers when they could earn their paychecks doing something else?

"Because the job has to be done," one mother replies. "Because I can't stand a dirty house," another says. "Because the fire will do much damage if it's not brought under control," explains a fire fighter. But the window cleaner sums up what all of them feel when he declares, "I like the satisfaction of seeing a job done well."

When Matt Fitzsimmons nosed his boat alongside a burning tanker he had no time to ask himself why he risked his life fighting fires in New York Harbor. The heat from the advancing wall of flame stung his eyes as he fought to steady his vessel so that his crew could rescue thirty-one men from the burning ship. "God keep me steady," he prayed as he gripped the wheel.

On the way back after a successful rescue, Matt thanked God that doing His will, while it wasn't always easy, brought peace and satisfaction to so many.

BREAD OF LIFE

Give us this day our daily bread. Matthew 6:11.

"Come, come!" the old monk reminded the children in his Bible class. "You must learn the rest of this prayer before you leave." But the children were tired, and reciting in Latin was boring. The monk scolded the children again, but the memorizing continued to drag. How could he make the task more fun? Finally he dismissed the children and determined to find a way to bring life into his teaching.

The next week he produced a little gift, or "pretiola," made from biscuit dough and shaped like a pair of arms folded across the chest in prayer. "This is for the children who remember today's scripture," he said. Everyone sat up and listened with sparkling eyes as the monk taught the lesson. The quick learners that day received a "pretiola."

The popularity of "pretioli" soon spread. Some enterprising person carried samples over the Alps into Germany, where people recognized a good thing. Soon glazed and well-salted "pretzels" became a staple food.

The monk's little gifts grew in popularity and spread to the United States, where Julius Sturgis first began to commercially manufacture them in the 1860s. From his little bakery in Lititz, Pennsylvania, the industry grew until today companies produce 300 million pounds of this bread "with a special twist" each year.

As you eat your meals today don't forget your spiritual bread. It is even more important to fill your mind with Bible lessons and store texts in your memory than it is to eat the kind of bread made from dough. You could give your spiritual bread a "special twist" by copying out a favorite text and sharing it with someone else. Corey and his brother Bobby made place mats by drawing pictures to illustrate their Bible texts. They gave them to a nearby nursing home to use on Easter morning. Why not take a text and give it your own twist today?

GIVE US THIS DAY

"Give, and it will be given to you. A good measure, pressed down, shaken together and running over, will be poured into your lap." Luke 6:38, N.I.V.

As you pray to God each morning do you usually have blessings you ask for? Do you pray as Jesus did, "Give us this day"? God wants you to take your needs to Him. He promises that your habit of unselfish giving is the measuring cup into which He pours His blessings. As you share with others God will overwhelm you with His generosity.

In a tiny community halfway between Wilmington, North Carolina, and Myrtle Beach, South Carolina, twelve girls set out to collect aluminum cans. The week before, their Sunday school teacher had taken them to visit the seaman's mission in Wilmington. Seeing the sailors from all over the world, the junior high school girls wondered what they could do to make such strangers to Wilmington feel at home.

Immediately they began baking cookies for the men. But they wanted to do something of lasting value. So they decided to raise money to buy Bibles to distribute among them. That's how they began collecting aluminum cans. Although they hated to see litter along the sides of the road, they found themselves wishing that people had thrown out more pop cans.

It was hard work, but the girls collected close to 3,000 cans, which they sold for recycling. The money they thus earned bought 450 complete Bibles in a wide variety of languages.

Why did they work so hard for people they hardly even knew? Not because they wanted something in return, but because they noticed a need. They gave themselves. This is the best kind of giving, and it hardly costs a cent. And the rewards they received surprised them. No, they did not stumble upon a treasure in the sand hills! But they made many new friends at the seaman's mission. They found the joy of doing something for others. And they forgot their own petty problems in working together.

BREAD FOR THE EATER

"So is my word that goes out from my mouth: It will not return to me empty, but will accomplish what I desire." Isaiah 55:11, N.I.V.

"Why don't you help out at Vacation Bible School?" the pastor asked Vicki. "We really could use a good pianist."

The girl thought about it for a long time. None of her friends were helping. They all had summer jobs.

"It would be a fun way to share your faith," the pastor added. "You'd really like it."

Vicki had felt guilty for some time because she did nothing to tell others about her faith. If I could share my faith by playing the piano, Vicki thought, this might be a good deal. At least she would get rid of her guilt feelings.

The first day of VBS was more fun than she expected. The kids tried to learn the songs, and some of the girls wanted to sit with her at storytime. But when the leader asked her to teach a class Vicki almost panicked. She had no time to say No. The leader thrust the flannelgraph pictures into her hands and pushed her toward ten rowdy little boys, five of whom the preacher's son had brought. What a handful! Vicki felt worn out but exhilarated by noon. Some of her boys had never heard of the Bible before. Two of them had never even heard of Jesus. Knowing that this might be the only chance they had to learn about Him, Vicki worked hard that night to prepare her lesson.

By the last day of VBS she realized that she loved her boys. They seemed to like her pretty well, too. Vicki set down her teaching aids and brought out her *Uncle Arthur's Bible Story Book* to illustrate her story.

"Oh, I know that man!" Kent exclaimed, excitedly pointing to the inside cover. "That's Jesus!" And the expression in his eyes told her that he had found a new Friend at VBS.

Vicki doesn't worry about her boys, whether they have forgotten what she told them about God. She trusts God to see that His Word will not return empty. For just as the rain does not return to the clouds until it has watered the earth "'so that it yields seed for the sower and bread for the eater, so is [God's] word that goes out from [His] mouth'" (verses 10, 11).

DAILY BREAD

Morning by morning, O Lord, you hear my voice; morning by morning I lay my requests before you and wait in expectation. Psalm 5:3, N.I.V.

How come parents and teachers are not supposed to show favoritism, yet they always have their pets? Tina sometimes feels a tinge of envy toward the people who seem to be teacher's pets. But she admits that she is something of a mother's pet herself. Why else would her mother share so many more secrets with her than with her rambunctious brother Bruce? Maybe it's because Tina likes to help mother in the kitchen. They talk as they work. On the other hand, you can't stop Bruce for 30 seconds to ask how his day went before he dashes off to do something else. So his mother can't share with him. He doesn't stop to listen.

Maybe God wasn't playing favorites either when He said that David was a man after His own heart. Maybe David just stopped by more often to talk. After all, God is available to each of us. He offers the same gifts of love and saving power to all. But some people take Him up on it. They set aside a regular time to speak to Him in prayer and a regular time to listen to Him as He speaks through the Bible. They ask Him for help and then follow His advice.

Have you thought of God as being like a baker? He stocks His shelves with fresh bread around the clock. The bread is free, and anybody may stop by and get what he or she needs. How foolish, then, to go starving because you are too busy to eat. Remember, the hungrier you feel, the slower you work. So it makes sense to stock up at the beginning of the day.

And just as you must have physical bread to keep your body growing, so you need spiritual food to help you grow in knowing God. The more you eat this kind of bread the better acquainted you become with God. So don't think that David was God's pet. He was His close friend just as you can be if you take the time to be with Him every day.

BURIED TREASURE

Thy word have I hid in mine heart, that I might not sin against thee. Psalm 119:11.

Danny loves the beach in summer. He likes swimming in the water and digging in the sand. Once when he was 9 he and a friend started digging their way to China. They got only four feet closer, but they had fun imagining themselves coming out on the other side. While they were digging they found an old pair of sunglasses wrapped up in a sandwich bag. That set them thinking about buried treasure. Danny never could figure out why people would hide it.

The psalmist says that he hid the Word of God in his heart. He meant that he stored it away in his mind. When you concentrate on learning something new, electrical impulses etch a record in the gray matter of your brain. Later, when you try to remember what you learned, the record becomes a little stronger. The more you review the information, the better you remember it. When you forget things, it is either because you did not concentrate on them enough in the first place, or because your brain computer has forgotten where it stored the information. Sometimes when you sit and think hard your mind's computer bank retrieves the data for you.

But why would you want to bury the treasure of God's Word in your mind? To forget about it? Or to keep it safe for when you really need it?

Long ago in Tanzania a mission doctor received word that an epidemic had begun to sweep the country. Many of the hill people had already died. So he ordered a massive supply of medicine to help his people resist the disease. One strong warrior proudly wore the medicine like a charm around his neck. "That won't do you any good on the outside," the doctor warned. "You must swallow it."

Carrying a Bible around in our pocket or keeping it beside our bed won't help us, either. But when we store God's Word in our minds we will learn what God wants us to do. It will save us from epidemics of sin and keep us on the right path.

SNAKES ALIVE!

"Which of you, if his son asks for bread, will give him a stone? Or if he asks for a fish, will give him a snake?" Matthew 7:9, 10, N.I.V.

I don't have anything against snakes—I just don't like them. Never sure if they're poisonous or not, I assume that they all are. I've seen cobras in baskets on the streets of India. A snake charmer crouches, sways beside the basket, and plays his bulbous bamboo flute. Crowds gather and watch as the cobra raises its hood and sways to the music. But I'm always scared that he'll lose his magic hold over the snake and someone will be bitten.

But according to the *Ranger Rick* magazine, the whole snake-charming act is a hoax. The lilting notes of the flute have no power over the cobra—for snakes are deaf. And the snake charmer replacing the lid on the cobra's basket needs neither skill nor courage. For he already has removed the snake's fangs. In fact, the snake is probably weak from lack of food, since its sore mouth allows it to drink only a little milk. And it raises its hood only as a defensive measure against the air from the flute that blows on its head. In a day or two it will die, and the snake charmer will find another to take its place.

The snake charmer's children know that the cobra in their father's basket is harmless. Even so, they would not be impressed if, when they asked for food, he gave them the snake. They would probably wonder how much he loved them. Human parents feel a natural concern for the well-being of their children. But how much better their heavenly Father understands their many needs. His Father heart is touched when a child goes hungry. But the only hands He uses to help them are ours.

I once read of a family that had no food left in the house. They prayed for some flour, and a few hours later a neighbor stopped by. God had impressed her to bring them some flour. Don't you wish the Lord would lead you to help people like that? He will if you keep listening and make yourself ready.

GOOD GIFTS

"If you, then, though you are evil, know how to give good gifts to your children, how much more will your Father in heaven give good gifts to those who ask him!" Matthew 7:11, N.I.V.

"Please come and visit my brother," the young teenager asked as she left the evangelistic meetings. "He is confined to his bed, but he wants to talk to a preacher." Struck down with polio at 14, David had not left his bed in four years. "Why can't God heal me?" he asked. "They say that God knows how to give good gifts. So why doesn't He do something for me?"

Only last week three teenagers lost their beautiful mother to a ravaging disease. Right up to the end they believed that God would intervene and heal her.

Joni Eareckson, after her paralyzing accident, had a friend offer to pray for her. "Do you really think God will make me walk?" Joni asked. Confidently the friend replied that he had faith enough for them both. But Joni doesn't walk. She probably never will.

Dave, Joni, and the other three must have asked, Why doesn't God keep His promise and give us the good gifts we ask for? Only God knows the answer to that question. But although He answered their specific requests with a No, He nevertheless gave them other precious gifts.

Joni is still discovering hers. First, she has found strength to learn considerable independence. She has discovered a wonderful ministry of speaking, writing, and painting—she holds the brush with her teeth. Even when everything seems to go against her Joni has learned to be a winner. And best of all she has found faith and happiness in Jesus.

When I was little I used to demand gifts from my parents. But I soon learned it was better to wait and see what they chose for me. That's how it is with God's gifts. We know He has good things in store for us. But let's not demand them. He gives good gifts. We don't always recognize their value, but in time we will, if we but trust His choice.

ALL YOUR NEED

But my God shall supply all your need according to his riches in glory by Christ Jesus. Philippians 4:19.

"When you are quiet we will have prayer," Miss Murphy said as she glanced around the room. Helen took a deep breath and waited for the signal. "Our Father," the class began their customary singsong chant of the Lord's Prayer. Helen thought longingly of her father. Where was he? Why had he not returned from his last sea voyage in March as he promised? Now it was June.

"Give us this day our daily bread." The familiar words jerked her mind back to the present. Would God really provide bread? After the other children had filed out of the room, she asked her teacher. "Where it says, 'Give us this day our daily bread,' does it really mean that God will give you food?" Miss Murphy smiled and told the girl about today's text: "My God shall supply all your need." "Things happen that test our faith," the woman said, "but God always provides. In fact, He says not to worry about food and clothes. He cares for the birds and animals. And He'll care for you, too."

That night Helen's mother placed five home-baked brown buns on the table. "Let's repeat the Lord's Prayer before we eat," she said. The girl thought about the words as she prayed. When they were done her mother explained that the buns were the last food in the house. "I don't know what we will eat tomorrow," she said sadly.

Then Helen reminded her mother of the words they had just prayed. "Don't worry, Mother," Helen concluded. "Let God do the worrying. He will provide."

They were still at the table when a neighbor arrived with a basket of food. "We baked all of this for a banquet tonight," the woman said. "But it was canceled. Send the boys with baskets up to the kitchen, and I'll fill them up. It will go to waste if someone doesn't use it."

"You were right," Helen's mother said, her face beaming. "No sooner had we given our worries to God than He sent us food for a feast. Isn't God good!"

BREAD AND WATER

Cast your bread upon the waters, for after many days you will find it again. Ecclesiastes 11:1, N.I.V.

If you eat store-bought bread, you probably find that it remains fresh for days because preservatives keep it from drying out. But homemade bread will dry out after a few days. If you must eat it, you might try to make it more palatable by spreading the butter thicker or by dunking it in milk. But I must warn you that soggy bread doesn't taste too good. I never could understand the raccoons that accepted bread from our cat—they stole it, actually—and "washed" it in his water dish.

But today's text is not talking about dunking that kind of bread. Bread here means whatever is necessary to sustain life. The wise man is saying that we should share even the things that we think we can't spare. Don't worry, he adds, for you will be surprised how the good that you do comes back to you.

The women on our street used to compete with each other by growing the most unusual plants and shrubs. One neighbor grew a beautiful double hibiscus that was the envy of all. But she carefully guarded her bush lest others take clippings from it and start bushes of their own. My mother was proud of a little yellow flower that provided a pretty border for her rose garden. When other people admired it she would offer them a root or two to start some for themselves.

One spring after a particularly harsh winter the gardeners on the street realized that they had lost some of their favorite plants. The lady with the hibiscus was devastated. Her bush died completely, and she could not replace it. Mother's border died also. But people with whom she had shared it returned a root or two until the border was soon as pretty as before.

When we share the love of Jesus, the Bread of Life, the blessing returns to us in unexpected ways. So try it today. "Cast your bread upon the waters." Share generously with others.

THE SECRET

"When you give to the needy, do not let your left hand know what your right hand is doing, so that your giving may be in secret." Matthew 6:3, 4, N.I.V.

Ever since Nancy could remember, she had dreamed of taking organ lessons. But when the family paid all its bills each month, nothing remained for the coveted lessons.

"Be glad that we can afford *piano* lessons," her mother often reminded the girl. "Your brothers don't even get that." Of course, Nancy appreciated her piano lessons, but she couldn't give up her desire to learn organ.

When Nancy went away to college her aunt agreed to meet the increased cost of piano lessons. And as a bonus she paid for organ lessons, too. "Thank you so much for making this possible," Nancy wrote to her aunt. "How can I ever repay you?"

"I'm glad to help," her aunt replied. "By playing for the glory of God, you will more than repay me."

But Nancy wasn't satisfied. Surely she should do something more to repay the debt to her aunt. And then Nancy read how a generous man once had loaned Carol Burnett $1,000 to launch her career. He stipulated that she repay the loan in five years and never reveal his name. And later when she was established she must help someone else in the same way.

Just imagine if every successful person reached out a hand to help someone else get started, Nancy thought. Doing good would surely snowball. But best of all, she liked the way Carol's benefactor helped make her famous without wanting to share the limelight.

As another version puts it: " 'When you give a gift . . . , don't shout about it as the hypocrites do. . . . Do it secretly. . . . And your Father who knows all secrets will reward you' " (verses 2-4, T.L.B.). As Nancy gave of her time, talents, and money without trying to get credit for doing good, she felt closer to God and to other people.

TRUST IN THE LORD

Whoso putteth his trust in the Lord shall be safe. Proverbs 29:25.

Have you ever found yourself in a tight spot when one person in the group offered to save the situation? "Trust me!" he said. "Just trust me!" And you knew deep down inside he was the last person you could trust?

I once read of a couple, Sandy and Joe, who found themselves in an extremely tight spot. An afternoon of sailing off Cedar Key on Florida's Gulf Coast had turned into a nightmare. All night huge waves smashed against their drifting boat, and the couple lashed themselves to the cockpit to keep from going overboard. Next morning they looked out on a terrifying sight—gray, choppy seas stretching to the horizon in every direction.

Through the day Joe rationed out their two cups of drinking water a sip at a time, while their dog lapped salt water from the bottom of the boat. With each passing hour Sandy's sense of panic deepened. But then, looking into the eyes of the dog crouched at her feet, she noticed peace and trust. Instantly she remembered God. If Jesus could calm the seas for His disciples, wouldn't He do it for them so that they could repair their damaged boat?

Five minutes after Sandy had prayed the sea calmed, and Joe hoisted the sails. Then the breeze picked up and sped them toward land.

Sandy's story reminded me of Doug Batchelor's experience. Sailing on a Mediterranean cruise as an atheist among a crew of confirmed atheists, he was amazed how everyone knew what to do when a serious storm threatened to capsize their boat. The lurching of the vessel had caused pandemonium down below, and seasickness gripped everyone, including the captain. The crew gave up all hope of survival, and one by one turned to God, promising to change their lives if He would save them. But when the storm blew over, they forgot their promises. Fear had driven them to God, but it could not teach them to trust Him.

Later Doug discovered the lesson that Sandy's dog helped her learn. "Whoso putteth his trust in the Lord shall be safe."

BEN'S BARLEY BREAD

"Here is a boy with five small barley loaves and two small fish, but how far will they go among so many?" John 6:9, N.I.V.

"Where are you going?" Ben calls to Josh from the doorway of his home. Josh shrugs his shoulders and points to his mother, who is hurrying ahead with his little brother. "She says the Master has crossed the lake, and we're going to see Him."

Suddenly Ben wishes that he could join the rush to find Jesus. His mother, understanding his need for adventure, hurriedly wraps him a meager lunch. Later, Ben is glad she did, for he is the only one who brought food on the long trek around the lake. They find the Master and gather on the hillside about Him.

After a while Ben wants to eat. But how can he, without offering some to Josh and his friend's mom and brother? He didn't bring enough to share. So he clutches his lunch and lets his tummy rumble. Then he overhears some disciples talking about food. Perhaps thinking that the disciples are worrying about feeding Jesus, he steps forward and offers Andrew his own small lunch—all of it. Then he hears Andrew say, "Here is a boy with five small barley loaves." His heart swells. He feels important. But his elation soon evaporates. "How far will they go among so many?" Andrew says disappointedly. Ben feels rejected. His gift isn't big enough.

And he doesn't miss the implication—what can you expect from a child! The boy bristles. Why does everyone always think he is only a child? But Jesus doesn't share Andrew's gloomy outlook. He takes the bread in His hands and commands everyone to sit down. Then He looks toward heaven and thanks God for Ben's humble barley bread. Ben can scarcely believe what happens to that bread in the hands of the Master. His gift grows and grows and grows until everyone is fed. Don't let anyone tell you that you are too young to work with Jesus. He can take your humble gifts and multiply them beyond belief if you give your whole self to Him.

A SPECIAL REASON

"Is there a man of you who by anxious thought can add a foot to his height?" Matthew 6:27, N.E.B.

Sandy Shelton grew up always feeling that she was a foot taller than other girls her own age. "Why is Sandy so tall?" people often asked. Embarrassed, she would scrunch down inside her jacket and try to shrink a few inches and not be noticed.

"You should be proud of your height," her mother said one day. "It's a gift from God."

Whenever Mother would launch into her proud-of-your-height speech, Sandy would chime in, "I know, it's a gift from God." But she didn't really believe it.

One Christmas when Sandy's two younger brothers didn't like some of the gifts they received, she realized what her mother was talking about. "People don't *have* to buy you gifts," Sandy scolded them. "And anyway it's the thought that counts."

And with a stab she realized that the way she walked showed God she didn't appreciate the gift that He had chosen for her. So instead of trying to deny her height, she began appreciating it. And that's when she discovered the secret of her gift. Sandy became an outstanding basketball player.

Sandy reminds me of Hebrews 10:35, 36, where it says, "Do not let this happy trust in the Lord die away, no matter what happens. Remember your reward! You need to keep on patiently doing God's will if you want him to do for you all that he has promised" (T.L.B.).

When Sandy accepted her height she was ready to discover God's plan for her life. Through academy she often led her intramural's team into the finals. In college she decided to become a physical education teacher so that she could help other kids like herself discover God's plan for their lives. She often tells a student, "When you realize what a blessing your height is, your whole life will change. Look what happened to me."

SOME DO; SOME DON'T

"Go home to your family and tell them how much the Lord has done for you, and how he has had mercy on you." Mark 5:19, N.I.V.

The bottom of the boat scrapes on the pebbled shore. Two of the disciples jump into the shallow water and push the vessel clear of the lapping lake. As the men walk up the deserted beach they wonder why Jesus wanted to stop in such a forsaken place. Suddenly they find themselves in an ancient cemetery, eyeball to eyeball with a madman. Warily the disciples inch backward toward the boat, but Jesus stands unflinching, gazing into the eyes of the unfortunate man.

Suddenly the man drops to his knees in front of Jesus and shouts, " 'What do you want with me, Jesus, Son of the Most High God?' " (verse 7). The love and sympathy in Jesus' eyes attract the man, but the anger in His voice startles him, as Jesus speaks to the devils tormenting him and orders them to leave. Granting the request of the demons, Jesus permits them to enter a herd of two thousand pigs. When the herd instantly charges madly over a cliff and into the lake, the herdsmen rush into the town to report the loss.

The townspeople have never heard such a story. They think only of the tremendous amount of money lost with the pigs, hardly noticing the man "dressed and in his right mind," sitting with Jesus. Urgently but politely they ask Him to leave. If He could cause this much damage in one morning, what might He do if He stayed all day!

The restored man is heartbroken. In that short time with the Master he has discovered the Bread of Life, and he doesn't want to let Him go. He pleads to get into the boat with Jesus. But Jesus gently pushes him back. "Go home to your family," he urges. "Tell them how much the Lord has done for you." The man senses Jesus' confidence in him. He accepts the challenge and sadly obeys. One man finds the Bread of Life and the others send Him away. What will you do with Jesus today? Will you accept Him and His gift of eternal life? Can you afford to turn Him away?

NOT BY BREAD ALONE

Jesus answered, "It is written: 'Man does not live on bread alone.'" Luke 4:4, N.I.V.

Carla was flattered when one of the junior counselors at Pathfinder camp showed her so much attention. What would Mark see in a skinny 11-year-old? She wondered more than once. Finally she concluded that her mirror had been lying. When Mark first suggested that she pop some pills with him, Carla wanted to refuse. But she hated to give up her newfound popularity. One thing led to another, and by the time she started school in the fall, she couldn't get along without drugs. How had she gotten started on a road that she knew led to addiction? "I let myself believe the lie that I would find something exciting," she says. "I put loving myself before loving Jesus. I have learned an important lesson."

Satan tempted Eve with a piece of fruit. It looked great, and she believed him when he said that she would learn more about good and evil if she ate it. She gave in to the temptation and discovered a good deal more about evil than she expected.

When Jesus went into the wilderness after His baptism, the devil came to tempt Him. But after forty days of talking with His Father He was ready for Satan. Knowing that Jesus had not eaten food during those forty days, Satan first tempted Him to turn rocks into bread. But Jesus recognized the trick. Satan was attacking at His weakest point—hunger. If he could get Jesus to work a miracle for Himself instead of trusting His Father to care for Him, Satan would have won an important victory. He would have come between Jesus and the Father—which is just what happened to Carla. But Jesus loved His Father too much to give in, even though He was starving. He used Scripture as a weapon. "'It is written,'" He replied, "'"man does not live on bread alone"'"—or on popularity. He needs spiritual food from God. You and I find it in the Bible.

A GIFT FOR THE GIVER

But the righteous give without sparing. Proverbs 21:26, N.I.V.

At the close of World War II much of Europe looked like a heap of rubble. From time to time the newspapers ran pictures of human misery, and the International Red Cross announced various drives to collect food and clothing to send to the needy.

When the church my family attended began its own drive to send a shipment of clothing, we talked about what we could donate. I gladly offered to send the clothes that I had outgrown and a Sabbath dress that I particularly disliked.

My mother had recently bought a lightweight wool suit, her first new clothes since before the birth of my brother. "To give something that you don't like wearing yourself isn't a sacrifice," she told me as she took the new suit from its hanger. "I have nothing else to donate but this."

Admiration for my mother filled my heart. I knew she had chosen well. "Do you mind if I give my favorite blue dress?" I asked. And I knew that I had given it from my heart.

I once read of a man who longed to give the Lord a large gift that would pay for a missionary to go to a foreign land. But his wife wanted to use their money to purchase a beautiful set of bells for the steeple of their family church. To keep the peace between them, the man grudgingly agreed to buy the bells. But the morning that the church dedicated them the man felt little pleasure in his gift. It had not come from his heart, because he would have preferred his money to win souls.

Several weeks later the church pastor visited the man and thanked him again for the bells. "They have been such a blessing," he said. "Only last week the bells led someone back to Jesus." And for the first time the man was glad for his gift. From then on the message of the bells encouraged his heart too.

When a righteous person gives without sparing, the Lord accepts and blesses that gift to the saving of souls—be that gift a simple Sabbath dress or a set of new bells.

LOVE BEFORE THINGS

"So do not worry, saying, 'What shall we eat?' or 'What shall we drink?' or 'What shall we wear?' . . . Your heavenly Father knows that you need them." Matthew 6:31, 32, N.I.V.

Jack was a young married college student when a letter from home asked him to give up his inheritance. College students need every penny they have to pay their school bills, and sometimes they worry about how they will ever save enough money to buy a house for their own families. So most students find it difficult to give up their inheritance. Such a request might even make them angry. But not Jack. Instead, he remembered all the love his parents had given him.

Jack and his many brothers and sisters had all been adopted into a loving home. Their parents called them "Sears and Roebuck babies" because each one had been chosen with love and care. After the brood grew up and Jack was in college, his parents discovered a handicapped child whom nobody wanted. But the judge ruled that before they could adopt the child they must rewrite their will, leaving everything to the infant. Because he was not normal, his future must be secure.

And that was why Jack agreed to give up his inheritance.

Sometimes newspapers report bitter struggles in the law courts over wills and inheritances. People who own thousands of times more than Jack did will battle over control of their parents' estate. Sometimes brother fights brother, or sister struggles with mother. In the end one party or the other gets the money at the expense of all the love and affection that the family had once enjoyed.

Jack's parents had taught him to put love before things. He remembered the love his parents had showered upon him and knew that another adopted brother would add love to their lives even if it didn't add up in dollars and cents. I wonder whether I'm ready to put love before things!

BASKETS WITH HOLES

Each one must do as he has made up his mind, not reluctantly or under compulsion, for God loves a cheerful giver. 2 Corinthians 9:7, R.S.V.

"Angie is so lucky!" Lisa sighed. "She keeps every penny she earns."

"So what does she spend it on?" Randy asked.

"I'm not sure," Lisa admitted. "But she spends all her time going through catalogs—all kinds of catalogs. I think she's fixing up her room."

A few days later her mother asked her to drop off a parcel for Angie's mom. And at last Lisa got to see what her friend was up to.

"So how was Angie's room?" Randy asked next day. "What does she spend her money on?"

Lisa thought for a long time. "It's hard to describe," she said finally. "She has matching wallpaper and drapes and a new carpet. But I liked the old one. I really think she's pouring her money into a basket with holes—there's not all that much to see for it."

Many teenagers, like Angie, have good summer jobs. They're hard to find at first, but then they pay well, and hard workers often find themselves with more spending money than their parents. Even after paying sixty percent of her earnings for tuition, Lisa had money for clothes. But whether buying clothes or fixing up a room, Angie and Lisa always need more, because money spent on one's self seems to disappear.

Paul suggests a good solution to the problem when he describes the generosity of the Macedonians. "Their overflowing joy and their extreme poverty welled up in rich generosity" (chap. 8:2, N.I.V.). In other words, they gave whether they could afford it or not. Our heavenly Father shares His bounties with us, but He expects us to pass on the blessings, or the source dries up. And as we share with others we discover that we seem to have more than ever to thank God for. Plug up the holes in your basket today—join God's cheerful givers.

MODERN MANNA

Then said the Lord unto Moses, Behold, I will rain bread from heaven for you. Exodus 16:4.

Biz Fairchild tells of a mission director's wife who reminded the mission family to remember God's promises and ask Him to "give us this day our daily bread." Drought had swept the area surrounding the central Angola mission in Africa. Crops had died in the ground, and water holes had dried up. The mission compound had exhausted all its stores of mealie meal, and nobody knew where to buy more.

As the prayer meeting broke up, the director's wife walked back to her house, deep worry lines creasing her forehead. If only her husband were here! If only they could find food! Then she remembered the courageous prayers of the people. How they thanked the Lord for His love and watchcare! She knew they were right. What was a little hunger compared to the peace and strength He provided day by day!

Just then an unusual sight caught her eye. Her 8-year-old daughter came into the house, eating. "What are you eating?" her mother asked in surprise. The little girl continued to munch in obvious enjoyment.

"I don't know," the little girl replied. "But it tastes good. Two men came up to me and said, 'God has answered your prayers. He has sent manna. You may eat it!' So I'm eating it."

Hurrying outside, the director's wife found small, irregular-shaped lumps lying about the cleared mission property. When the mission director arrived back he was amazed, particularly since this manna did not spoil overnight. For three nights it fell, and for three days everyone harvested it and stored it away.

Later the director took some with him to the committee meetings in South Africa. Nobody could doubt his story after they tasted it. And what did it taste like? Everyone agreed with the director's 8-year-old daughter, who said, "It tastes like honey."

What a thrill to know that God loved them enough to care for their daily needs!

Adapted from "Miracle From the Sky," *Guide*, April 20, 1983.

WHAT IS A FAST?

Is it not to deal thy bread to the hungry, and that thou bring the poor that are cast out to thy house? Isaiah 58:7.

When I was a girl we used to fast at least once a year on the last Sabbath of the Week of Prayer. We went to Sabbath school without eating breakfast—which wasn't hard to do. But after church, instead of dashing home to dinner we stayed for an extra prayer meeting. The pastor explained it this way: "Today we will starve our tummies so we may feast on God's Word." And the Lord blessed in a special way on fast days. Once the church all around the world fasted and prayed for an end to persecution in a South American country. And the Lord heard and answered.

People don't seem to fast much anymore. So maybe Isaiah is talking to us when he tells us what is involved in real fasting. Not just starving yourself, it's also giving to feed the poor. Some Christian youth wear T-shirts that say "Let It Growl." They give to famine-relief funds the money that a day's food would have cost. That's the true spirit of fasting.

You probably don't know any starving people who need bread, but if you open your eyes you might recognize someone starving for love. Like Chad. Every afternoon when the schoolchildren walked up his street in a laughing group, he walked behind—alone. Chad was starving for friendship.

As Valentine's Day approached he decided to make valentines for everyone in his class. Every evening he worked away with colored paper, rickrack braid, and glue. On Valentines' Day morning he set out with thirty-one original valentines. That evening he returned—alone, behind the happy throng. His mother opened the door, thinking he would burst into tears. But he rushed by her smiling. "I made thirty-one hearts, and there were thirty-one kids in my class."

Sharing his love with others had filled Chad's own lonely heart. Let's love those starving for friendship, so our hearts can open to receive God's blessings.

WAY TO SHINE, LONNIE!

And if you spend yourselves in behalf of the hungry and satisfy the needs of the oppressed, then your light will rise in the darkness, and your night will become like the noonday. Isaiah 58:10, N.I.V.

" 'This little light of mine, I'm going to let it shine,' " Laura sang as she sat close to the campfire, its glow warming her cheeks. Only minutes before she had sat in the dark, shivering with uneasiness at the strange night sounds. What a difference that one match had made as it ignited the paper, then the dry twigs. Now even the eucalyptus logs were blazing. "Let it shine, let it shine, let it shine"—the words burned into her consciousness. She had never thought much about the song before. After all, it was just a ditty to amuse cradle roll children. But she couldn't get the words out of her head.

That morning the visiting youth leader had said that part of being a disciple of Jesus Christ was telling others about His love. "You can't keep the good news to yourself," he had said. "You have to let your light shine." But Laura couldn't think of any way to let her light shine.

Maybe you share Laura's problem. You want to witness for Jesus, but you don't know how.

Lonnie found the solution one December. The love of Jesus touched his heart; he wanted to do something to help. So, when the Pathfinder leader asked him to go Ingathering, he went. Lonnie didn't especially feel as if he was lighting up the Calverton neighborhood as he went from door to door. But he trusted Jesus to use his witness. All he did was smile at each person and ask people if they would like to give to the needy. I know, because he came to my door. I could see the love of Jesus shining in his eyes. Though he only asked me to help and then thanked me, he warmed my heart with his love. The money Lonnie collected was used to send medical supplies and food to people who really needed it. And, according to Isaiah, that's a good way to shine.

ANYONE CAN HONK

Out of the most severe trial, their overflowing joy and their extreme poverty welled up in rich generosity. 2 Corinthians 8:2, N.I.V.

I was waiting to enter a busy highway, but the timid driver of a car bearing a bumper sticker that read "Honk if you love Jesus" blocked my progress. I love Jesus and I wanted to honk, but I knew that just then the driver would not have appreciated it.

Another bumper sticker reads: "If you love Jesus, tithe—anyone can honk!" When I first read that, I laughed. But then I simply nodded my head. It was another way of saying, Put your money where your mouth is. For you don't really love someone unless you give them a little of yourself. A smile or a wave isn't enough to keep a friendship alive. You have to give friends time and attention. At appropriate occasions you also give them gifts—tokens of your love.

And Christians who love God will gladly give Him those same things. At least ten or fifteen minutes a day is not too much to devote to a friend who means as much to us as He does. He also asks for one day out of our week. A day set aside in honor of Him. A day when we can be alone with Him a little longer. We also give Him our attention by listening in church. Furthermore, we pray every day in thoughts—not just words. And we read His Word and concentrate on the meaning. But above all, we return to God His share of our hard-earned money. We don't give it grudgingly, but because our love and joy "well up in rich generosity."

A group of citizens in our town is concerned about saving an old landmark—an old tavern. Every month that the building remains standing it costs the owner thousands of dollars in taxes and insurance. I often wonder why the group fighting to save the tavern doesn't go ahead and raise the money to pay the taxes. Wouldn't they do that if they loved it as much as they said?

On Sabbath morning does the gift you place in the offering plate give a true picture of the love and joy that wells up from inside you?

WHAT IS A BIBLE?

The entrance of your words gives light; it gives understanding to the simple. Psalm 119:130, N.I.V.

"This is a perfect day for fishing," someone commented as the children climbed into the car. "It's a perfect day to begin a Vacation Bible School, too," Mrs. Sattlemeier reminded them, and the happy carload of children agreed.

Everyone enjoyed the VBS program, and all the way back they discussed the features they liked best. As Mrs. Sattlemeier backed out of the last driveway she noticed a little boy sauntering down the road, a fishing pole in his hand. He must have been from one of the vacation campsites near the lake. She stopped the car beside him. "Here's something you might be interested in," she told the boy. "You could meet lots of children your age at Vacation Bible School. I hope we see you there tomorrow."

Jeff did come the next day—and he never missed a meeting. He enjoyed the songs and stories. On the last day he brought 15 cents to spend at the trading post. A local religious bookstore had donated many little items for the children to purchase. Jeff chose a bookmark and proudly showed it to Mrs. Sattlemeier. He had no idea what one used it for, but had chosen it for the pretty picture.

"You should keep it in your Bible," Mrs. Sattlemeier said.

But Jeff looked confused. "What's a Bible?" he asked.

Not wanting to embarrass him over the fact that he had not yet learned what it was, she carefully explained that it is a book with God's words printed in it.

"You mean there is a book that will tell me God's words so I can read it for myself?" Jeff asked, excited by his discovery. Mrs. Sattlemeier rushed around and found her own copy of the *Good News Bible* and gave it to him. Now he not only knew what a Bible was, but he had one of his own.

Are you excited knowing that you can read God's words every day? I am. And the more I read them and think about them, the more interesting they become.

FRIENDSHIP FORMULA

It is more blessed to give than to receive. Acts 20:35.

"I'm 13 and in the eighth grade. I get on well with the other kids and get included in most of the activities. So I'm not complaining because nobody likes me. But I'd like to know why I don't have any really close friends.

"Sometimes I go around with a fellow a lot. But after a while I get friendly with someone else. And I do a lot of things with that person. But I don't ever feel like I know that person very well or that we are close friends. Is something the matter with me? How can I build some close friendships? And how can I make them last?"

Kerri discovered an important clue to friendship when she was only 8. Badly wanting to make friends with Holly, she decided to buy her a birthday present. Mother helped with the shopping, but Kerri wrapped the gift by herself. "When is Holly's birthday?" Mother casually asked. "Were you invited to the party?"

Kerri went on wrapping in silence. Finally she replied, "It's today, but she couldn't invite me. Her mother said she could have only eight girls, and she invited the new girl instead of me."

"Then why are you buying her a present?" Kerri's older sister Becki demanded.

"Because she's still my friend," came the brave little answer.

When you can risk giving something knowing you'll receive nothing in return, you are on your way to lasting friendships. Here's a true-false quiz to help you discover how good a friend you are:

T or F Jesus knows that you need friends.
T or F Friends are for keeping you happy.
T or F Belonging to a big gang guarantees close friendships.
T or F Close friends always like the same kinds of things.
T or F Real friendship means never saying, "You're wrong."
T or F Close friends never need to forgive each other.*

* Only the first statement is true.

TILLIE'S DREAM

"From everyone who has been given much, much will be demanded; and from the one who has been entrusted with much, much more will be asked." Luke 12:48, N.I.V.

People called her crazy because she determined to grow *pomodori,* a type of tomato until then raised only in Italy. Soil experts and agriculturalists agreed that pomodori could not thrive in the United States. But Tillie believed that God was guiding her and it could be done.

She traveled to Italy and studied the manufacturing process. Then with $10,000 and a bag of seed she returned to start her own operation. First Tillie persuaded farmers in the San Joaquin Valley of California to plant the seeds. A canning factory agreed to process the fruit but demanded a $10,000 deposit. And finally Tillie persuaded wholesalers on the East Coast to place orders for her pomodori.

The farmers who had at first grumbled about raising "eyetalian" tomatoes soon reported a beautiful crop. The tomatoes ripened and the processing began. God blessed Tillie's operation. She tried always to remember that "'from everyone who has been given much, much will be demanded.'"

Tillie understood that principle when she paid her employees a generous wage. She wanted them to share in her blessing. And they in turn multiplied her blessing the year of the strikes. Many canneries closed because, just when the tomatoes ripened, the workers went on strike for better wages. But Tillie's employees knew that she had treated them fairly, and they refused to shut down the plant.

"WHEN HE HAD GIVEN THANKS"

The Lord Jesus, on the night he was betrayed, took bread, and when he had given thanks, he broke it and said, "This is my body, which is for you; do this in remembrance of me." 1 Corinthians 11:23, N.I.V.

"Where are you going?" I asked Carla. "Church isn't finished. What about Communion?"

She gave me a one-raised-eyebrow quizzical look that said, "Don't you know what a bore Communion is?"

Reluctantly I let her go and returned to participate in the foot-washing ceremony and the Lord's Supper.

After the congregation had reassembled in the church, the pastor stood and read, "'The Lord Jesus, on the night he was betrayed, took bread.'" In my mind's eye I could see the twelve seated about the table with their best Friend. As Jesus spoke, His words etched themselves into the disciples' memories.

"'And when he had given thanks.'" It is the night before He must face the vast unknown of death. But He is thankful—thankful for bread—thankful for life, though He is about to lose it. "'He broke it and said, "This is my body, which is for you; do this in remembrance of me."'" Christians for two thousand years would celebrate joyously the birth of a tiny Baby—God's best Gift to man. But the Gift was not complete until Jesus willingly gave Himself up to cruel men to die for our sins. And as a symbol of that complete gift, He holds up a piece of bread and breaks it.

As I sat there in church by myself thinking about the Giver and the Gift I prayed, "Give us this day our daily bread." And I knew I would never skip Communion again.

Break Thou the bread of life,
  Dear Lord, to me,
As Thou didst break the loaves
  Beside the sea;
Beyond the sacred page
  I seek thee, Lord;
My spirit pants for Thee, O living Word!

THE BETTER WAY OUT

Who is a God like you, who pardons sin and forgives the transgression of the remnant of his inheritance? Micah 7:18, N.I.V.

"To my dear Mom," Melissa began as she sat in the sunshine near the railway tracks back of her rural Maryland school. "You always asked if there was anything wrong. I always said, 'No, I'm OK.' Mom, I wasn't telling the truth. I was never OK. I am now pregnant. I ran away from all of my problems. And now I'm taking the easy way out."

Melissa shared some sandwiches with her cousin Pearl, drank a bottle of wine, and popped a few pills. At twelve minutes to noon she saw a faint speck far down the railway line. Amtrak 141 was on schedule. As the train approached she ran to the tracks and knelt between the rails, her hands clasped in prayer. The train engineer saw Melissa cross herself, and though he applied the brakes at once, 14-year-old Melissa and her unborn son died instantly.

"Mom, please don't have a nervous breakdown and be crying all the time," Melissa had written. "I want you to live forever and ever, the way you want to, and I will always love you very much. Please try to forgive me. Love, Melissa."

What made Melissa, an average student who loved life and people, end her own life before she had finished eighth grade? What makes thousands of teenagers every year take their own lives? Loneliness, pressure to achieve, and an inability to face their problems are major causes. Although Melissa was nine months pregnant, she refused to admit it. Right to the end she denied that her most obvious problem existed. And although her school employed a psychologist and two counselors, she never asked them for help.

Our mistakes and the problems they cause can grow between us and God. If we don't confess them and seek forgiveness, they squeeze all the love of life from us. Jesus promises to blot them out and gives us courage to start over when we ask forgiveness. And He gives us the courage to start over. Now, isn't that a better way out?

HOW TO FEEL FORGIVEN

If we confess our sins, he is faithful and just and will forgive us our sins and purify us from all unrighteousness. 1 John 1:9, N.I.V.

Jill loved Jesus and knew that someday she would ask to be baptized. But often when she knelt down to pray she wondered whether God even heard her, for she had an unconfessed sin nagging at her conscience. When Jill was only 8 she had helped herself to a diary while browsing in a bookstore waiting for her mother. But she had never been able to enjoy it and kept the diary hidden away in her purse.

From the start Jill was afraid to acknowledge that she was a thief. Her parents would be disappointed. But the longer she left the matter unforgiven, the harder it was to confess. She must now acknowledge that she is both thief and coward.

At last, when Jill was 14 and lived clear across the other side of the country, she decided to write to the store and send a dollar bill to make things right. She was glad she did and felt better at once. But sometimes people worry because they don't *feel* forgiven.

Do you ever not feel forgiven although you can't think of a single unforgiven sin? Unfortunately no magic formula will produce the feeling of forgiveness. But whether or not you *feel* forgiven is not important. After all, what if Miss America doesn't feel beautiful? Does that alter her looks? And if the Super Bowl champions don't feel like winners, does that change the outcome of the game? Is Mrs. Reagan poorer because she doesn't feel rich? Do grades switch on a clever student's report card because he feels dumb?

God says, "If [you] confess [your] sins, he is faithful and just and will forgive [them]." So you are forgiven. That's it! Being forgiven does not depend upon what you have done or how you feel, but upon what God has done. He died on the cross to save you from sin. And He would have died, by the way, had you been the only sinner. So forget about the feelings and claim His promise. You are forgiven because He says so.

CORRIE FINDS FORGIVENESS

You will again have compassion on us; you will tread our sins underfoot and hurl all our iniquities into the depths of the sea. Micah 7:19, N.I.V.

Corrie ten Boom suffered much in prison camps during World War II. One day as she sat in solitary confinement in her little cell, the food hatch opened and banged shut and a letter fluttered to the floor. After opening it, Corrie read of the death of her father. Filled with grief, she needed to share her pain with someone. But the guard who answered her call for help showed no pity. "Forgive me for craving human sympathy," Corrie prayed. "I have You, Lord. I need no other shoulder to cry on."

Later when Corrie and her sister were reunited they learned the name of the man who had turned them in for helping homeless Jews. Hatred toward the traitor so filled Corrie that she could not sleep for several nights. "Doesn't it bother you?" she asked her unperturbed sister.

"Oh, yes!" Betsie replied. "I feel for that poor man. I pray for him constantly." Corrie knew that in God's sight she was no better than the traitor. But fortunately, God "treads our sins underfoot." And when she broke down and asked the Lord's forgiveness she felt His peace again.

After the war Corrie set up a home to care for those whose lives had been scarred. She raised money for it by telling her experiences and urging people to forgive those who had treated them harshly during the war. After one such meeting one of the guards who had roughly treated her sister Betsie came forward to shake Corrie's hand. But she could not give him her hand. Frantically Corrie prayed for love to forgive the man, but she could not. "Jesus, I can't forgive him," she desperately prayed. "Give me Your forgiveness." Only then did love well up into her heart and down her arm as she grasped his hand. His forgiveness, not ours, is what heals the past. He does not stay angry forever, but delights to show mercy (see verse 18).

THE GAME'S NOT OVER

Remember not the sins of my youth and my rebellious ways; according to your love remember me, for you are good, O Lord. Psalm 25:7, N.I.V.

In the book *Another Chance,* Haddon Robinson tells how, as the men filed into the locker room at halftime, they slumped down on the benches around the room. Pulling his blanket around his shoulders, Roy Riegels sat down in a corner and, face in hands, sobbed like a baby.

It was New Year's Day, 1929, and the University of California was playing Georgia Tech in the Rose Bowl. Just before halftime Riegels had recovered a fumble for California, but raced back sixty-five yards toward the wrong goal. One of his own teammates finally brought him down just before he scored for the other team. And when California tried to punt, Georgia blocked the ball.

When the coach entered the locker room for his usual halftime speech, he said nothing until it was almost time to return for the second half. Finally he said, "I want the same team who played the first half to begin the second." The men began to file out, but Riegels did not move. When the coach called to him he still didn't budge. Tapping him on the arm, the coach repeated his message: "The same team will begin again."

"Coach, how can I face everyone?" Riegels asked. "I've let you down. I've disgraced the name of our school. I've ruined my own name. How can I face that crowd?"

"Come on," the coach replied, "the game's not over." And Riegels played that second half like a different ball player.

In the game of life perhaps you have taken the ball and run in the wrong direction. Perhaps you haven't run as fast as you should, or you have fumbled the ball and wonder if you can face the crowd again. But Jesus assures you that the game isn't over. With His help you can go back out there and play the best ball of your career. But first you must let Him help you forget the mistakes of the past and make a fresh start.

BLANK PAGES

He forgave us all our sins, having canceled the written code, with its regulations, that was against us. Colossians 2:13, 14, N.I.V.

In Bible times when a contract between two people was canceled it was "crossed out." Someone drew a big X from corner to corner across the page. But when Paul told the Colossians how God cancels out our sins, he used a word that means "to wash over," or to whitewash. The ink used in his day consisted of soot mixed with glue and water. By taking a wet sponge, one could completely wipe the writing away.

Judson Cornwall tells of a man who had fallen into sin and had to leave his job. Filled with shame and sorrow, he moved to another town and found work in a lumberyard. Cornwall often talked to the man about God's love and forgiveness, and gradually the man recovered his self-esteem.

But he could not believe that God had forgiven him enough to let him work for Him.

One day as he knelt praying for the man, Pastor Cornwall dreamed that he was in a large library. On one shelf he found a book marked with his friend's name. Taking down the book, he leafed through it. He found a complete history of the man, written like a diary. The first page told about the man's birth. Another described his childhood, and yet another his courtship and marriage. I wonder what it says about whatever he did that got him fired, Judson thought and turned to the year when it happened. But he found the whole page blank. Looking closely, Pastor Cornwall saw that the page had once contained writing, but it had been erased. So were the next several pages. Then he found those that recorded how the man had come back to the Lord.

Rushing to the telephone, Judson told the man what he had seen. Not only had God forgiven his sins, but He had canceled them. He washes yours out of remembrance, too, when you pray for forgiveness.

HUMBLE APOLOGIES

"Blessed is the man whose sin the Lord will never count against him." Romans 4:8, N.I.V.

"Let me tell you a story," the pastor said during one of his frequent visits to the court of the king. Being of a poetic nature, the king readily gave his whole attention, expecting a pleasant diversion from the problems of government.

"There was once a rich man who wanted to make a feast for friends," the man of God began. The king nodded. He also liked to entertain his friends.

"He decided to kill a lamb," the storyteller continued. "And all would have been fine except that, instead of choosing a lamb from among his own numerous flocks, the rich man took the only lamb of his poor neighbor."

"Oh, come now!" the king exclaimed indignantly. "I see that this thing has actually happened. You did well to tell me. Name this undeserving person, and he shall be punished.

"It is Your Majesty," the prophet said.

Suddenly King David realized that God had sent the prophet to point out his sin. For David had taken another man's wife and in order to make it seem all right he had sent her husband to the front lines of battle. When word came that the man was dead, David had married the woman. But God sorrowed over the matter.

The Israelite ruler admitted his guilt. "'I have sinned against the Lord,'" he confessed to Nathan (2 Sam. 12:13).

Then Nathan replied, "Yes, but the Lord has forgiven you." Although David had spoiled his reputation and dishonored God by his sin, the Lord was prepared to forgive him. The king humbled himself and accepted God's forgiveness. In Psalm 34:18 he wrote, "The Lord . . . rescues those who are humbly sorry for their sins" (T.L.B.). If something you did long ago still bothers you, talk to Jesus about it. Tell Him you are humbly sorry and He will take away the memories of it. Remember: "Happy is the man (or woman, boy, or girl) whose sin the Lord will not hold against him."

HERMAN'S PEACE

"Blessed are they whose transgressions are forgiven, whose sins are covered." Romans 4:7, N.I.V.

In the book *Another Chance,* William Merrill tells of a young man who grew up in Detroit's "Black Bottom" ghetto. Herman Heade attended church every week and sang in the choir. But when he was 17 he and his dad disagreed over a girlfriend who was being a bad influence on him. Heade left home, and after graduating from high school, joined the Army. After an early discharge he found a good job—the first black in the drafting department at North American Rockwell. But he fell in with a fast crowd and wasted himself with drinking and drugs.

Needing more money to support his drug habit, he held up a store and then a bank, and landed in jail. He was paroled early, and given a job as a correctional officer in the hope that it would help him stay straight.

But Herman wasn't changed inside, and before long he was back behind bars. For ten months the guards did not allow Herman out of his cell. But one day the prison librarian brought along some books for the men in Herman's block. The first book Herman picked up was *Peace With God,* by Billy Graham. He didn't want anything to do with God, so he threw the book down. But another prisoner handed it back to him. Herman threw it back over his shoulder and forgot about it. But later that afternoon he noticed it and picked it up, began reading, and was born again. Heade found God and the forgiveness he so badly needed. His remaining years in prison he used to gain a college degree and to help others find Jesus. Though he was behind bars he was free—free from the weight of guilt he had once carried. Are you one of those who have found happiness, whose sins are forgiven? All you need do is tell God you are sorry. He is waiting to forgive and give you the peace that Herman found.

PEACE ROSE

He who conceals his sins does not prosper, but whoever confesses and renounces them finds mercy. Proverbs 28:13, N.I.V.

Every time Mike walked past the McClintocks' yard he admired their roses. Possibly he would not have noticed them in the first place except that his mother pointed them out to him. His mother loved roses, but Mike's dad didn't have any luck growing them.

"I'll grow roses for you when I grow up," Mike promised, but the words sounded hollow. How long might his mother have to wait? Ten years? Mike knew that he couldn't hurry his growing up, but he resolved to pick his mother one of Mr. McClintock's peace roses so she wouldn't have to wait. One day as Mike ran home from the store in the rain he found his opportunity. He quickly snatched a peace rose and broke off its stem. But when he presented it to his mother she looked suspicious.

"Where did you get this?" she asked. A telephone call saved Mike from answering right away, but he knew his mother would not forget to ask again. When Mike's dad came home he sent Mike on an errand. On the way back Mike met Mr. McClintock. For one embarrassing moment their eyes met and Mike felt a jab of conscience. He had stolen and would have to make it right.

"I see you like roses," the man said.

"Mr. McClintock, I helped myself to one of your peace roses," Mike stammered. "I picked it for my mother. She loves them. I want to grow roses for her when I'm older."

"You have good taste in roses. Let me cut some for your mom," Mr. McClintock said. When Mike arrived home with a whole bunch of cut roses, he felt strangely lighthearted. He had confessed his sin, and Mr. McClintock had shown mercy and generosity. Furthermore, Mike had a permanent job helping the man with his roses and learning how to grow them. It's true, Mike thought. "He who conceals his sins does not prosper, but whoever confesses and renounces them finds mercy."

Adapted from *Guide,* May 5, 1982.

JULY 9

YOURS FOR THE ASKING

"When they could not pay, he forgave them both." Luke 7:42, R.S.V.

According to the grown-ups in town, nobody could throw a party like Si. His guests usually clamored for his recipes and would discuss his flower arrangements and table service for days afterward. If Si had a party, he did it right. Of course, at the last minute he usually called in two or three friends to help.

"This is probably the most important event ever," he told Mary when he asked her to help. But when Mary saw the guest list she shook her head. "You don't know what you're getting into, Si," she tried to say. "Your fancy food won't impress Him." But Si wouldn't listen.

From the start of the dinner Mary couldn't keep her mind on what she was doing. So as soon as everyone was served she slipped into the room and poured a box of precious ointment over Jesus' feet and washed them with her tears. But the rich perfume gave her away, and soon everyone turned disapprovingly to her.

If Jesus is God, how come He let a woman like Mary touch His feet? Simon thought. But Jesus turned to him and said, "Simon, a certain rich man lent money to two men. He lent $50 to one and $500 to the other. When neither could repay his debt, the rich man forgave them both. Now which debtor will love his benefactor more?"

"The one who owed more, I suppose," Simon replied slowly.

Jesus nodded and turned to Mary. "Her sins, which are many, are forgiven, for she loved much," He said. "Mary, your sins are forgiven. Your faith has saved you."

If you worked for the rest of your life, you could never make up for your sin. But God offers to forgive all—to cancel your debt. But you must reach out and accept His love and forgiveness as Mary did. It's yours for the asking.

FOUR HUNDRED AND NINETY TIMES

"Lord, how often shall my brother sin against me, and I forgive him?" . . . Jesus said to him, "I do not say to you seven times, but seventy times seven." Matthew 18:21, 22, R.S.V.

As you probably know if you have any at your house, younger brothers can be quite a trial. As Claire lay on her brand-new beach towel soaking up the late-summer rays, she dreamed of the mean tan she would show off at the Student Association picnic the first week of school. But her little brother dumping ice water on her back interrupted her thoughts.

"You wait!" Claire yelled, trying to be a good sport about it. But by the third repeat performance she had had enough. "I don't have to take this anymore," she told herself. "I'll have to teach him a lesson." But teaching Cal anything proved impossible. She couldn't catch him, and he was too big for her to dunk under the waves anyway.

As she lay on her wet towel, brooding over the injustice of not being an only child, all the sunshine went out of her day. She knew Cal would not have started with the water treatment if she had gone surfing with him when he asked. And now that he had started on his ice-water war, nothing would stop him.

"Claire, could you lend me money for a snow cone?"

"You know you don't deserve a snow cone," she replied coldly. It was her chance to get even. But Claire felt unhappy about it. And what made it worse, Cal didn't ask again. He sauntered off to sit alone in the sand.

Well, how many times does he expect me to take his fooling around, anyway? she thought. Then she remembered how she used to bother her dad when he lay on the beach. What if he had not forgiven her over and over again?

"Here's your money, Cal," she yelled. "And don't worry about paying me back!"

REDISCOVERING THE WHEEL

"For if you forgive men their trespasses, your heavenly Father also will forgive you." Matthew 6:14, R.S.V.

We use wheels in so many ways that we can hardly imagine how people managed without them. Historians believe that man's first wheels were rolling logs—a clumsy way to move things. But then someone thought of slicing up a log and attaching two circular sections to an axle. Thus he invented the first cart. The Romans hollowed out their chariot wheels and wrapped them with leather thongs. Today we depend on wheels to carry us about and minimize our work.

Imagine a country deciding to live without wheels. Their children, having never seen a wheel, would have to rediscover it for themselves. Think of all the time and effort they would waste when they could learn from past experience. But sometimes people waste much time and happiness rediscovering spiritual "wheels." The won't learn from the experience of others but want to find out for themselves. This can be disastrous, especially where it concerns forgiveness.

The Old Testament uses the word *forgive* twenty-seven times. Jacob first mentions it when he tells his sons to ask Joseph to forgive them. But Jesus first links forgiveness with a forgiving spirit. He spells out the truth that to enjoy forgiveness, a person must know how to forgive. Not because God *won't* forgive someone who remembers past wrongs, but because He *can't*. It is like the little boy with his hand stuck in the neck of a vase. Nobody, not even the doctor, can get that hand out while it clutches something in the vase. But when the boy lets go of the marbles, his hand slips out. Should the boy's hand remain in the vase for years, it would grow stunted and deformed. And so it is with forgiveness. Failing to forgive now will be disastrous later on. It could make you unhappy and rob you of friendship and contentment. Let's learn to forgive today, and not wait to rediscover the wheel.

FORGIVING TO DO

"And out of pity for him the lord of that servant released him and forgave him the debt." Matthew 18:27, R.S.V.

Let's compare the kingdom of heaven to a king who wished to settle accounts with his servants. Each person probably negotiates a timetable for repaying his debts. But one man attracts much attention and sympathy from the king. Earning a modest salary, the man asks for time to repay his debt. "How long would it take if he repays his whole check each week?" the king asks his adviser.

"Oh, many lifetimes, your Majesty."

Out of pity for him the king forgives the servant his enormous debt. The man enthusiastically expresses his gratitude and hurries home to tell his wife the good news. On the way he meets someone who owes him a few dollars. Grabbing the unsuspecting debtor by the throat, the unjust servant demands that he pay up at once. Since he can't, he winds up in jail.

When the king hears what happened he calls in his servant. "You wicked servant," he says. "I forgave you all. Why did you not have mercy on your fellow servant? You also have some forgiving to do!"

You see, God cannot forgive us our sins unless we in turn forgive—not because He doesn't want to, but because an unforgiving person simply cannot accept forgiveness.

Like Angie. She liked to keep score of all the times her parents favored her little brother Tom. "They think his is the only brain in our generation," she complained to her friends. "When he mispronounces a word it's cute. But when I do, I'm an air head." When Angie realized that she had some forgiving to do toward her parents, she grew up and learned to accept God's forgiveness. Have you some forgiving to do today?

BURY THOSE APPLE CORES

"And whenever you stand praying, forgive, if you have anything against any one; so that your Father also who is in heaven may forgive you." Mark 11:25, 26, R.S.V.

"What does your fortune cookie say?" Graeme asked excitedly. Nicole drew the paper from hers and read it aloud: "To forgive is to forget."

"That's true," she said."If you really forgive, you shouldn't remember what people do to annoy you."

"Just because it's written in a fortune cookie doesn't make it true," Graeme challenged. "If you forget everything, how will you learn from mistakes?" Nicole shrugged. Graeme always had to have the last word. And besides, hadn't he said only yesterday, "How come you remember every little thing that happens?" Maybe she did have some forgetting to do. But knowing you should forgive and forget doesn't mean you know how to do it.

Several years later Nicole visited her big brother at college when she recognized a girl they had both known years before. "Shall I call her over?" Graeme asked.

Nicole shook her head. "You know, she once put her big, fat, juicy apple core into my locker when I wasn't looking. It stained my things, and she never said she was sorry."

Graeme looked at his sister with a twinkle in his eyes. "Remember the fortune cookie?" he asked. "Didn't you ever forgive her?"

"She didn't ask."

"That's her problem. Besides, remember all the fun we used to have playing with her? Are you going to let an apple core wipe that out?" Nicole felt ashamed, but in her heart she knew she needed to bury some apple cores. Next time she met an old friend she wanted to remember the person, not an unforgiven act. "Lord, please teach me to forgive, and please bury those apple cores for me," she prayed. And she meant every word.

RIPE TOMATOES AND FORGIVENESS

And forgive us our debts, as we forgive our debtors. Matthew 6:12.

"Rob, do you want to do something fun?" Dave called. "Meet me at the corner in ten minutes." Wondering what he had found interesting, Rob sauntered down to the corner where Dave and Jerry stood with a half bushel of ripe tomatoes. He felt uneasy as he joined the half-dozen boys walking through town toward the lake turnoff. At the corner of Canal Road and Main Street they crouched behind a white picket fence.

"What are we planning?" Rob asked. "I thought you were going to make tomato sauce."

Dave slapped his knee and laughed heartily. "We're going to pelt cars," he whispered.

"What if someone recognizes us?" Rob wasn't sure he wanted any part of it. But Dave reassured him by explaining that they would only pelt the big cars from the lake resort as they made a left turn onto the road for Philadelphia.

"Wow! Traffic's heavy tonight!" Jerry yelled as the fifth car slowed for the turn. But instead of speeding on when hit, the white Cadillac stopped and a middle-aged black woman stepped out.

"You boys should be ashamed of yourselves!" she scolded in a low voice. But her statuesque form presented a target the other boys couldn't resist.

"Maybe fifteen tomatoes found their mark before she climbed back into the car and drove away," Rob said later. "I felt embarrassed. She was a much finer person than we were. And I knew that had I stepped forward and apologized, she would have forgiven us. I wish that lady knew what a lesson I learned from her."

LOST BOOTS AND FROSTBITE

Therefore confess your sins to each other. James 5:16, N.I.V.

Jim and Al had enjoyed an hour of skating on the frozen pond. But when they came to change into their boots, Jim's were missing. "Someone must have stolen them," he said. Another newer pair of boots stood nearby. "What's the difference?" He muttered, trying to convince himself that it was OK to wear the other boots. "Someone took mine, so I'll have to wear these. Besides, Mother will never notice." After checking one more time for his own, Jim wore the newer boots home.

The next morning the news was all over the school that Billie Powers was in the hospital with frostbite. "Someone took his boots," the teacher said. "He had to walk home in his socks, and he may lose a toe."

Jim felt terrible when he heard the news. At recess he and Al decided to pool their savings and buy a book for Billie to read in the hospital. "We're awfully sorry to hear what happened," they told him when they visited the hospital after school.

"There was an old pair of boots I could have worn," Billie said. "But I thought that would be stealing to wear somebody else's." Jim cringed. He wished he'd had such strong convictions before he took Jim's.

On the way home Jim and Al checked out the hut where they had left their things the night before. There stood Jim's boots in the corner where he had put them. And because of his mistake Billie Powers might lose his toe. After talking things over with his Sabbath school teacher, Jim asked Billie's forgiveness and offered to help him catch up on his schoolwork.

Jim took three steps to forgiveness. First, he confessed his sins—admitted to himself and to God that he had made a mistake. Second, he said exactly what the mistake was. And third, he asked the other person for forgiveness. Those steps helped him face God and Billy and the rest of his classmates. They'll help you, too.

Adapted from *Guide,* Joan Martin, "The Stolen Boots," Jan. 6, 1982.

WASHED IN THE BLOOD

How much more, then, will the blood of Christ . . . cleanse our consciences from acts that lead to death, so that we may serve the living God! Hebrews 9:14, N.I.V.

If you have cut your knee recently, you probably remember how careful you were to clean up after the bleeding stopped. And if only a tiny drop splashed onto your shirt, your mother probably washed it out carefully with cold water because blood stains.

Ancient religions recognized blood as a purifying agent. That was why they sacrificed animals. The blood was supposed to wash away the uneasiness you felt after doing something wrong. But blood isn't our idea of a cleanser. If you have a tooth pulled, you take great care to rinse the blood out of your mouth to keep your breath fresh. So when the Bible says that the blood of Jesus cleanses us from sin it doesn't make much sense.

That's because we don't understand blood, says Dr. Paul Brand in his book *In His Image*. Blood cleanses your body. If you want to *feel* that cleansing action, ask someone to wrap a blood pressure cuff around your upper arm. Have a friend pump it up to about 200 milimeters of mercury. That should stop the flow of blood to your lower arm and feel uncomfortably tight. (Don't keep the pressure on more than a few moments, however. Stopping the circulation can be dangerous.) Open your fingers and close them to make a fist about ten times.

"No trouble!" you say as you make the first few fists. But suddenly you will feel weak. If you do another couple it will begin to hurt. You probably won't get to ten because of the pain. Now comes the fun part! Loosen the cuff and feel the relief flood down your arm as the blood moves back into the closed-off blood vesels. You see, the poisons collecting in your muscles caused the pain. But as soon as the blood returned to wash them away you felt the relief.

Sin has a way of clogging up your conscience. It makes you irritable and unhappy. But Jesus can cleanse away the guilt of sin and free you from its habit. How do you come under His cleansing flood? Ask Jesus for forgiveness. Accept His offer to come into your life today. And feel the relief He brings.

CRANK CALLS

"But if you do not forgive men their sins, your Father will not forgive your sins." Matthew 6:15, N.I.V.

When Jack was just a boy a neighbor's dog bit him. So vicious was the attack that the dog had to be destroyed. Its owner blamed Jack and never forgave him. She began to pester his family with anonymous phone calls. Jack grew up and married, and still the crank calls persisted. When he could stand it no longer he called the police. The woman was tried in court and jailed for three months. But as soon as she came out the phone calls resumed.

After many years the woman was to have gone to court again. But the judge postponed the hearing because the woman, now 84 years old, had just gone into a nursing home. A few nights later she somehow found a telephone, and—you guessed it—Jack had nine anonymous calls.

After all those years that woman has still not learned to forgive. Forgiveness doesn't make a lot of sense to many people. Christians teach it, but even boys and girls who love Jesus sometimes find it hard to do. Like Terry and Mike. They were best friends except for one Saturday night at the Y. They began fighting by the edge of the pool. The lifeguard separated them and asked them to sit on either side of his chair. After ten minutes he got down and asked the boys if they would like to shake hands to show that there was no bad feeling. But they refused. "Well, either you sit here until you can or else you go to the locker room and get dressed," he said. Terry chose the latter.

"You must feel pretty bad about it," Terry's dad said, coming into the locker room. "You probably wish that I would go beat up on his dad." Terry had to laugh at the thought of two grown men not forgiving each other. But it isn't funny—it's sad—when a person carries a grudge for forty or fifty years. If only the old lady knew that.

LOST CHILDREN

"'Let's have a feast and celebrate. For this son of mine was dead and is alive again; he was lost and is found.'" Luke 15:23, 24, N.I.V.

Joan Baez, the famous folk singer, once attended a moving ceremony conducted in a desolate corner of a large South American city. Far from the flashy signs of the prosperous and fashionable areas of town she found a leveled area that once had been crowded slums. The only building left standing was a crooked little church. Five families gathered there for a private ceremony in which they said their last farewells to their children. The children had not died. They had disappeared along with thousands of other men, women, and children—victims of their repressive government. The parents, having done all they could to find the missing children and afraid to ask more questions, simply decided to end the search by celebrating a farewell mass.

The priest had to pause between sentences to keep from crying. And Joan, a seasoned performer, felt her voice choke when she came to sing.

Some stories of lost people end happily as with the lost sheep and the prodigal son. Others have no ending—the grief and suffering just don't stop. I read of parents in northern California who preserved things just as their son had left them when he disappeared just before Christmas. His gifts remained unopened year after year. He was a teenager when he finally walked into a police station and asked to go home to the parents he loved. But he was one of the lucky ones—he was found.

There's something sad about lost people—especially when they knowingly lose the way back to their heavenly Father. But He never loses track of them. Sometimes you may feel lost and far from God. Remember that He still loves you and grieves for your return just as human parents do. He will never say a last farewell as long as you live.

NO CONDEMNATION, LARRY

Therefore, there is now no condemnation for those who are in Christ Jesus. Romans 8:1, N.I.V.

When you have done something really stupid, do you feel like Larry? For several days he had known that Luke and Roger had a magazine that was not allowed in the dorm. At first he had no desire to see it. But the more the other fellows sniggered and whispered about it, the more he wondered just what could be so interesting. On the fateful evening Larry discovered that one of his roommates had the book. What would it hurt to take a look! No sooner did he have the magazine in his hand and turn a few pages—very slowly—than the dean appeared at the door. Quickly Larry lifted the corner of his mattress to hide the book. But it was too late.

Quietly the dean removed the magazine and looked reproachfully at him. What could Larry say? "It's not mine"—and tattle on the others? "I don't usually read bad magazines"—who'd believe him? So he hung his head and said nothing. For the rest of the school year he felt uncomfortable every time he saw the dean.

He had asked God to forgive him, and he believed he was forgiven. His problem was that he couldn't forgive himself. But when Larry discovered Romans 8:1 all that changed. When he realized that God did not condemn him, he knew he should not condemn himself. After all, why should he be harder to please than God? Larry knelt beside his bed and poured out his heart in prayer. "Lord," he said, "I feel embarrassed about being caught with that magazine. I don't normally read stuff like that. But You let the dean catch me, and he probably thinks that I bought it. Please forgive me and help me to forgive myself. Help me not even to think about it again. Amen."

Like Larry, we may "set our hearts at rest . . . whenever our hearts condemn us. For God is greater than our hearts, and he knows everything" (1 John 3:19, 20).

GOD'S FORGIVENESS

"Lord, do not hold this sin against them." Acts 7:60, N.I.V.

In the days when the Christian church had grown to the point where the apostles were too busy both to preach and look after the distribution of funds to the poor, it chose seven deacons to help with the latter. One of the new deacons was Stephen, a man full of grace and power. The Holy Spirit worked through him, doing signs and wonders.

But enemies of the growing church took Stephen before the high priest and accused him of trying to change the Jewish customs. When the council members turned to ask him if it was so, they noticed that his face shone like an angel's. Stephen gave a long defense trying to point out how God had led the Jewish nation out of Egypt and how He promised to send Jesus. The leaders could not answer his arguments, but instead they ground their teeth and covered their ears. They dragged him outside the city and began to throw rocks at him.

With his dying breath Stephen prayed aloud, "'Lord Jesus, receive my spirit.' Then he fell on his knees and cried out, 'Lord, do not hold this sin against them.' When he had said this, he fell asleep" (verses 59, 60).

What a lovely spirit of forgiveness Stephen showed! It reminds me of Jesus' prayer on the cross: "'Father, forgive them, for they do not know what they are doing'" (Luke 23:34). And Moses, pleading on behalf of his willful people: "'But now, please forgive their sin—but if not, then blot me out of the book you have written'" (Ex. 32:32). Have you ever felt that kind of forgiveness toward someone who did something to make you angry? I know that I can't forgive like that. So today my prayer will be, "Father, give me Your forgiveness when I need it today."

ANYBODY HERE PERFECT

My dear children, I write this to you so that you will not sin. But if anybody does sin, we have one who speaks to the Father in our defense—Jesus Christ, the Righteous One. 1 John 2:1, N.I.V.

When the Pathfinder leader said that he would put a flagpole right where the two rows of tents came together to form a V, Kent ran to find something with which to dig the hole. But Mr. Thomas, to Kent's amazement, said that he would raise the pole without any digging. He tied three lengths of rope to the top of the pole and stretched each out along the ground so that they were spaced an equal distance apart. Then he and two counselors each took a rope and began to pull. First one rope pulled the pole upright. Then the other men tightened the other two to provide just the right tension. The pole could not be pulled forward by any one rope because the other two held it firm.

Do you sometimes feel like that pole? The knowledge that Jesus loves you and died for you pulls you to your feet. But the idea of becoming like Jesus adds a tension to your life. You get excited because He forgives your sins and frees you from feeling guilty. Thus you feel a tug to depend wholly upon Him. But then you feel the balancing tension of the other ropes—your need to keep close to Jesus and to reach for the goals He sets for you.

If you continually feel the tension between what God does for you and what you want to accomplish for Him, then today's text is for you. The apostle John writes, "So that you will not sin." And lest you think you have to be perfect, he adds: "But if anybody does sin . . ." You could say that John really understands people. He knows about the tension you feel between what you want to do and what you actually do.

The good news is that as you walk with Jesus you learn one by one to overcome the bad habits in your life. Sometimes you slip and make a mistake you're ashamed of, but as John seems to say, "Hey, nobody's perfect. It's not the length of your step that matters so much as the direction in which you are walking."

THE CANCELED DEBT

"I canceled all that debt of yours because you begged me to. Shouldn't you have had mercy on your fellow servant just as I had on you?" Matthew 18:32, 33, N.I.V.

Evelyn Waugh tells the story of a wealthy man who left his family and church to marry another woman. Cordelia, his youngest child, suffered most on account of her father's actions, but she steadfastly refused to condemn him or to give up hope of his return to God. When at last he came home to die, she hoped he would make things right with God. But the old man refused. "Was it so bad, what I did?" he asked.

"Yes, Father," came Cordelia's painfully honest reply. Finally, just before death, he asked forgiveness. Should God forgive and wipe out his sin in one stroke after all those years of stubborn disobedience?

Freda worked harder than almost anyone else in the college cafeteria. The first time I met her I knew she was a special person. Goodness just seemed to ooze from her. And with it flowed love and understanding. If you'd had a hard day you didn't have to tell Freda. She sensed it and did all she could to make you smile again.

One day I stopped by her room. On her dresser stood a framed photograph of a radiantly attractive couple. "Who are they?" I asked.

"That's my husband and me," she said simply. Then she told me how he had divorced her when she accepted the Seventh-day Sabbath. And now she was trying to earn her way through college so that she could start a new life.

"Didn't you hate him for doing that to you?"

"At first I didn't want to be totally forgiving," she confessed. "My husband had done wrong and deserved to be punished, didn't he? But you have to forgive."

Today's text assures us that God cancels our debts of sin. So why do we sometimes not want to see Him forgive somebody like Cordelia's father? As His love shines into our hearts He makes us merciful and forgiving as Freda was. Let's open our hearts to His love today.

THE SMILE OF FORGIVENESS

Be kind and compassionate to one another, forgiving each other, just as in Christ God forgave you. Ephesians 4:32, N.I.V.

Judy and Pat were my best friends in third grade. But you might not have known that had you seen us at recess. One or another of us was forever "getting the pip" with one or both of the others. In south New Zealand where I grew up, "getting the pip" meant that you disagreed with someone and, instead of forgiving and forgetting, you gave him the silent treatment for a day or two. Getting the pip belonged almost exclusively to third- and fourth-grade girls. It didn't infect boys because they couldn't ever remember from one recess to the next who had made them mad.

You may have heard one of the girls say, "Enid's got the pip with me," but not "I've got the pip with Enid." Getting and giving (though nobody ever admitted to giving) the pip provided us an opportunity to revel in self-pity. Being mad at someone tasted like unsweetened chocolate—bitter—but you ate it anyway.

Growing up helps us laugh at the way we behaved in third grade. But once in a while teenagers and adults can learn from third-grade mistakes. What was it that we indulged when we went pippy? Pride, selfishness, obstinacy? And what did we do that changed our childhish habits? We learned to forgive.

Have you heard it said that to err is human, but to forgive is divine? Randy discovered this truth when he smashed up the family car. Mother needed milk for breakfast but didn't want to go out in the cold to get it.

"I'll go," Randy offered, glad for an excuse to drive the car. "And I promise to take care."

But not one block from home a camper skidded on the icy road. The driver, unaccustomed to icy conditions, jammed his foot on the brake and slid right toward Randy. And though he turned off the road and onto somebody's front lawn, the camper hit the family car, denting the rear door.

Randy hated to drive the car home. What would his mother say? Would she ever trust him to drive it again? But when she heard his story she hugged him and said, "I'm so glad that you're all right." And Randy knew that forgiveness was from God.

LOST AND FOUND

"There is rejoicing in the presence of the angels of God over one sinner who repents." Luke 15:10, N.I.V.

When anyone lost in sin finds repentance the angels rejoice as heartily as you do when you find something important that you have lost.

When Kerri landed in Antigua, smartly uniformed Pathfinders saluted her and her friends from Takoma Academy as they crossed the tarmac. Quickly Kerri pulled out her camera to capture the scene forever. "I hope these pictures come out," she giggled. "Between my flight bag and document folder, I can hardly raise my arms."

The group soon set up camp and familiarized themselves with their duties. Kerri's assignment involved working on the roof of the new school building. She learned to nail the beams, spread the tar paper, and lay shingles. On the third day she discovered that her document folder containing a copy of her birth certificate was missing. Without the certificate she could not reenter the United States the following week. Frantic, she began to search for it. Every member of the team assisted her. Where could she have left that folder? The last place she remembered seeing it was the airport. So Pastor Gainor drove her out there to look for it, but without success. They contacted the American consulate. "We'll discuss your problem over lunch and let you know if anything can be done," the consul said. The girl groaned. She could just see her team returning home without her.

Everyone prayed earnestly over her problem. That evening one of the national pastors asked, "What is it you are missing? A folder? A black one? I picked up something at the airport the day you arrived." When Kerri opened it and found her precious documents she felt like dancing.

Now Kerri knows how the angels in heaven rejoice when we turn back to God after letting ourselves get lost in busywork. She resolves not to get lost again.

FORGIVING IS FORGETTING

"Forget the former things; do not dwell on the past." Isaiah 43:18, N.I.V.

"When I'm a father I'll love all my children the same," 11-year-old Stanley muttered. He felt sure that his dad knew how his stepmother picked on him. "How come he doesn't stick up for me?" he yelled as he kicked the garage door in frustration.

That afternoon Stan had been playing catch with Al, his teenage neighbor, when little Timmy, Stan's half brother, came out to join the fun. Not realizing that Tim couldn't catch a ball yet, Al had thrown him a gentle catch. But the baseball caught Tim on the chin, and he set up a howl just as his mother stepped into the yard.

"That's no way to treat your brother," she yelled. Stan hated her. Not even asking what happened or who threw the ball, she grounded Stan for the rest of the day.

That evening Mrs. Grady fixed all Stan's favorite dishes for supper. If his heart had not been so full of anger over the earlier unfairness, he might have realized that she was trying to say that she was sorry. Years later, Stan's anger still weighed like lead on his spirit. He made friends with his parents, and after he had a home of his own, he often returned to visit them. But he never forgot all the times when his stepmother wrongly accused him and how his father didn't stick up for him. Somehow he couldn't let himself love them fully. He didn't like himself either.

One day Stan talked over his problems with a counselor, who helped him see that he needed to forgive his parents. "It's OK to dislike what happened to you," the counselor said. "But you must forgive them for it. And that means you must let it go—forget it all." Together Stan and the counselor asked Jesus to give him a forgiving spirit. Stan is a different person now. You can see the happiness in his eyes. But he wishes he'd known as a boy how to forgive and "'forget the former things,'" and not dwell on the past.

FOR MY OWN SAKE

"I, even I, am he who blots out your transgressions, for my own sake, and remembers your sins no more." Isaiah 43:25, N.I.V.

Jay Robbins had broken the law, and the authorities had caught him. A judge sentenced him to two years in prison. Then a marshal handcuffed him with two other prisoners and drove them to a Federal correctional institution in Texas. One of the other prisoners, a Mexican, sat reading a New Testament. He looked like a decent man, Jay thought.

At lunchtime the marshal parked the police car outside a restaurant and unlocked the handcuffs on the prisoners. "We'll get a bite to eat," he said. "But don't any of you try to run for it. I'm a mean shot."

"Don't worry," Jay replied. "I broke the law and I figure I'll take my punishment like a man." For the first time the Mexican prisoner raised his eyes to Jay's. "It's not punishment you need," he said quietly. "You need forgiveness." All the way to prison Jay remembered those words: "You need forgiveness." What did it mean? Jay remembered dozens of wrongs he had committed. The only way he knew to make up for them was by punishment.

By the time the prisoners had been processed it was late. A guard took him to a cell, and Jay climbed up to the vacant top bunk, where he lay on his back. The lights went out, but sleep would not come.

His mind wandered back to his childhood. During those years his father had deserted the family, and his mother was often too drunk to care about him. At age 11 he had stolen for the first time. It seemed that from there his life had gone steadily downhill. Now his life was ruined, and nobody cared. But I love you; I care. Startled by the thought that was as real as if spoken, Jay responded, "Is that You, God?" Next morning he met Eric, his cellmate. And Eric introduced Jay to Jesus Christ. "He can rid you of guilt," he said. Jay's journey to forgiveness took time, but today he rejoices in God's promise: " 'I, even I, am he who blots out your transgressions.' "

Adapted from Jack C. Waldon, *Joy Ride to Freedom.*

PAYBACK

Do not take revenge, my friends, but leave room for God's wrath, for it is written: "It is mine to avenge; I will repay," says the Lord. Romans 12:19, N.I.V.

David Kale worked for the government at Mount Hagen when he became a Seventh-day Adventist Christian. The happiness that he found was too good to keep to himself. His people also needed to hear the good news. So David and his wife, Mary, left their well-paying jobs and returned to the simple life of the village, where each family grew its own food and their needs were few. As soon as the Kales had planted their garden they laid plans for the village.

David began by organizing a Pathfinder group. At first only a few children joined. "We have our own church," the others said. But before long the Pathfinder troop grew until most of the village children belonged. The appreciative parents helped build a large thatched meeting place and a house next door—in case the mission sent them a pastor. But just as the work was progressing well and all the village attended morning and evening worships, David found himself involved in an accident. A minibus he was driving rolled off the road, killing a passenger. David was jailed, not because he had caused the person's death, but because his society demanded that the passenger's relatives seek revenge. The authorities jailed him for his protection.

Many societies practice revenge. People thus live in constant fear. For revenge may strike an innocent relative instead of the intended culprit. The Mafia operates on this basis; so do street gangs. Many religions allow for revenge. But in this respect Christianity differs. Jesus said, "Vengeance is mine; I will repay" (K.J.V.). At first it might seem cowardly to do good for evil—as if forgiveness is easy. But in truth it takes courage to break the "payback" system, as they call it in New Guinea. It's always easier when you are angry to strike back. Of course, you wouldn't stab anyone. Or would you? Sometimes we stab people in the back with malicious gossip.

Jesus says, Forgive and forget. I'll take care of injustice and anger. Turn your problem over to Me.

COALS OF FIRE

But I say unto you, Love your enemies, bless them that curse you, do good to them that hate you, and pray for them which despitefully use you, and persecute you. Matthew 5:44.

On the streets of New York, where Jim Finley grew up, not many people had heard of heaping coals. During Jim's first day in one new neighborhood, five boys on the street beat him up because he spoke with a southern accent. He limped home, sick and bleeding. But his stepfather wouldn't let him in until he went back and took revenge on the boys who had bullied him. Spying a skinny boy leaning against a wall, Jim took out all his anger and frustration on him. When he had bloodied up the boy he felt a glow of superiority.

Some time later, after he had moved to another neighborhood, a street bully took a ball from Jim's buddy Donald. "Why did you do that?" Jim demanded. Whereupon the bully called all the kids on the block to come see him teach the new boy a lesson. Jim clenched his fists as the larger boy lunged for him. Two hard punches and he had knocked the bully out cold. This time Jim felt no sense of accomplishment. He hadn't wanted to fight.

Many years later, after joining the Navy and leaving New York, Jim built up a respectable life for himself and his family. For twenty years he worked night and day to establish a thriving manufacturing business. When he was ready to retire he sold out to a younger man. Jim required no down payment, only light monthly installments. But the buyer took over the business and pushed Jim out without ever paying him a cent.

Remembering the skinny lad he once had bloodied and the bully he had fought, and how revenge had brought him no happiness, Jim asked God to help him understand and love the man who had taken away his business. And it worked. It did not restore the money Jim had lost. Neither did it shorten the difficult months of starting another business from scratch. But it filled him with a peace and a sense of closeness to God that money could never buy.

DONNY AND THE DART BOARD

In him we have redemption through his blood, the forgiveness of sins, in accordance with the riches of God's grace. Ephesians 1:7, N.I.V.

At the previous house his family had lived in, Donny kept a dart board in the garage. The wall around the board was peppered with tiny pricks from stray darts. But when his family moved back to the mission field, they left the dart board behind.

In the closet of his room in the mission house, Donny found a box containing drawing pencils, an old compass, and a pair of dividers with sharp points that reminded him of darts.

Without considering the difference between a closet door and a garage wall, Donny paced backward and threw the opened dividers. They landed with a delicious *zup*. So did the compass, except that it struck about five inches to the left of the spot he had aimed for. Figuring out how to correct his aim kept him busy until supper.

"Oh, no!" his mother moaned when she first noticed the door. "Surely we don't have wood borers in this house!"

Donny hadn't realized before how much he had peppered the door. What should he do? If he told her of his makeshift darts she would probably ground him for a couple of days. So he said nothing. But somehow he didn't feel right inside.

That evening his dad came in to inspect the door. "It looks like somebody played darts," he muttered to himself and then looked at Donny. "Son, do you know anything about this?"

The boy hung his head. Keeping the truth to himself didn't feel so good, so reluctantly he told the truth. "I used it for a dart board," he said, handing his father the pencil box. "I'm sorry I've spoiled the door."

Slowly his father put down the box. "I'm proud of you for confessing," he said. "You must feel—"

"Sort of stupid." Donny finished the sentence himself. And looking into his father's eyes, he saw nothing but love and forgiveness. That's the kind of forgiveness Jesus offers. Forgiveness from the heart. Forgiveness for whatever we may have done. Forgiveness that's free, because He paid the price on the cross. And remembering that makes us truly sorry as Donny was.

THE COMPASS

As far as the east is from the west, so far has he removed our transgressions from us. Psalm 103:12, N.I.V.

I don't remember how it got there—that compass in my crayon box—but having it was like magic. No matter which way I turned that little round box, its needle pointed north—except when Billy Hutchins brought his magnet. Then the needle pointed to him. I used to imagine myself trekking up the slippery edge of the world, following the direction of my compass. How would I know when I had reached the pole? "Oh, easy!" Billy said. "As soon as you step your foot past the north magnetic pole, your compass needle will swing back in the opposite direction."

You have no way of knowing when you arrive at east or west because there's no east or west pole. If you live in Maryland or New Jersey, you think that California is west. But if you are in Hawaii, California is east for you. And if you fly east, you will never arrive at a place from which you can't keep going east.

King David possibly didn't know much about flying east around the world. But he knew a lot about forgiveness. He had committed almost every sin in the book—including murder. And he experienced forgiveness for every one of them. God said of David, "He's a man after My own heart."

With his heart overflowing in love and gratitude to God for His mercy, David wanted to share the good news about forgiveness with everyone. But how could he explain it? Like God taking your sin far away. How far? Well, how far is east from west?

It's like you draw a straight line on a piece of paper. Close your eyes and imagine how that line continues on in both directions straight and true forever—into infinity. Now imagine your sins on the line. They move along the line to the left. They will never stop moving away from you. Put yourself on the line and imagine yourself moving to the right. Though you travel until you die you will never meet those sins again. *That's* forgiveness! And it's yours today for the asking.

LET US RETURN

"Come, let us return to the Lord; for he has torn, that he may heal us; he has stricken and he will bind us up." Hosea 6:1, R.S.V.

Jerry didn't exactly enjoy his reputation as a bully. Most of the times when he had hurt children he had not meant to. Like the time Kay had begged him to push her swing. He had shoved so hard that she fell off. But he was only trying to help. And he couldn't even remember what had happened to Donny. Somehow in a rough-and-tumble game Donny had gone home crying that Jerry was a bully, and the name had stuck. He hated it.

Then one afternoon as Jerry sauntered past Donny Jones's place, 4-year-old Shane came rushing across the front lawn and out onto the sidewalk.

"Shane, stop!" Jerry yelled, but the child kept going. In an instant Jerry lunged at Shane and grabbed his legs. The boy fell hard and split his lip on the curb. Just then a huge tractor-trailer thundered by.

"You'd have run in front of the truck," Jerry said as he helped Shane up. "I didn't know any other way to stop you." But the child didn't listen. Already he was wailing loudly.

"What did you do to Shane?" Mrs. Jones called from the porch. "Are you bullying him again?"

"I saw what happened, Mom," Donny called from the side of the house. "Shane would have run in front of the semi." He turned to Jerry. "Good thinking," he said. "You saved Shane's life."

Sometimes you and I get so busy doing our thing that we don't realize we are headed down a path that leads to disaster—that separates us from God. In order to open our eyes to the danger, God uses some kind of tackle. We may get angry as Shane did, or we can admit our guilt and ask forgiveness, saying, "'"Come, let us return to the Lord; for he has torn, that he may heal us; he has stricken and he will bind us up. . . . Let us press on to know the Lord"'" (verses 1-3).

NOT INTO TEMPTATION

"'And do not bring us to the test.'" Matthew 6:13, N.E.B.

I used to puzzle over Jesus' prayer in which He said, "Lead us not into temptation." I knew that God would not involve us in temptation. In fact, James 1:13 reminds us that He never tempts anyone to sin. So I thought that the text probably meant, Help us to avoid temptation.

Like Ed. Ever since he was small he would become angry and impatient during the half hour before lunchtime. Thinking that Ed could learn to keep calm if he knew why he felt angry, his mother would say, "Now, Eddie, your blood sugar is low; you're hungry." She could have given him a snack to solve the problem. But eating between meals would have left him feeling more cross than ever by midafternoon. So instead, she would help him find something he liked doing and encourage him to wait. Ed would not have learned to control his feelings had his mother removed the temptation. Instead, she assisted him in developing patience. Knowing that his hunger wouldn't last long aided him in handling it.

Ed is grown now. Suppose that he had never learned to control his feelings when he was a child. He might still act like a child. Can you imagine his wife and children running to hide from him if supper is late? Did you ever think how lucky you are that your parents learned patience when they were your age?

It's like hiking. Trails that always go downhill soon lose their challenge. So if you would grow into a strong, mature Christian, you sometimes need a stiff climb. God challenges you to tackle the steep, difficult trails so you may feel the satisfaction of developing strength and enjoying a better view. And just as you know that it's suicidal to walk where loose rocks might carry you sliding over a precipice, so you should pray that God will help you avoid unnecessary enticements to sin. As you walk with Him today, ask Him to help you meet the tests along the way.

GOD WILL PROVIDE

By faith, Abraham, when God tested him, offered Isaac as a sacrifice. Hebrews 11:17, N.I.V.

When Doug started school he looked forward to bringing home a report card full of A's. But it turned out that his school didn't give grades during the first two years. When at last he brought home a third-grade report card he was shocked to find only a few A's. "Never mind," his mother consoled. "You work really hard, and I am sure you could get more A's." But the same thing happened all through grade school. Things improved a little in high school, but always Doug knew he could do better if he tried harder. In college he decided to show everyone what he really could do. Every afternoon after class he went straight to the library and studied. And at last he made all A's. Doug had passed the test—the goal he had set for himself before he ever started school.

God's tests aren't like the goals we set to try ourselves against. He examines our hearts. Abraham was a friend of God. When God said, "Leave home and go to a land that I shall show you," he went. He entertained angels once and talked to God. When God gave him a son in his old age, his joy knew no bounds. He loved that son very much—naturally. Maybe God wanted to see whether Abraham loved Isaac more than Him. He tested Abraham's love by asking him to sacrifice Isaac on Mount Moriah. As they climbed the mountain together the young man asked where the lamb was for the sacrifice. "God will provide," his father assured him with aching heart. You know the rest of the story—how at the last minute when Abraham raised the knife, God called a halt to the test. Abraham had passed with flying colors. Temptations are unexpected tests of our loyalty to God. And you can be sure of passing God's tests if you trust Him as Abraham did.

THE PLAN UNFOLDED

And Abraham said, My son, God will provide himself a lamb for a burnt offering. Genesis 22:8.

An old man could have been excused for giving up. "Sorry, Lord," he might have said. "I was physically unable to make it to the top of Mount Moriah. If You really meant for me to sacrifice Isaac, why didn't You make it easier?" But Abraham wasn't a quitter. Neither did he ask, What kind of God commands a father to slay his son? Instead, he remembered all the good times—all the blessings—he had shared with God. Perhaps, he reasoned, the Lord would raise his son from the dead or work some other miracle.

But by the time Abraham had tied his son to the altar and raised the knife, his heart was breaking. "I don't understand the reason for this terrible thing, but Your will be done," he prayed.

Then the Lord did just as Abraham had said He would. He provided a ram, caught in a thicket. As Abraham and Isaac joyfully sacrificed the animal they could not know that all heaven was rejoicing with them. For as the angels watched the drama unfold, they had no idea how it would turn out. They were as relieved as Abraham when the ram appeared in the bushes. And suddenly the truth dawned on them. God would not let men die without hope of a resurrection. Jesus Himself was to be the Lamb who would die for the sins of the whole world.

Harold Richards learned the meaning of that lesson one summer day when he was teasing his kid brother mercilessly. "Next time you do that you will have to spank me," his mother said. Harold forgot the warning and soon set upon his brother again. "All right," his mother said, "go bring a switch." Harold loved his gentle mother and could not bring himself to strike her. Seeing how upset he was, his mother took him in her arms and explained how our sins wound the Saviour. Suddenly Harold realized that Jesus' death on Calvary delivered him from sin. It delivered you, me, and Isaac, too.

BUT JESUS WOULD

Some time later God tested Abraham. Genesis 22:1, N.I.V.

People carefully counted every penny when I was a girl. One day while shopping with my mother I found some small balloons. Balloons had not been available in Australia since before World War II, and I didn't remember ever having one of my own. Once at a picnic I had seen a little girl playing with one. My friends and I gathered at a safe distance, watching in envious silence.

And now here I was face to face with a whole packet of balloons. Wanting to see me experience something that every child should have known, Mother asked the clerk the price. "They're twopence," she said after checking the price on the packet.

So my mother bought the balloons, but insisted that I wait until after supper to open them. When she brought them out that evening she noticed that the price on the package read twopence per balloon and not per package.

Mother was prepared to pay twopence for the whole package but not for each balloon. "You may have one," she explained. "Choose which color you want. But we'll take the rest back to the store."

"Oh, Mother," I begged, "don't do that. Nobody will ever know."

"That's right," she agreed. "But Jesus would. And we don't want to disappoint Him."

So we returned the balloons to the clerk. She seemed impressed that we had taken the trouble. "I've made mistakes before," she said, "but nobody ever returned when the mistake was in his or her favor. Why did you bring back the balloons? Nobody would have known."

"Yes, but Jesus would," Mother said with a smile.

Years later while shopping with my daughter for clothes, we selected three T-shirts. But the clerk charged us for only two. After we had pointed out the error and she corrected it, we turned to leave. "Why did you tell her?" Julie whispered. "She wouldn't have known." And she answered her own question: "But Jesus would." And like Abraham, Mother, and me, Julie has learned to meet the test.

EGG TEETH AND EIDERDOWN

"God has come to test you, so that the fear of God will be with you to keep you from sinning." Exodus 20:20, N.I.V.

The mother killdeer prepares her nest and lays her eggs according to the manner of her species. Nobody taught her what to do. But God placed within her the ability to follow a built-in pattern of behavior. When enemies endanger her young she pretends to be injured, and lures the enemy away from her nest. She did not think up the tactic—it came by instinct. God thus provided for the killdeer's self-defense before ever it needed protection.

The killdeer chick grows within the strong protection of its egg until the time comes to break out. Its mother does not wait around to assist her weak offspring. The killdeer chick doesn't need help. Its egg teeth—tiny white projections on its beak—aid it in chipping away at the shell. And as it chips, it develops strength. When the shell finally cracks open, the chick has passed its first test of endurance.

Iceland's gray eider ducks begin to nest in early May. The female lines a hollowed-out space in the ground with soft, downy feathers from her breast, and lays her eggs. In spite of the cold, two weeks later farmers rob the nests of some of the down. The eiders soon replace the stolen down, which the men will sell for hundreds of dollars a pound. Why do the farmers steal the down when the baby chicks need it? Because otherwise the eider will not produce more.

God did not protect the children of Israel from the sound of His voice when they trembled with fear at Mount Sinai. He knew that this test of endurance, as they experienced His nearness and awesome presence, would develop in them a new respect for their mighty God and for the seriousness of sin. Likewise, the tests you meet today will help you develop an inner strength as you learn to stand up for the right. And you may be sure of success as you ask God to strengthen you.

DOES GOD TEMPT PEOPLE?

When tempted, no one should say, "God is tempting me." For God cannot be tempted by evil, nor does he tempt anyone. James 1:13, N.I.V.

Michelle learned to love food when she was only 10. At a time when most of her friends were refusing to eat because they didn't like vegetables, Michelle happily devoured anything placed before her—and much more. "If you keep on, you could be unhappy with yourself by the time you are 14," her mother gently reminded her. "Weight is easy to put on, but ever so hard to take off. So let's be careful now." And she and Michelle decided on a course of action. Today if you offer Michelle chocolates she will say, "Oh, you shouldn't *tempt* me like that!" And her friends know that she means that she has a weakness for chocolate candy.

After Jesus' baptism He went into the wilderness for a time. Matthew says that "Jesus was led by the Spirit into the desert to be *tempted* by the devil." Does that mean that Jesus had a weakness for sin just as Michelle has for chocolate? No, indeed. Jesus was not born with a weakness for sin as you and I were. But He was severely tested all the same. And He could have weakened and given in to Satan. Knowing this, He did not run away from the tests, but neither did He go looking for them.

I once heard of a little boy who hung around the corner fruit stand. His hands would hover over the bright-red apples. "What are you doing?" the vendor asked. "Are you trying to steal my apples?" The little boy straightened up quickly.

"No, Sir," he answered in all seriousness, "I'm trying not to!" Wasn't that a strange way to avoid temptation? Why then did Jesus go where He knew temptation awaited Him? Because He knew the best way to stand firm against the evil one was to stay close to His Father. He went into the wilderness to pray for forty days. Then He was ready for the test when Satan came to Him, and didn't try to avoid it.

And Jesus withstood temptation in the strength of the Holy Spirit—the same way you and I may be victorious Christians. Don't forget to ask for that power today.

A WAY OUT

But when you are tempted, he will also provide a way out so that you can stand up under it. 1 Corinthians 10:13, N.I.V.

"Mary Trim tells of jumping out of bed the morning of her school's track-and-field day. It was her last chance to win some trophies for the shelf above her bookcase. "If only I win at least one trophy!" she sighed.

By the time Mary arrived at the track, people were beginning to find their places in the stands. Mary complimented a long-legged junior who was effortlessly practicing hurdles. "Thanks," the girl responded. "I train at the athletic club on Saturdays. You should come too."

"I can't," Mary said. "I'm a Seventh-day Adventist. I go to church on Saturdays."

"Well, you should see your priest about getting permission to work out at the club," the other girl replied. "It would make a big difference to get some good coaching."

As Mary prepared for her long-jump event, the idea tempted her. With good coaching she would surely win that trophy. But she refused to think of it, deciding instead to concentrate on doing her best. When she won first place Mary again resisted the temptation to wish that she could have better coaching.

The next day in PE class the coach from the club offered to train all those who had won a place the previous day. Mary could hear herself refusing his offer before he had finished his speech. But to her surprise the coach announced that his training sessions would convene each afternoon after school. God had provided a wonderful way out.

After two weeks the coach announced a Saturday morning meet. "This is good experience for you," he said. And when Mary declined to attend, he seemed to understand. However, she was able to participate in a weekday track meet just before school ended. "Thank You for giving me one more chance to compete," she told the Lord. And she resolved always to look for His way out of tempting offers.

BEND IN THE ROAD

Lead me, O Lord, in your righteousness because of my enemies—make straight your way before me. Psalm 5:8, N.I.V.

That rainy October evening of her sixteenth year, Helen thought her world had come to an end. Numb with grief, she stood by the window and thought of the pleasant paths by which the Lord had led her. She saw herself walking with the family to church on Sunday mornings, dressed fit for the fashion page and holding her head high.

But without warning her father had died, leaving the family without support. As Helen gazed out the window she realized that she must give up her dreams for studying law. Instead, she would accept a job with the Ohio Public Service Company and stay close to home. Although she couldn't see it at the time, her life had come to a bend in the road. She put her trusting hand into the hand of God and carried on.

As she began the various tasks required in her work Helen determined to learn all she could about her work. As chairman of a women's committee she received her first invitation to speak at a convention. When she stepped to the podium her mind went blank. "Your heavenly Father knows what you are going to say," a voice reminded her. With a sigh of relief Helen asked the Lord to help, and she delivered the speech flawlessly. The audience enjoyed her talk, and word of her speaking ability soon spread. Conventions throughout the country invited her to lecture to them.

Her world almost ended again when her husband died. But the experience proved to be another bend in the road. The Lord led her into a whole new writing career. These words by Helen Steiner Rice may help you next time a crisis blocks your way:

"So rest and relax and grow stronger.
Let go and let God share your load.
Your work is not finished or ended.
You've just come to a bend in the road."

"I'VE BEEN BITTEN"

Now the serpent was more subtil than any beast of the field which the Lord God had made. Genesis 3:1.

When Louis Morton picked up the plastic bag and hoisted it to his shoulder that April night, he probably gave no thought to the danger it contained. Louis, a Washington, D.C., seventh-grader, was used to handling snakes. He had once kept a copperhead and a water moccasin in aquarium tanks. But his mother refused to let him enter the house again until he got rid of them. What Louis planned to do with the two deadly Gaboon vipers in the plastic bag is not altogether certain. But no sooner had he slung the bag over his shoulder and sauntered up 15th Street than he came running back.

Leaning on the door of the bus, he announced, "I've been bitten by a snake." When Jane White, the bus driver, noticed the two red punctures in Louis' jacket, she radioed for help. Louis was whisked away to Children's Hospital while antivenom was rushed in from the zoo and later from zoos all around the country.

The Gaboon viper is one of the deadliest snakes in the world, according to snake expert Dr. Dale Marcellini, of the National Zoo. It is also one of the most spectacularly beautiful—and stupid. The Gaboon viper lies around a lot. But if aroused, it rears up and "strikes with tremendous force." Its venom attacks the circulatory and nervous systems, bringing death in minutes.

By the time Louis arrived at the emergency room his blood pressure had dropped dangerously and he felt "nauseated, lethargic, and incoherent," according to the Washington *Post* account.

Sin intrigues us the way snakes did Louis. We think we can handle the danger. But harmless though it at first appears, sin eventually raises its ugly head and strikes. The best way to avoid the terrible scars of sin is to leave it alone—avoid the temptation. But if you do wander carelessly into the viper's nest of sin, never forget that Jesus provides the antivenom—free. He waits to forgive and to heal.

FENCES

Keep your servant also from willful sins; may they not rule over me. Then will I be blameless, innocent of great transgression. Psalm 19:13, N.I.V.

An ounce of prevention is worth a pound of cure, says the proverb. Better to build a fence at the top of the cliff than keep an ambulance at the bottom! Not only is it wise, but it is also efficient. I guess that's why my doctor didn't think too highly of my last health-insurance company. They would pay in full for every doctor's visit when I was sick. But they refused to reimburse for *keeping* me well, though it would have saved money in the end.

Fortunately God is both wise and efficient. He provides a cure for the sin-sick. And because Jesus paid an awful price for our sins, it hurts Him when we keep on sinning. That's why He goes to great lengths to help us gain the victory over sin. His commandments are meant to hedge us in so that we will avoid sin. They are like the fence at the top of the cliff. We willfully set them aside and do as we please only at great risk.

Bosco was only a macaque monkey with no idea of what was expected of him around people. He demanded to be the center of attention all the time. When he could not be with people, he liked the attention of other pets. He slept at night with a stray kitten, who fortunately liked Bosco's companionship. But Sheba, the school lamb, thought otherwise. She did not appreciate Bosco riding on her back.

Dorothy Eaton Watts tells how as the monkey grew older his natural curiosity got him into trouble. He stole tubes of toothpaste from the neighbors' open bathroom windows and took medicine and food. He scared innocent children by dropping out of trees onto their unsuspecting heads and once he even tried to kidnap a baby. He needed a good strong fence to box him in, but he hated his new cage and cried to be let out. One day he pried lose some bricks in the cage wall and ate a packet of rat poison. Bosco died a few hours later. If only he had realized what fences and cages were for!

WHATSOEVER THINGS

Whatsoever things are true, whatsoever things are honest, whatsoever things are just, whatsoever things are pure, whatsoever things are lovely, whatsoever things are of good report; if there be any virtue, and if there be any praise, think on these things. Philippians 4:8.

"What's full of holes, but holds water?" Carl teased as he clutched his *World* magazine to his chest so his brother couldn't see the answer. "Nothing!" Brucie declared confidently. "It's impossible."

"Nope! It's an animal that lives in the sea. But it has no eyes or ears, or mouth or brains. As a matter of fact, it doesn't have a heart, stomach, or legs," Carl added after checking the magazine again.

"Well, thanks a lot!" Brucie retorted. "Now I know that it can't walk. It probably doesn't eat, either."

"Wrong!" Carl said with a grin. "He doesn't chew, but he eats. All animals have to take in food. Plants make their own. Remember?"

"How long does this animal live?" Brucie was looking for hints.

"Oh, anywhere from ten to fifty years. They attach themselves to things under the sea. The water enters through little holes or pores. The animal filters food and absorbs oxygen from the water before forcing it out through a large opening. Divers harvest them. They are used to wash things." Carl was going to say that they came in different colors, too, but Brucie suddenly interrupted him.

"It's a sponge," he said excitedly. "There's one in the bathroom."

Carl looked a little deflated at having his brother guess so soon. "They used to be found in the bathroom," he corrected, "but nowadays people use plastic sponges—they're cheaper."

Have you ever thought how sponges are like your mind? They soak up anything they touch. Your mind absorbs and stores away everything it sees and hears, as well as all your thoughts. That's why you should reread today's text and determine to soak up only the very best.

PROVE IT!

And this he said to prove him: for he himself knew what he would do. John 6:6.

When I was 10, Doug was the orneriest character on our block. Anything that we had learned to do, he already did better. Not only was Doug older and bigger than we were; he was infinitely smarter. (At least he thought he was.) I thought I had Doug when I casually suggested one day that although he usually won our arguments, girls as a whole were smarter than boys. But Doug squelched that triumph with two swift words: "Prove it!"

While silently admitting defeat, I recognized a brilliant new weapon against his smart tactics. Whenever he slipped in some new information to impress us, I would demand, "Prove it!" Maybe that's when I came to like science classes. They gave us endless opportunities to prove things. For instance, you can *prove* that air expands and contracts (shrinks). You need two pop bottles, two balloons, a pan of ice water, and one of hot water. Fit the balloons over the pop bottles and place one bottle in each pan. Watch what happens. The balloon that flops over limp has less air in it because the air in that bottle contracted. The other balloon will inflate because the expanding air in the other bottle filled it out. But you'll have to perform your own experiment in order to prove which expanded the air—the heat or the cold.

Did you know that God sometimes chooses to prove people? When the five thousand followed Him and listened to Him all day, He wanted to feed them before sending them home. He asked Philip (who came from that area) where would be a good place to buy them food. He asked not because He didn't know, but because He wanted to prove the disciple—to see what he would say. And Philip demonstrated that his faith was small. He didn't think Jesus could afford to feed so many people. When Jesus did feed them all from one little boy's sack lunch, He showed what faith can do. And Jesus wants to help you use today's bothersome experiences to expand your faith and love.

A GRIZZLY TRIAL

"Today, if you hear his voice, do not harden your hearts as you did . . . during the time of testing in the desert." Hebrews 3:7-9, N.I.V.

The six-hundred-pound grizzly bear snoozes in the warm sunshine as her three yearling cubs explore the nearby woods. One cub stretches his nose into the wind and smells fresh meat. The other two cubs soon pick up the scent and scurry after their brother. Over fallen logs and through sticky brambles they race, lured from the protection of their mother. They find a half-buried carcass, but do not see the four wolves moving in to attack. The wolves spring, and frightened cries soon bring the mother grizzly. The wolves include her in their attack, trying to separate her from the cubs.

No sooner have the bears fought their way to the safety of a nearby hill but the smallest and weakest of the cubs deliberately ignores the wishes of his mother and returns to the half-buried carcass. Within seconds hungry wolves surround him. Should the mother again expose herself and the other cubs in order to save the disobedient cub? She has no other choice.

The leader of the wolf pack distracts the mother's attention away from the cubs. But she soon realizes that the other wolves are concentrating their attack on her weakest cub. Breaking away, she charges furiously into their midst, swinging her powerful paws in self-defense. With the same fury she swats both cubs and drives them bawling before her toward the safety of an icy stream. The weak cub hesitates on the shore, but, showing no mercy, she pushes him into the stream. Does he understand the necessity of his mother's stern actions? Or does the trial of the freezing water block out his memory of the wolves? Can you "greatly rejoice, though now for a little while you may have had to suffer grief in all kinds of trials" (1 Peter 1:6)? "These have come so that your faith . . . may be proved genuine" (verse 7).

PROVE YOURSELF

Examine yourselves, whether ye be in the faith; prove your own selves. 2 Corinthians 13:5.

If you are small for your age you can sympathize with Lennie. Since before he could remember, people had pinched his cheek and told him how cute he was. Valuing height above cuteness he began to work out with weights, building his muscles and hoping to grow taller. But although Lennie couldn't change his height, he did develop into a fast sprinter.

At the school Sports Day he hoped to win the 440-yard sprint, though he would compete against fellows much older and faster than he. Hoping to use this opportunity to prove himself to the whole school, Lennie had trained for months.

Lennie started well. Taking an early lead, he gradually increased the distance between himself and the rest of the pack. The enthusiastic cheers of classmates assured him that at last he had captured their attention. But soon the cheers sounded more frenzied, and he guessed that someone was gaining on him.

That must be Bruce, he thought. Bruce wouldn't let a lowly sophomore win without a good fight. Determined to draw on all his speed to keep ahead, Lennie lost concentration for a split second and fell heavily on the cinder track. The crowd echoed the disappointment he felt.

But instead of despairing over his lost chance to prove himself, Lennie jumped to his feet and, ignoring the blood oozing from his knees, raced down the track. Drawing on his reserve strength, he ran faster than he had ever run in his life. He caught up to and passed the stragglers. The cheering turned to screams as Lennie sped after the leader.

"Had the race been one hundred yards longer you might have won," the dean said later. "That was the most thrilling race of the day." And though he didn't win, Lennie knew he had proved himself. As we run the race of faith today, let's prove ourselves, as Lennie did.

THE ROCK

The Lord is upright: he is my rock, and there is no unrighteousness in him. Psalm 92:15.

Has anyone ever accused you of having rocks in your head? Even though you sometimes act without thinking, you don't like people to suggest that your brain has frozen solid. But maybe a rock in the head is not such a bad idea—if it is "the" Rock.

Did you know that rocks can be useful—on the inside? Crocodiles swallow rocks. That's probably why they can lurk just under the surface of the water with only their eyes and a little strip of snout showing. The weight of the stones in its stomach keeps the top-heavy and tail-heavy croc from flipping over and floating on its back. The rocks also make it easier to submerge with a struggling antelope and lie on the river bottom until the unfortunate dinner drowns.

Penguins also eat rocks. As with the crocodile, the rocks go to the penguin's stomach—not to his head. Most birds eat gravel to help digest the hard seeds that they swallow. But penguins eat only soft food. They don't need the rocks to aid digestion. Scientists think that the weight of the rocks makes swimming and diving easier for penguins. And it helps them right themselves in the surf.

Sometimes when storms of trouble blow about me I am glad that I have a Rock. When I keep in touch with Him He helps keep me upright. Even when some weakness of mine gets the better of me and knocks me over, the Rock reminds me that I may be down but I'm not out. He helps me bounce back and reminds me to keep my mind fixed on Him.

If you wish you could bounce back more quickly when something makes you feel down in the dumps, don't start eating rocks. Eat *the* Rock. How do you do that? By Bible study and prayer. As your eyes "eat" up the words on the page, the ideas you learn help to bring your mind in touch with Jesus, *the* Rock. If you study something until you understand it, we say that you have "digested" that information. The *Reader's Digest* often makes articles simpler—easier to understand. Prayer helps you digest the great truths of the Bible. And the more you read and pray, the better you understand and love the Rock.

OUT OF THIS WORLD

"My prayer is not that you take them out of the world but that you protect them from the evil one." John 17:15, N.I.V.

The story is told of a master violin maker commissioned to fashion a brand-new violin. Wishing to find exactly the right material for the instrument, the man chose wood from a gnarled old tree that had withstood many a battering by wind and rain, instead of one that had grown in the shelter of the forest.

Through the years some Christians have sought to avoid the temptations of the world by locking themselves away. Simon Stylites perched high atop a rock, hauling up his food and water on a rope. For more than thirty-five years he sat unprotected from the weather and unpolluted by the joys and sorrows of the world.

In Jesus' day the Jews did not associate with or speak to Samaritans. As far as possible, they avoided mingling with Gentiles so as to avoid the temptation to follow their gods. But this was not Jesus' idea when He taught the disciples to pray, "Lead us not into temptation." In His final prayer in the garden Jesus said, "'My prayer is not that you take them out of the world but that you protect them from the evil one.'"

One summer I received a beautiful azalea plant. I read with great interest the explanation that came with it, for I wanted to put it in a sheltered spot near the house. The slip of paper stated that the azalea had grown in a hothouse where light and temperature were carefully regulated. But I was instructed not to plant the azalea outdoors—its life in the hothouse had unfitted it to withstand the winter. The azalea never bloomed again, because I couldn't simulate the hothouse conditions. Eventually I threw it out.

Knowing that hothouse Christians will never mature into the men and women who will change this world, Jesus does not promise to remove temptations. But as you walk day by day with Him He will help you to choose wisely so that you may bravely resist the storms of temptations from the evil one and grow into a victorious and useful Christian.

THE MAN UPSTAIRS

Keep me from the snares which they have laid for me. Psalm 141:9.

Today's text reminds us that with temptations, as with any kind of trouble, prevention is better than cure. It would make a good prayer to begin every day: "Keep me from the snares which they have laid for me." If you were a spy setting out on an important mission, wouldn't you make sure that you had everything you needed before you started? You would not wait until you found yourself in a tight spot before asking for the key to decode your instructions. So it is today. You have a mission. Nobody else can carry it out for you. So why not check the Bible, your instructions book. And since you'll need all the help you can get, kneel beside your bed and pray, "Lord, keep me from the snares today." Then go out, holding your head high. Yours will be a successful mission today.

As the teachers in a large public school sat around planning a field trip, somebody asked about the weather forecast for the day of the trip. "Wouldn't it be a disaster if it rained," he said. "We cannot reschedule the trip. So if it rains the whole thing is off for this year."

Then the principal turned to me and said, "You'd better talk to the Man upstairs. Tell Him we need a good day." I smiled to myself and wished I could think of a way to tell him that, while God cares about little things and answers prayers, I can't manipulate Him into answering my prayers. And I can't just do whatever I like without consulting Him and then expect that He will arrange good weather for me when I ask. But when I pray, "Keep me from the snares," I know that I will do all in my power to stay away from the snares—the bad shows on TV, the cheap, trashy books, and the dirty jokes. You have your own list of snares. God will help you stay away from them and protect you from the pitfalls you aren't aware of. Yes, the Man upstairs hears, and cares, but you can't use Him just the day of the field trip. You must ask Him to keep you from temptation if you want deliverance from evil.

SAYING NO

We know that suffering produces perseverance; perseverance, character; and character, hope. Romans 5:3, 4, N.I.V.

Have you ever noticed how 2-year-olds like to say No? My brothers and I used to deliberately ask questions of a 2-year-old. "Do you like me?" we'd ask.

"No!"

"Do you like yourself?"

"No!" No is a 2-year-old's favorite word.

I guess you and I were once terrible twos, reveling in our newfound power to refuse. But something happened along the way. "Let's skip class," Norm whispers. You don't really want to, but it *is* warm. Besides, can you imagine a whole year of being on the wrong side of Norm? Suddenly No is difficult to say.

It hurts to say No. Your friends get offended. They accuse you of acting stuck-up, and leave you out of their activities. But Paul helps you look at it another way: Saying No hurts, but it helps you stand for the right. Standing for the right helps you stiffen your backbone—other people will say you have "character." And people of character have hope (faith). So in the end you feel happy about yourself. You know that you and God can do great things.

If you find it hard to say No, remember that saying No to a bad idea is the same as saying Yes to being in charge of your own life. It's like saying, I want to be me. And saying No to temptation is saying Yes to God. So don't waste time wondering what you missed by saying No. Concentrate instead on what you gained by saying Yes. Saying No to drugs is saying Yes to good health and to winning. Saying No to bad magazines can be a Yes for reading a true adventure story. Next time you say No to setting up a dumb practical joke, say Yes to a clean one that won't hurt anyone.

Saying No is not all bad. Sure, it hurts sometimes, but each No makes it easier for the next. And being in charge of yourself makes you feel free and grown-up. It's a whole new way of life. And it begins each morning with Jesus. He has the power to help you say No.

ALICE'S TEST

The testing of your faith develops perseverance. James 1:2, N.I.V.

"Can you do addition?" the White Queen asked. "What's one and one and one and one and one and one and one and one and one and one?"

"I don't know," said Alice. "I lost count."

"She can't do addition," the Red Queen interrupted. "Can you do subtraction? Take nine from eight."

"Nine from eight I can't, you know," Alice replied readily. . . .

"She can't do subtraction," said the White Queen.

As you already know, life is full of tests. You have taken timed tests, achievement tests, intelligence tests, reading tests. Some tests, like the one that Alice faced in Lewis Carroll's *Through the Looking Glass,* frustrate you. People sometimes even have bad dreams about tests—like one adult student who dreams that he gets into the test room late for an important exam. All the other students are busily writing when he finds his seat. He opens the booklet only to discover that every page is blank.

You have probably already discovered that tests are not the end of the world. In fact, they can be a way to grow. You ask your friends after a test, "What answer did you give for number 4?" and discover that yours was wrong. But after the class brain explains it, you never again forget the correct answer. So tests can help you learn.

One lesson I'll never forget came the day I completed a forty-minute test in fifteen minutes. Mr. Gifford corrected my paper immediately and gave me 100 percent. "Why don't you try this sixth-grade test while you wait?" he asked. But I didn't have a clue as to how to pass it.

In the game of life the important tests are easy at first, but they get harder. You don't pass all of them the first time. But as you keep at them with Jesus' help, your faith grows. In the final examination at the end of time, your passing it is assured if you learn to depend on Him now.

DOG DAYS

Dear friends, do not be surprised at the painful trial you are suffering, as though something strange were happening to you. 1 Peter 4:12, N.I.V.

August in Washington, D.C., is a sizzling month. That's when people talk of dog days—not that dogs enjoy this weather. Because Sirius, the Dog Star, seemed to rise with the sun during July and August, the ancient Greeks spoke of dog days. By the way, Sirius is the brightest star and radiates about thirty times as much light as our sun, but it's too far away for its heat to reach us.

Scott thinks the name dog days fits because of how an August day leaves him feeling grumpy. He snaps at his sister for no particular reason. "It's because you feel hot," his mother explained. "When you're uncomfortable your patience wears thin." The boy knew that—why else would he have let fly with a shoe when his sister made him mad? "Well, why did you bring us to Washington?" he demanded when his mother scolded him. "The weather makes me do it."

In today's text the apostle Peter says, "Do not be surprised at the painful trial you are suffering." Don't give in to it. He goes on to suggest that trials and temptations might be good for us if we use them as a way to grow up. After all, that is the way to learn. When a mouse cannot get to the cheese because of an obstacle in his way, he looks for a way to get around (or over or under) it. When he finds a way, he has learned something. Next time he meets that obstacle, he knows what to do.

So what will you do when temptation comes to you today? Don't use August's dog days as an excuse to give in. But with God's help, turn the temptation into a learning experience.

Many children from Christian schools across America have discovered something to improve their attitudes. They spend from ten to twenty minutes each morning in a quiet time with the Lord. "You can't have a good day without it," they say. And you can't. Are you trying it?

LOOKING FOR TROUBLE

Be sure your sin will find you out. Numbers 32:23.

Have you ever been tempted to get into trouble? I doubt it. The serpent could never have persuaded Eve to eat the fruit if he had told her a fraction of the problems it would bring. "Here, taste this; it won't kill you right away," he might have said. "You'll enjoy the flavor at first, but it will bring eventual misery and death." Eve was too smart to fall for a story like that. So Satan lied instead. And he's been lying ever since.

When Cain got mad at his brother he might have checked his anger had he known how lonely he would be, a murderer sent away from home.

Pete and Charlie didn't realize that the temptation to disobey Mother and go wading in late October was an invitation to strep throat and missing three days of school. Had they known, do you think they would have been so eager to get their shoes and socks off?

You can probably name all kinds of temptations that you have fallen for, only to discover yourself stuck with the consequences—some sort of trouble that you hadn't bargained on. The Bible warning "Be sure your sin will find you out" is another way of saying that sin spells trouble—eventual embarrassment and pain.

Frankie and Dan couldn't resist the temptation to skip Friday evening vespers and explore the attic upstairs. "No one will know, and it will be such fun," they reassured each other. It may have been. But Dan stepped from the supported walkway onto the soft ceiling tile. The smiles were all on the faces of the people sitting in chapel when they saw his body dangling above them. I hardly think any argument could have convinced him to miss vespers had he known the consequences in advance.

Next time you suspect that you are being tempted to do something you shouldn't, remember today's text. Though sin may look ever so attractive, in the long run it "will find you out"—and let you down badly.

THE TASTE TEST

Taste and see that the Lord is good. Psalm 34:8, N.I.V.

"I'm going to give you a taste test," Miss Rogers told her class. "Each of the ten vials is numbered. Remove the cap and smell the contents. Then write down what you think you smell."

The class buzzed with excitement as they opened and cautiously sniffed each tiny bottle. Linda easily identified the first sample and wrote "ammonia" at the head of her list. She wasn't sure of the fifth one. It seemed familiar. If only she could see what color it was, but each specimen looked the same—a damp cotton ball in a clean bottle. Was it mouthwash, toothpaste, or peppermint food flavoring? Linda fished out the cotton ball and touched it to her tongue. Mouthwash, she decided. Number eight posed a problem. The cotton ball clearly looked wet but had no odor at all. Linda knew she couldn't go tasting all of the samples. So she took a chance and wrote "water."

God knows that, like Linda, you and I trust our sense of taste. So He set up a test of His own, and He challenges you and me to "taste and see that the Lord is good."

If you are growing up in a family that doesn't take God too seriously, you may be afraid of His taste test. You feel uncomfortable because you don't know what you are getting into.

Or perhaps your parents love God and urge you to make Him your friend too, but you don't know if you'll like it. You should do as you would with new foods. Some people say, "Try it, you'll like it." If you trust their judgment you'll at least taste it. You know it can't hurt you.

And when you take God's taste test by reading the Bible and praying every day, you're in for a surprise. Like Timothy. He started smoking when he was 9. But at 17 he saw a Stop Smoking-clinic advertisment in a Detroit newspaper. Tim attended and finally kicked the habit. "I didn't know that food could taste so good," he marveled. After God's taste test, life seems better too.

PREVENTIVE MEDICINE

Because thou hast kept the word of my patience, I also will keep thee from the hour of temptation. Revelation 3:10.

Paddling is one effective but unpopular method of keeping children from temptation. According to James Hunt, principal of Booker T. Washington Junior High, school paddlings are on the increase. Mr. Hunt claims to have administered 874 paddlings in one year—an average of five per day. He states that paddlings are popular with parents and don't put students behind in their schoolwork.

"I like paddles," says Minerva Straman, seventh-grade teacher for sixteen years. "My classes like them too. In fact, at the beginning of each school year my students clamor to see my fifty-three-paddle collection. They get a kick out of The Killer, The Judge, The Sting, The Vice President, The Song Leader, The Butcher, and the four-paddle set: Eeny, Meeny, Miney, and No Mo." Usually Mrs. Straman allows her class to choose twelve paddles to hang in the classroom. "I've never used any—YET! I appeal first to pride and then to hide!" she says with a twinkle. Fortunately her students prefer to get their own act together. "It's a matter of self-control," one of her former students says. "I learned to ask myself: Can I handle this situation? Usually I decided that I could. But if ever I needed help, she was there." Students in Mrs. Straman's classes enjoy her sense of humor and her no-nonsense approach to work.

Does God believe in paddling? I'm sure He does—but only as a last resort. His first plan is to help me take control. And He wants to help me learn. He assists me in reaching my goals and then whispers that He has big plans for me. God teaches me to pace myself, and above all He trusts me. I feel bad when I let Him down, but He helps me in getting my act together and starting over. When I read the Bible and pray, He keeps me not only from trouble but also from its consequences—like the paddle. That's why I'm starting out with Him today.

CONSENT THOU NOT

My son, if sinners entice thee, consent thou not. Proverbs 1:10.

The morning's devotional text was so easy that Kevin had it memorized in no time flat. He understood what it meant, too. But he didn't think he was likely to be enticed to do something wrong, because he would be too busy. After school he had promised to baby-sit his 2-year-old sister, Betty Ruth, while his mother attended the mothers' club meeting.

Kevin felt good about his decision as he waved goodbye to his mother and began playing with Betty Ruth. Her laughter filled the yard so that Kevin almost missed the familiar whistle that called the boys of his team to their evening ball game.

At first the boys teased Kevin for insisting that he must stay home and watch Betty Ruth. Then they suggested that they play on the vacant lot next door so that he could watch his sister in her playpen at the same time. Reluctantly Kevin agreed. During the first inning he watched her often. Then he became absorbed in the game until he heard a sudden screech of brakes on the road. A quick glance at the playpen confirmed his worst fears. It was empty. He had forgotten how well Betty Ruth could climb.

When Kevin ran to the road, he found her crumpled in a heap. Fortunately his father came home just then, and hurried her off to the hospital. Apart from a broken arm she was OK, but her mother had to stay with her that night.

"I guess we men will have to look after ourselves," Kevin's father said when he came home. At eight-thirty as they were saying Good night, his dad asked him to review his memory verse one more time. Kevin hung his head as he remembered it: "My son, if sinners entice thee, consent thou not."

Suddenly Kevin felt bad. He had let God down—his dad, too. As the tears flowed down his cheeks, his father held him close. "You failed the test, but with Jesus' help I know you really learned the lesson," Dad said. And he was right.

Adapted from Lois Christian Randolph, "Betty's Brother," *Guide*, April 16, 1969.

LET IT GROW

For when the way is rough, your patience has a chance to grow. So let it grow, and don't try to squirm out of your problems. James 1:3, 4, T.L.B.

When 13-year-old Heidi Jaeger woke up at five o'clock that summer morning she felt a cold breeze on her neck. The girl remembered how snug she had felt the night before with little Susie beside her and Joe on the other side of Susie. But where was that cool breeze coming from? Reaching behind her, she found a large hole cut in the back of the family tent and Susie's sleeping bag empty.

After waking the rest of the family, Heidi helped search their campsite in the predawn darkness. If only God would send the light so they could see!

But daylight brought no clues. Susie had disappeared without a trace—except for her stuffed animals lying on the ground outside the tent.

For the next sixteen dreary months Heidi and her family hoped and prayed and worked to find the child. Many times the trial seemed more than Heidi could bear. Sometimes when she saw the sadness in her parents' eyes or felt the emptiness in her own heart, she would find a quiet place to cry all alone.

Heidi could have turned to alcohol or drugs to hide from this trial, as other children of her age sometimes do. Or she could have given in to the anger that she felt. But she wisely listened to her mother's counsel and trusted Jesus to help her face one day at a time.

When Susie's body was found and her abductor arrested, Heidi and her family were so filled with the love and patience of Jesus that they forgave the man. "We would never ask to go through a trial like that," Heidi's mother said. "But out of our darkness God brought the light of Jesus' love. In the rough times God helped our patience grow."

TAR IN THE BASEMENT

"Watch and pray so that you will not fall into temptation." Matthew 26:41, N.I.V.

"What's in the basement?" Manfred asked as he explored the family's new house.

"I wanted to talk to you about that," his mom replied. "You may go down and take a look, but don't touch anything." Carefully the children climbed down the steps and looked around. "Wow!" Manfred exclaimed. "See how clean it is." No soot from the furnace darkened the walls. Not a drop of paint marred the concrete floor. It was the cleanest basement he had ever seen. In one end of the basement stood piles of clean lumber, cans of paint, and a large black drum with a tightly fitted lid.

"Please, don't ever touch that drum," Mrs. Schmitt said as she joined the children. Immediately Manfred wanted to know why, but his mother refused to say any more about it. Often after that Manfred wandered down to the basement. And always he ended up standing beside that drum. By tapping the side, he established that it was full of something. If only he could take a peek!

Then one afternoon he could resist the temptation no longer. With great difficulty he used a large screwdriver to pry the lid from that drum. And when he did, the most awful-smelling, thick, black goo oozed out and onto the clean floor and ran in a stream that inched its way toward the wall. "Tar!" he yelled in horror. Instinctively he knew that no one could ever wash the mess away. The basement floor was permanently spoiled. "I'm in trouble for sure!" he cried, tears splashing down his face.

"It didn't turn out so bad," he told me recently. "I wasn't spanked. But I will never forget the horror of seeing that tar ooze from the open drum, and knowing that what I'd done could never be erased." Sin leaves permanent scars on our hearts, too. God blots out the blame for what happens, but we have to live with the consequences of our mistakes. How much better to seek God's help to avoid temptation in the first place.

KEPT ON YOUR TOES

Test me, O Lord, and try me; put my heart and mind to the proof. For thy constant love is before my eyes, and I live in thy truth. Psalm 26:2, N.E.B.

The cod fishermen of Maine equipped their boats with holding tanks, which they filled with seawater. When they made a catch, they would put the cod into the tanks to keep the fish fresh until they were ready to head for land and the fish markets.

The idea seemed good, but it did not work. When the cod went into the holding tanks, they just lolled around on the bottom and lost their body tone. Their flesh went flabby and produced soft meat for which buyers would not pay well. The fishermen discovered that by adding a catfish to the holding tank, the cod kept constantly moving. Their natural enemy made them active.

You and I have a tendency to become spiritually flabby when our lives run smoothly all the time. Perhaps God allows irritations to come our way to keep us on our toes.

Chaim Potok tells the story of Rueven Malter, a Jewish boy who visits his friend Danny one Sabbath afternoon. Danny's father is a learned rabbi who subjects his son to an unusual weekly test. Before a synagogue full of people, the rabbi begins to expound Jewish law, quoting many learned scholars. When he finishes he expects his son to tell him if he made any mistakes. Danny must also comment on the argument and quote other learned scholars.

Rueven is impressed with Danny's memory as he shows where his father misquoted a scholar and where he disagrees with his father's interpretations. The men in the synagogue enjoy the exchange of ideas. But afterward Rueven tells Danny that he thinks a public test like that is cruel and unusual. "Oh, it's not so bad," the other defends. "I don't mind it. Besides, it keeps me alert and thinking."

When difficulties come to you today, treat them as something to keep you on your toes—a test of your constant love for God.

TO CATCH A THIEF

Submit yourselves, then, to God. Resist the devil, and he will flee from you. Come near to God and he will come near to you. James 4:7, 8, N.I.V.

"Oh, it's easy," Herbie whispered. "I'll show you what to do." Looking over the toy cars that the salesman showed him, he then asked to see a model not on display. As soon as the man went to get it, Herbie slipped behind the counter and helped himself to a model from under the counter. He gave Manfred one also. Both boys stuffed their loot into their pockets before the salesman returned.

"I told you it would be easy," Herbie gloated as the two of them walked home. But Herbie didn't say anything about the horrible feeling that would come with the stolen car. Manfred couldn't show his to anyone for fear they would ask where he got it. But he went on stealing anyway. In the months that followed, Manfred became alarmingly adept at stealing anything that pleased him. He just couldn't stop himself.

One day as he was buying something for his mother at the candy store, Mrs. Moore, the owner, turned to serve another customer. Automatically Manfred reached for a handful of jelly beans. The owner turned around while his hand was still in the jelly bean dish. She didn't say a word, but Manfred felt awful. For the first time he had been caught. Mrs. Moore knew he was a thief. All the way home his conscience bothered him. Manfred knew he was powerless to break the thieving habit. Suddenly he remembered how his grandmother had told him of the power of prayer. Maybe with God's help he could break the awful habit. "Dear God, I can't stop taking things," he prayed. "Please take away the desire to help myself to anything I see. Amen." The next time he walked into a store he realized that he didn't have to steal anything. God had answered his prayer. "But I couldn't have resisted the devil on my own," he tells boys and girls today. "First I had to give in to God."

OVERCOMER'S BLOOD

Because he himself suffered when he was tempted, he is able to help those who are being tempted. Hebrews 2:18, N.I.V.

The famous mission doctor Paul Brand tells how an epidemic of measles struck Vellore, India. When his older daughter contracted a severe case, he feared for the life of his younger infant daughter. A pediatrician advised Dr. Brand to obtain some convalescent serum. So the word went out that the Brands needed the "blood of an overcomer"—someone who had been infected with measles but who had fought it off. The blood of someone who had struggled with mumps or malaria would not help. The person must have produced the antibodies to fight measles.

When the doctor found the blood and let the cells settle out, he injected convalescent serum into the child. With the borrowed antibodies the child suffered no ill effects from the measles. She fought off the measles not by her own strength, but because someone else had previously battled the illness.

This story suggests that perhaps blood becomes more valuable after it has fought off disease. For that reason Terry knows he cannot get mumps again. His glands swelled up until they nearly closed his eyes. But his blood fought off the infection and built up antibodies that now protect him from coming down with the disease again.

By coming to earth, Jesus went out of His way to expose Himself to temptation. He encountered the same stress and strain that temptation brings us. By so doing, He developed "Overcomer's blood" that can save us from temptation. Do you suppose that's the reason he did not try to avoid the temptation in the wilderness?

Next time you go to Communion, remember that the grape juice represents Jesus' blood—Overcomer's blood that can save you from sin. And "because he himself suffered when he was tempted, he is able to help those who are being tempted." And that means you and me.

THE TRANSFUSION

Jesus said to them, "I tell you the truth, unless you eat the flesh of the Son of Man and drink his blood, you have no life in you." John 6:53, N.I.V.

"She looked like a waxwork madonna or an alabaster saint statue in a cathedral. Her lips, too, were pallid. . . . She did not seem to be breathing, having long before passed through the desperate phase of heavy breathing. I felt sure she was dead.

"Then the nurse arrived with a bottle of blood, which she buckled into a high metal stand as the doctor punctured the woman's vein with a large needle. They had mounted the bottle high and were using an extra-long tube so that the increase in pressure would push the blood into her body faster. The staff told me to watch over the emptying bottle while they scurried off for more blood.

"Nothing in my memory can compare to the excitement of what happened next. Certainly the precise details of that scene remain vividly with me to this day. As I nervously held her wrist while the others were gone, suddenly I felt the faintest press of a pulse. Or was it my own pulse? I searched again—it was there, barely perceptible but regular, at least. The next bottle of blood arrived and was quickly connected. A spot of pink appeared on her cheek, and spread into a beautiful flush. Her lips darkened pink, then red, and her body quivered in a kind of sighing breath.

"Then her eyelids fluttered lightly and at last parted. She squinted at first, as her pupils adjusted to the bright lights of the room, and at last she looked directly at me. To my enormous surprise, in a very short time she spoke, asking for water." *

If Jesus were here today and he wanted to describe to us the way He delivers us from evil, don't you suppose He would do so in terms of a blood transfusion? Dr. Brand thinks He would. Sin has drained away our right to eternal life, but Jesus waits to hook us to a supply of His life-giving blood. He doesn't fuss with plastic tubes, though. All it takes is a prayer to get hooked up.

---

* As appeared in *Christianity Today*, adapted from *In His Image*, by Dr. Paul Brand and Philip Yancey. Used by permission of Zondervan Publishing House.

THE CATERPILLAR SNAKE

Being then made free from sin, ye became the servants of righteousness. Romans 6:18.

"It's just like a miniature buzz saw slicing away the leaf," Gary exclaimed, his eyes wide with wonder. "I can't see his jaws chomping, and I don't hear the saw, but look how the leaf keeps disappearing with each turn of the caterpillar's head."

That's how it is with sin. You can't always see it eating on you, but it slices away your reputation and your character. Have you noticed how some caterpillars—the hairy-looking type—look evil? You don't trust them, so you squish them. But others look so pretty that you can't believe they would do any harm. But I've seen harmless-looking caterpillars strip the leaves from an oak tree, thus depriving the tree of its food.

An enterprising type of caterpillar found in the Amazon rain forest protects itself from natural enemies by sucking in air and swelling out the front of its body. Its head thus becomes triangular like a snake's. Two black markings on either side of the head resemble sinister eyes. The dark skin of its back and lighter underbelly make it appear like a deadly tree snake that no bird wants to tangle with. So the caterpillar is safe. When danger passes, the fake snake lets the air out and goes its way.

Sometimes sin looks no more dangerous than a fake snake. Clever advertising makes smoking and drinking look harmless—even beneficial. TV cartoons show lying and stealing as clever tricks used by intelligent children to achieve popularity and independence. You and I cannot appreciate the greatness and goodness of our holy God until we recognize that even the most attractive-looking sins weaken and separate us from Him.

The good news this morning says that Jesus came to free us from sin so that we could serve Him in rightdoing. But first we must recognize sin's destructive power and our need of His help. As you walk with Him today, ask Him to make you a servant of righteousness, free from the caterpillars of sin.

FAST WORK

Turn, O Lord, and deliver me; save me because of your unfailing love. Psalm 6:4, N.I.V.

If you have been praying the Lord's Prayer lately you have probably noticed how that saying "Our Father" reminds you of the love of God. In His model prayer Jesus teaches us to pray for the really important things. Do you remember what they are?

First, you pray for His kingdom of love; second, for understanding of His plan for you; third, for the basics: food and shelter. Fourth, you admit that you aren't perfect and ask forgiveness. And lest you fall into the same mistakes again, you ask for strength to resist temptation. And now comes the part of the prayer that seems most important to people your age: "Deliver us from evil."

Little children often think of prayer as asking for *things*. But by now you have more important concerns: the scary, fearsome things you have seen, heard, or read about. And so you come to think of prayer more as a cry for help, a lifeline to save you from pain, embarrassment, unhappiness, and death.

That's why teenagers sometimes say, "God doesn't answer prayer anymore." They forget that feeling God's love and knowing His will are themselves answers to prayer. And so are the food and clothing He provides and the closets full of toys. When we look only at the ugly things that Satan has caused, it's easy to blame God and think that He no longer answers prayer.

So when we pray, let's remember all of the Lord's Prayer. If we aren't interested in His kingdom or His will, is it fair to expect Him to deliver us from evil? Like the boy who cried because he was tripped up when he would have run into the path of an oncoming truck, we sometimes don't recognize deliverance when it comes.

Irwin had given up praying because He couldn't see that it did any good. But when he was kidnapped at gunpoint and forced to drive two criminals to Florida, he felt the overpowering urge to pray. An attendant at a service station noticed the blood on Irwin's head and alerted the State troopers. Irwin knows that not only did God answer his prayer, but He worked fast. He always does, but sometimes it takes much longer to appreciate His answer.

A CLOSE CALL

Call upon me in the day of trouble: I will deliver thee, and thou shalt glorify me. Psalm 50:15.

When the family drove to Sydney for their annual seaside vacation, Mary's parents insisted on leaving her pets at home. But the girl fretted until eventually her father telephoned home to ask someone to bring Ajax, Mary's golden-haired dog.

The day Ajax came bounding over the garden fence, the vacation began in earnest for Mary. Suddenly she enjoyed swimming in the quiet inlet in back of the house. One morning she awakened early and decided to tiptoe through the house without waking anyone. She would enjoy an early swim on her own. Quietly she unlatched the back door without waking the dog and ran down through the back garden.

The tide was out, and the water lay oily smooth. The sun had not yet risen when she dived in and began swimming about. After a while she decided to head for shore. When she turned back, she noticed to her surprise how far from shore she had come. As she began to kick toward home, she realized that the tide was still going out. She could not move against it. Remembering how futile it is to fight the tide, she rested on her back, wondering what to do. Suddenly she thought of the sharks that sometimes swim into the inlets around Sydney Harbor and wondered whether she might drift out to sea before anyone missed her. Then she remembered her dog. "Ajax!" she called, as loudly as she could.

Within seconds she saw a golden spot bound across the distant beach and melt into the water. Another dot then appeared and launched a dinghy. Later Mary's father told her how he had to pull both Mary and Ajax into the boat together because he couldn't pry her fingers apart from around the dog's neck. The animal's alertness and devotion had saved her life.

Most of us do not have dogs to appear miraculously when we are in trouble. But today's text reminds us to call upon the Lord. His deliverance comes in different ways. Sometimes not quite as we expect. But trust Him—His deliverance is sure.

TO SEEK AND TO SAVE

For the Son of man is come to seek and to save that which was lost. Luke 19:10.

More than eighty years ago Alex, a Scottish farm boy, noticed a young man in difficulty swimming in a lake. Immediately he dived in and brought the swimmer to shore. The parents of the rescued youth showed their gratitude by offering to pay for Alex's education at a top medical school in London.

He did well in his studies and majored in bacteriology. Later he became a professor at the same school. After the first world war Alex began to search for a substance to kill the germs that infect wounds. For nine years he experimented without success. One day while working the doctor noticed a plate of staphylococci that a mold had contaminated. As he picked up the plate and carried it to the sink to wash it off, he noticed that the mold was destroying the staphylococci. He had discovered penicillin—a substance that kills bacteria. Dr. Alexander Fleming's name soon became famous.

Many years later, during the second world war, the British Prime Minister, Winston Churchill, lay seriously ill with pneumonia in Teheran, where he had gone to meet Stalin and President Roosevelt. His staff radioed an urgent request to London: "Send penicillin." Dr. Fleming himself flew to Teheran with the antibiotic. When Churchill was out of danger, he called in the doctor. "This is the second time you have saved my life," he said. Dr. Fleming nodded. He was happy to have been able to help.

Jesus has a wonderful solution for the sin that threatens our spiritual lives. It is not clear like penicillin, but blood-red. He shed His blood on the cross so that you and I, by believing on Him, may be saved. And He does not leave it to chance that we will find the cure. He actively searches us out. No matter where we go or how bad we are, He lovingly searches us out. He came to seek and to save the lost.

TAKING HOLD

But let all those that put their trust in thee rejoice: let them ever shout for joy, because thou defendest them. Psalm 5:11.

One Christmas Eve Henry Carter sat at his desk trying to think up a special Christmas sermon. A light rap at the door interrupted his thoughts. The floor mother from the home for emotionally disturbed children beckoned him to follow her. He knew that Christmas Eve frightened the few children who did not go home for the holiday. This time it was Tommy. He refused to come out from under his bed.

As Henry entered the upstairs bedroom he noted the six empty beds. Where was Tommy? The floor mother pointed, but he could detect no sign of the boy. So he began talking to the cowboys on the bedspread. He told them about the six-foot Christmas tree in the lobby and the gifts for Tommy packaged underneath. Silence under the bed.

Kneeling down, the minister peeked under the fringe of the bedspread. Two large frightened eyes peered back. Henry knew that it was no use dragging the child out. Somehow he must coax him to come out on his own. Thinking that he might lure Tommy out by food, the man described all the delights waiting on the table downstairs. But if Tommy heard, he didn't care. With one last thought for the sermon he should be preparing, Henry crawled under the bed and lay beside the orphan, reminding him of the songs that he had learned for the evening program. When he ran out of things to say, he just lay there. At last Tommy's cold little hand crept into Henry's big one. After another pause the pastor suggested that they both go out where they could stand up. This time Tommy crawled out.

That night Henry talked about how God called to us from heaven, but we were afraid. How He sent messengers, but we would not listen. But when He came down Himself in our place, we trusted Him enough to take hold of His hand. And now we stand side by side, unafraid of whatever this day holds for us.

ONE LESS THROW

Though he fall, he shall not be utterly cast down: for the Lord upholdeth him with his hand. Psalm 37:24.

It is Jenny's first game of tennis. Her foursome has only two balls. Scott serves the first ball into her court, but she concentrates so hard on hitting it that she sends the ball high into the air and over the fence into somebody's backyard. "Oh, no!" everyone groans. "What did you do that for?" Jenny wishes she could shrivel up and blow away. Sometimes our embarrassing mistakes are more serious than Jenny's. They let other people down. That's when we need lots of determination to get up and keep going.

Larry Ritchey was out snowshoeing on his own when he fell fourteen feet through crumbling ice and rock into an underground cavern. After exploring by the light of a candle, he realized that the only way out was the way he had come in. But he could not climb the sheer rock walls. Then he remembered a thirty-foot rope he carried in his pack. Tying a rock to the end of the rope, he aimed for the narrow oblong opening and threw with all his might. The rock disappeared through the opening. But when he pulled on the rope, the rock came hurtling back through the hole. Larry wished that the rock would anchor itself on something. Twenty times Larry hurled the rock, only to have it pull back inside. Then he turned and threw so that the rock flew out the opening in a different direction. After twenty more attempts, he rotated his body a little before each try, hoping that by so doing, the rock would land some place where it would catch. Once Larry thought it held, but by the time he had climbed halfway to the opening it gave way and he fell back. By now he felt like giving up. "Once more," he told himself. This time the rock anchored in the roots of an old fir tree, and he managed to climb out.

The psalmist says that "though [you] fall, [you] shall not be utterly cast down." So don't stay down. Get up and, like Larry, try again.

THE RUNAWAY

Blessed is he who has regard for the weak; the Lord delivers him in times of trouble. Psalm 41:1, N.I.V.

"Brent! help me down. I'm stuck," 7-year-old Barry yelled from the willow tree. Brent paused under the basketball hoop long enough to see his little brother standing high in the tree.

"You're always getting into something you can't get yourself out of," Brent called as he dunked the ball for the third time in a row. "Figure a way to get down yourself. After all, you got yourself up there."

As Brent continued shooting baskets he could hear Barry sniveling in the tree. Poor kid, he must be scared, the older boy decided at last. And he propped a ladder against the tree and helped his brother down.

Mrs. Woodbury noticed what her son had done and commended him later. "Don't be embarrassed about helping someone who is weaker than you," she said. "It's one way to practice the golden rule."

Over dinner she told the boys about a power company foreman in southern Colorado who was driving a half-ton truck over dangerous mountain roads when a car passed him at top speed. Realizing from the frantic wave of the car's passenger that the vehicle was out of control, the man accelerated until he had passed the car.

Then by slowing down gradually, he let the car catch up until its bumper met his. He slowed both vehicles to forty miles per hour before slamming his brake to the floor. The vehicles stopped just before a sharp curve that the runaway car could not possibly have negotiated.

"Why would a complete stranger risk his life to save someone he didn't even know?" Brent's mom asked. The boy shrugged his shoulders. He didn't understand the man's action, but he admired his courage.

The psalmist says it this way: "Blessed is he who has regard for the weak; the Lord delivers him in times of trouble." Jesus doesn't keep score of how many times you help someone before he agrees to answer your prayer for help. But doesn't it seem unfair to your Elder Brother if you don't also help where you can?

KEEP SWIMMING AROUND

"Do not let your hearts be troubled. Trust in God; trust also in me." John 14:1, N.I.V.

"Why do I feel like this? Anyone would think I was scared of the dentist," Nigel muttered.

"Well, aren't you?" his mother asked without taking her eyes from the road. "You know that you will come out alive, but you are afraid of the unknown—whether or not it will hurt much. Almost everyone is."

Have you experienced fears like that? Some people fear the future; some fear evil that hasn't happened yet. Many people, reading in the Bible of a time of trouble, lie awake at night worrying about it. They let it make them feel gloomy. Jesus said, "Don't worry! Trust Me. I'll help you when the time comes." Well, you worriers are probably saying, "How will He help me?" Nobody can answer that, but a wise person once said that God helps those who do what they can while they wait. That reminds me of "The Optimistic Frog":

Two frogs fell into a deep cream bowl,
One was an optimistic soul.
But the other took a gloomy view;
"We shall drown," he cried without more ado.
So, with a last despairing cry,
He flung up his legs and said,
"Goodbye."
The other frog, with a merry grin,
Said, "I can't get out, but I won't give in.
I'll swim around till my strength is spent,
Then I will die with more content."
Bravely he swam till, it would seem,
His struggles began to churn the cream.
On top of the butter at last he stopped,
And out of the bowl he easily hopped.
What of the moral? 'Tis easily found!
If you can't hop, keep swimming around.

—Author Unknown

MARYBETH'S ANGELS

The angel of the Lord encampeth round about them that fear him, and delivereth them. Psalm 34:7.

I once heard of a little girl named MaryBeth who was returning with her grandmother from choir practice when all at once she met the four things she feared most—a thunderstorm, darkness, the unknown, and cows.

The thunderstorm came first. It looked so awesome that MaryBeth's grandmother decided to take the shortcut home. But another car forced them off the road, and Grandma's car overturned in a ditch. Fortunately, neither of them was badly hurt. The accident pinned her grandmother beneath the steering wheel, but MaryBeth was able to crawl out of the window.

Afraid to walk on her own through the gathering darkness and pelting rain, the girl hesitated to go for help. But praying that God would send His angel with her, she plucked up courage and walked toward the only light she could see.

Stumbling through the darkness, she heard an even more terrifying sound than the storm—the lowing of cattle. And before she could change direction she found herself surrounded not by angels, but by cows. She might easily have wondered what kind of deliverance her prayer had brought.

But the cows turned out to be part of the answer. The way they clustered curiously about MaryBeth attracted the attention of the farmer. And in no time deliverance was on its way to her grandmother, too. But what if Marybeth had stayed in the car and only prayed? How could God have answered her prayer?

My friend Helen and I were driving to Benton Harbor, Michigan, when her new car ran out of gas. Helen pulled off the road and emptied a can of gas into the tank. But still the engine wouldn't start. "Why don't you pray?" our two boys insisted. So we did. But still the car wouldn't start. Finally Helen took out the manual and read the appropriate section. Following the instructions, she had the car on the road in no time. Did God answer the boys' prayer? Of course He did—but Helen, like MaryBeth, had to do her part too.

RIGHT-HAND MAN

I have set the Lord always before me. Because he is at my right hand, I will not be shaken. Psalm 16:8, N.I.V.

Early one sunny Sunday morning my husband and I were walking across an empty parking lot. Nearby stood one lone car; a young man was changing its right front wheel, assisted by his wife and 3-year-old son. "Where's the wrench?" the man said. "Here it is," his wife responded, placing it in the hands of the 3-year-old. "Here it is," the little fellow echoed, handing it to his daddy. Just as I was thinking about what a wonderful father he was to let his little boy help like that, the father said crossly, "Look, I can finish this much quicker if you two would just leave me alone."

Maybe you remember times when you wanted to help but someone did not appreciate your thoughtfulness. You weren't "big enough" to help. But has it ever occurred to you that sometimes parents feel the same way? They could help you solve problems if you would only ask them.

One stormy night Carolyn and Ed Miller couldn't sleep, though it was past two o'clock. Dennis, their teenager, had not come in yet. Finally Ed dressed and drove around looking for his son. He found him and his friends trying to get the front wheels of his car onto the road from where they were stuck in the soft mud of the shoulder. They kept breaking their thin rope when they tried to tow the car. "Why didn't you call me?" Ed asked. "You know I keep a towrope in my car." With a shrug Dennis mumbled that he had not wanted to wake them up. "Besides," he added, "I thought we could get it out."

Ed felt hurt that his son hadn't called him, but he often did the same thing with God. Though God is at your right hand, do you often ignore Him? "Oh, it's not important enough to bother Him with," you say. "Besides, I can do it myself." God wants you to develop independence, but remember, it's when you work with Him as a team that you succeed.

WHOSE FAULT?

Ask, and it shall be given you; seek, and ye shall find; knock, and it shall be opened unto you: for every one that asketh receiveth; and he that seeketh findeth; and to him that knocketh it shall be opened. Matthew 7:7, 8.

I used to think this passage meant that if I wanted something, I needed only to pray and it would be mine. Once when I was 13, Mother sent me straight home after church. She knew that she would be late, and rather than have the food spoil in the oven, she sent me to remove it. I knew my task was urgent, so I ran almost all the way. But I left without the key to the front door. As I stood on the doorstep trying to figure how to get inside and save the lunch, I remembered Jesus' words, "It shall be opened unto you." Right there I told God that I believed Him and asked Him to open the door. But I was still standing there praying and trying the door when my family returned from church with the key. That incident puzzled me for years until I realized it was for my own good God answered that prayer with a No. Had He opened the door for me I might never have learned to remember my keys.

There are certain prayers that Jesus always answers with Yes. They are the ones He hopes we will pray often—because they ask for the most important things in life: love, forgiveness, and knowing and believing Him.

Mr. Fortner's class once prayed an important prayer: that their Sabbath school would grow until every chair was filled. The following week when Mr. Fortner stood up to speak, all twenty-eight chairs were taken. But before the boys could bow their heads in thankfulness, more arrived. The boys kept coming until Mr. Fortner removed all the chairs and the boys sat on the floor. When still more continued to arrive, Mr. Fortner looked plainly distracted. "It's all my fault," a voice called from the back of the room. "I asked God to send fifty!" And that was the exact number that came to Sabbath school that morning! Don't forget to pray for the truly important things this morning.

WHEN LOVE GOES

Children, obey your parents in the Lord: for this is right. Honour thy father and mother; which is the first commandment with promise. Ephesians 6:1, 2.

Debbie Jahnke hated her dad. Ever since she was 4 he had beaten her regularly. When she was 17 her brother Rick, 16, executed their father with a shotgun. Had he missed, Debbie was waiting in the house with a .30 caliber carbine. Their mother testified in court that Mr. Jahnke seldom ate meals with the family and repeatedly abused the children. Her husband had forbidden them to bring their teenage friends to the house, threatening to throw them out if they came.

When Paul told children to love and honor their parents, did he include parents like Mr. Jahnke? Could you love a father like that? Do you think God loved him?

I don't like what Debbie and Rick did, but I try to put myself in their place. What might I have done? It's difficult enough to get along with loving parents. Paul understood this when he said in verse 4, "Fathers, provoke not your children to wrath." And that's probably why he added three key words—"in the Lord"—to today's text. Parents and children working prayerfully together usually can work things out. But some teenagers find themselves caught in life-threatening situations because parental love has gone. Perhaps that's how it was with Debbie and Rick.

Why didn't their mother help them? Probably because she didn't know what to do. Should they have run away? No, that usually exchanges one set of problems for another. I wish that they had spoken to their guidance counselor at school or to a teacher or pastor. Or they could have called the local children's protective society, which has offices in most counties and which promises to help within twenty-four hours.

Aren't you glad for your parents? Remember, when you can't communicate with them, your heavenly Father knows and cares. Keep in touch with Him, and He'll help you find a loving way to get along.

IS THE LIGHT OUT?

Have mercy upon me, O Lord; for I am weak: O Lord, heal me; for my bones are vexed. Psalm 6:2.

Nine-year-old Marty was the spitting image of his dad. The two of them often did things together. Whenever anyone asked Marty what he would do when he grew up, he would proudly answer, "Be a preacher like my dad." But that never happened. He contracted leukemia and died when he was 11.

"Why me?" the boy once asked his dad. "Why would God let me get this awful disease?"

Pastor Henry loved his boy. He loved his girls, too, but he especially looked forward to seeing Marty grow up and learn to do all the things his father did well—like waterskiing, and leading people to Jesus. And though Marty didn't know it, his dad often paced the house late at night wrestling with God over the same questions that bothered his son.

"Why Marty, God? Why did it have to be him?" And out of the darkness God seemed to say, "Isn't that a selfish question? Is it all right when other children die of leukemia, but not when it's Marty?" And through the pastor's suffering and prayer he found the answer in time to help his son.

"God loves you," he said. "You know that, don't you?" Marty nodded. "Who brought evil into the world? Did God?" the boy shook his head. He knew that when Adam and Eve disobeyed they opened the gates for the flood of evil that troubles our world to this day.

"Jesus came to earth to bring us hope and to show us that God really cares about us," Marty's dad continued. "When we hurt, He hurts too. God isn't punishing you, son, and He doesn't want you to die. But this is a wonderful opportunity for you to let your light shine."

And Marty bravely let his light shine to the end. And now that Marty is gone, does that mean that the light is out? No, it shines brightly in the memory of all those who remember him.

THE TRADE-OFF

Give thanks to the Lord, for he is good; his love endures forever. 1 Chronicles 16:34, N.I.V.

Italo Patinella, the owner of a car dealership, couldn't believe his ears when Pamela and James Green offered to trade their 14-month-old son for a $9,000 car. Wondering what kind of people could do such a shocking thing, Patinella pretended to go along with the deal. But, unknown to the parents, he contacted the police. At first Patinella had thought of keeping the child. He had lost his own son, daughter-in-law, and grandson in a dreadful fire. Missing them greatly, he felt angry with those who did not love and cherish their own child. "What would this baby do when he grew up and discovered that he was traded for a car?" Patinella angrily asked after the parents walked out, leaving the child on the showroom floor. "They didn't even kiss him goodbye."

Had you been one of the policemen who arrested Mr. and Mrs. Green, what would you have said to them? Do you ever trade anything truly important just for the sake of getting more things?

Donny grew up in a loving family. Sometimes his parents teased him about how they found him under a cabbage leaf. And they often boggled his mind by naming enormous sums of money—billions and trillions of dollars—all of which they would turn down rather than sell him. The boy felt secure in God's love, too. He knew that though earthly parents sometimes get mad at kids and human love wears thin, God's love endures as warm and forgiving as ever.

For a while, when Donny was 13, he traded in his love for God and his family—all for popularity. When Cal and the others invited him to join them in vandalizing the old school, he saw a chance of getting in with their gang. He had always wanted to be friends with Cal, and now was his chance. Never mind that he didn't particularly want to smash things. "I'm glad we got caught," he said later. "I'm sorry for the embarrassment it brought my family, but it brought me to my senses. Popularity is a poor trade for love and trust."

THOSE ABLE TO HELP

And in the church God has appointed first of all apostles, second prophets, third teachers, then workers of miracles, also those having gifts of healing, those able to help others. 1 Corinthians 12:28, N.I.V.

You have probably noticed that everyone at your church has a special work to do. Pastor Tokkon preaches, Mrs. Joy plays the organ. Some of the men collect the offering, and Mr. and Mrs. White greet the visitors. What do you do? You can't preach, and they don't ever ask you to take up the offering. So maybe you feel unimportant—like nobody needs you. But that's where you are wrong. Just by sitting quietly, taking part in the service, and singing the hymns, you are helping. Did you notice in today's text that helping others is one of the special gifts given to church members?

When Corrie ten Boom was imprisoned during World War II she had no idea how she could help win the war. The authorities assigned her to work in the prison factory fitting together relay switches for radios that would be used in Nazi fighter planes. "Dear watch lady," the foreman whispered to her one day, "can you not remember for whom you are working?" And Corrie realized that she could help the Allies by not working so hard on the switches.

A little group of prisoners in Czechoslovakia "helped" the war effort by leaving out the explosive charge in antiaircraft shells. Elmer Bendiner tells of an American B-17 crew who returned from a run over the German city of Kassel where antiaircraft flak had hit the plane's gas tank. Next morning the pilot asked his crew chief if he could keep the shell that hit his gas tank. He wanted a souvenir of his miraculous escape. The chief told him that the repair crews had found not one shell but eleven in the tank—eleven unexploded shells. Any one of them could have downed that plane. The shells were sent to be defused. But not one of them had an explosive charge. One contained a tightly wadded scrap of paper. On it was written in Czech, "This is all we can do for you now." Thank God for "those able to help."

AND HEALED THEM

Then they cried to the Lord in their trouble, and he saved them from their distress. He sent forth his word and healed them. Psalm 107:19, 20, N.I.V.

The lesson for the day had covered Elijah's choice of a successor, the chariot of fire, and the bears that taught some impudent young men a lesson. "Now what do you know for sure about you and God?" I asked the class after we had recalled the stories.

Our class always gets into that question after the lesson story, so they know to be thinking about the answer. Some clever children know that my question means Why did I tell you this story? and that the answer appears at the beginning of each lesson, right after the memory verse, where it says Lesson Aim.

But I always like best the answers that come right out of somebody's head. That's why Janee's answer (which was really another question) excited me. "Can we have our prayers answered like Elisha's when he struck the river with Elijah's coat?" Janee thought that God didn't perform miracles anymore. Tod said God answered prayer all the time, but people often don't notice. And Malini suggested that we should explain to God our problems and let Him show us the solution instead of trying to tell Him what to do.

That reminded Darien of a story he had read. "Once there was an old woodcutter," he began. "Walking over a steep hill with a load of wood on his back, he felt so tired and sore that he found a rock to sit on and rested his load beside it. I wish I were dead, the old man thought.

"Just then the skeleton of death walked by and asked the old man what he had said. Realizing that the skeleton could be himself if his wish were granted, the old man replied, 'Oh, nothing! But I wish you would help me hoist this bundle onto my back.' And after the load was adjusted he walked happily away.

"And that just goes to show," Darien concluded, "that you should not complain about what God has given you, because if He had not answered your prayers the way He did, you might be far worse off." I think Darien was right, don't you?

DELIVERANCE

From the Lord comes deliverance. May your blessing be on your people. Psalm 3:8, N.I.V.

Sally feels like a phantom rising from the shadowy depths of the Mariana Trench (the deepest spot in the ocean) as she breaks through the surface of sleep. Flailing her arms, she swats the button on her alarm clock, and the buzzer stops. Although she wants to snuggle back beneath the blankets, her sleepiness dissolves instantly as she remembers that today in chapel the awards will be given out for yesterday's sports day. Sally will receive five or maybe six blue ribbons. Also she may win the coveted best sportsperson award. Now she springs out of bed, glad to be alive. Everything looks great, from her sunny room to her little brother, who bursts into the room without knocking.

At breakfast the family pauses for worship. The devotional is about deliverance. A little girl named Anna runs away from home. "I ain't never going back," she declares defiantly. "And don't take me to the police either, because I'll never tell where I come from!"

I'm so lucky! Sally thinks as the steam from her oatmeal warms her chin. Maybe when I grow up I'll adopt someone like her. Sally breathes a silent prayer for children everywhere who need deliverance from poverty and neglect. And secretly she's glad that she doesn't need deliverance from anything.

At seven-forty-five she is ready to catch the school bus. But as she kisses her mother goodbye she notices her brother sneaking out the door with her baseball mitt. "Oh, no, you don't, Buddy Boy!" she yells. "You bring that mitt back. And next time, you ask first!"

Now she feels miserable. Deep down she knows that it wouldn't hurt to let her brother borrow her mitt. She's just jealous because he's getting to be a better catcher than she is. And suddenly the truth hits so hard that it hurts. "Lord, please deliver me from jealousy," Sally whispers as she runs for the bus. "And help me never again to be so smug that I think I can manage without help."

STILL WATERS

He leadeth me beside the still waters. Psalm 23:2.

I would like to visit the town of Somerset, Wisconsin, on a hot summer's day because I've heard that the town has lots of traffic, but not on the streets. You may find it on the Apple River, which flows by the town. The traffic consists of people tubing.

Everyone wears his swimming gear and old sneakers—the river is not very deep and the riverbed is rocky. He also takes along an inner tube. Groups of people tie their tubes together for the two- to three-hour trip. Some, like 12-year-old Suzie, lie back gazing at the treetops while their tubes and the river carry them along. Todd remembers when he used to travel along with his tube tied to his mother's. But now that he is 11 he likes to go on his own.

The Baileys have a cooler of canned drinks that floats in its own inner tube. Mrs. Bailey usually takes the cooler with her when she leaves the river at the first sign of white water. Lisa used to stay with her mother. But after seeing how much fun people had on the rapids, she decided to try them. Now she says that, though it is scary, it's the best part of the trip.

When the psalmist wrote, "He leadeth me beside the still waters," he wasn't wishing that his life were one peaceful tubing party down the Apple River. Nor would he want to miss the white waters if it were. David was a man of action. He didn't know how it would turn out when he took on Goliath. But after his major battles, when he felt tired or discouraged, the thought of restful waters cheered his soul.

Sailors assembling for their weekly yachting on the Potomac River near Washington, D.C., were glad for the brisk winds that tugged at their spinnakers. But the unexpectedly violent squall that suddenly ripped through the area caused concern, as many boats capsized. During such times of distress still waters sound inviting even to sailors. Aren't you thankful today for the calm that Jesus brings into the waters of your life?

READY FOR COMBAT?

Therefore put on the full armor of God, so that when the day of evil comes, you may be able to stand your ground. Ephesians 6:13, N.I.V.

One overcast day in October, 1979, Stanislav Levchenko, a Soviet spy, asked for political asylum in the United States. Within five hours the American Government had granted his request, and Levchenko found himself flying to the United States. He expected to face rough treatment from American intelligence people trying to get information from him. But the courteous reception he was given pleasantly surprised him.

In the years since then Stanislav has learned to adapt to American ways. But when a Washington reporter met with him recently, he noticed that some habits are slow to change. Levchenko insists on deciding at the last minute just where he will meet a reporter, and he likes to sit facing the door so he can see who enters. In restaurants he eats quickly and "cleans his tracks" when he leaves. The former spy says that he likes to remember that he is in a "combat situation." If his enemies could, they would kill him.

In a sense you are in a combat situation too. Your struggle is not against spies but against Satan. Paul warns, "Be strong in the Lord and in his mighty power" (verse 10). And how can you be strong in the Lord? By putting on "the full armor of God." In the fight against Satan we don't just pray and then sit back and let the Lord do everything. We must be alert to our danger and follow certain precautions just as spies and soldiers do.

For example, we must buckle up with "truth" and wear a bulletproof vest of "righteousness," and running shoes fitted from the "gospel of peace." Also we should carry the "shield of faith" (which absorbs the devil's lasers of temptation), wear the "helmet of salvation," and carry the "sword of the spirit" (verses 14-17). And where do we get outfitted with all that gear? From God. He promises the best protection money can buy. How could we dare go out without it?

THE MAGNET

"But I, when I am lifted up from the earth, will draw all men to myself." John 12:32, N.I.V.

The ancient Greeks of Magnesia supposedly discovered and gave their name to the rock lodestone, which attracts small pieces of iron. Thus the Greeks called any metal that attracted other metals a magnet—for Magnesia. They explained magnetism by saying that magnets have minute hooks that catch hold of tiny rings on the surface of certain metals, such as iron. Scientists today smile at that simple theory. It makes about as much sense to them as saying that sugar magnetizes ants, or candlelight magnetizes moths.

You may create a magnet by stroking a small piece of iron with another magnet. If you keep the strokes all going in the same direction and use the same end of the permanent magnet to make them with, the iron will soon be magnetized enough to pick up a pin or a paper clip.

You may make a simple electric magnet by winding two layers of insulated wire around a flat iron bar bent into a flat-bottomed U. Cover only the curve of the U with the wire and leave the wire long enough at both ends to attach to a small battery. Strip the insulation from both ends of the wire before connecting them to two posts of a dry-cell battery. Test your magnet by holding it near some nails, paper clips, or the refrigerator door.

Magnetic force reminds me of the love of Jesus that attracts us to God. Everywhere Jesus went on earth His love captivated children. His healing drew the sick; His forgiveness, sinners. But the act that attracts people right down through the ages is Jesus' death on the cross. He died for our sins so that we might enjoy eternal life with Him in heaven. That's why He said, "'I, when I am lifted up from the earth [on the cross], will draw all men to myself.'" Now *that's* magnetism. Magnetism that delivers you from the pull of sin. But you can't be magnetized against your will. Are you ready to allow yourself to be drawn to Jesus? Tell Him you accept His love and forgiveness and discover the difference it makes.

THE ROCK

The Lord is my rock, my fortress and my deliverer; my God is my rock, in whom I take refuge. Psalm 18:2, N.I.V.

What is a rock? To Timmy it was something to collect. His dad often bundled him and his friends into one of his antique cars and trundled them over rutted roads to a windswept hill dotted with rocks of all descriptions. Soon Tim became adept at identifying agates for his collection. But to Terry and Howdie rocks were for throwing at crows to keep them away from the ripening corn. And to Julie and Mark they were something with which to build a fort, especially after their parents took them to visit a real one chiseled out of the sheer rock cliffs of western India.

Rocks were once of utmost importance to soldiers. To them a simple cave carved in a rock face was a stronghold, a refuge, a fortress. Imagine yourself in David's army. Perhaps your strength and bravery have earned you a place among his inner group. As you flee from Saul and his armed men you begin to tire. "Where can we rest?" you ask. David points ahead to a rocky crag rising high above the land. It will be a tough climb, you know. But up there is a cave where you may safely pause without fear of Saul's forces surrounding you. "Many times I have fled to the refuge of that cave," David says. "It's the only place a fellow can feel safe." And as his legs keep churning toward that stronghold he begins to chant tunelessly: "I love you, O Lord, my strength" (verse 1).

Aha! you think. That's the secret of this man's endurance. The Lord is his rock—for the same word translated *strength* means "rock." Again you listen to David's chant. "The Lord is my rock, my fortress and my deliverer." Later as you claw your way up the cliff face and finally rest in the shelter of the overhang, you remember Moses striking the rock that represented Jesus, the Rock of our salvation, the One who delivers us from sin. And as you look fearlessly down at the tiny cloud of dust Saul and his men raise on the plain below, you feel safe and secure, and praise God for a new understanding of rocks.

AND SO DO I

Commit your way to the Lord; trust in him and he will . . . make your righteousness shine like the dawn. Psalm 37:5, N.I.V.

Life had been tough for Red Evans. All the world had been against him—except his grandmother. His only comfort, she loved him fiercely. When it seemed that everyone else was mad at him, he could count on Grandma to make him feel loved and valued. But when Red was 13, she became ill with cancer. Red encouraged her with his belief that God wouldn't let her die. When the old woman did die, he felt betrayed. Why had God turned his back on Grandma? With nobody to comfort him and explain His love, Red turned against God. Bitterness filled his heart. Nobody cared whether or not he tried to be good, he decided. God did not exist anyway. So he turned to crime and violence and soon found himself in prison.

During his last prison stay Red formed a gang that he called the Aryan Brotherhood. Through fear and his gang, Red managed to control much of what went on behind the bars of that institution.

Red particularly hated a little band of prisoners who worshiped God on Saturdays. When Jay Robbins, a promising new member of the Brotherhood, refused to beat up on the Adventists but joined them instead, Red decided to kill him. Finding Jay alone one evening, Red grabbed him by his shirt and shoved him into a corner. "Are you ready to become an Adventist martyr?" he asked menacingly. But Jay was not afraid. He surprised his attacker by dropping to his knees—not to pray for his own deliverance, but for Red's. Suddenly Red's murderous intentions melted. He wept as he remembered his grandmother's love. Right there he gave his heart to God. All because Jay Robbins had committed himself to the Lord and trusted Him.

If the shadow of evil should cross your path today, be it through the death of a loved one or the threat of a bully, don't doubt God's goodness. And don't blame Him for evil. Instead, ask Him to lead the way. Then trust Him—He knows the way.

TRACY FINDS MERCY

Because he turned his ear to me, I will call on him as long as I live. Psalm 116:2, N.I.V.

Six weeks into the sixth grade Tracy had to leave the cozy church school where she knew everyone and attend a large public school in a distant city. "I soon got used to the tough way the other students spoke and acted," she says. "But I never quite lost my fear of the teachers. They yelled at kids instead of requesting us politely to do things."

Tracy's homeroom teacher had a reputation for strictness. "In the afternoons when we marched to Mr. Hall's room for a science lesson, his class would pass us on their way to English literature with our Miss Jones. You could see the fear in their eyes," she remembers.

When the sixth-grade teacher who taught girls' needlework became ill, Miss Jones took over the sewing classes. And nobody could please Miss Jones. She demanded that the girls pull stitches out and do hems over. Since Tracy had started the year late, she was behind in her sewing, and Miss Jones threatened dire punishment if she did not complete her blouse and skirt in one week. Frantically the girl sewed at home, trying to catch up. "But as I worked I knew that I could never please Miss Jones," she says. "I had visions of her taking my work and ripping it apart."

So it was with trepidation that she timidly presented her neatly pressed garments to Miss Jones at recess time on the day of the deadline. Wearily Miss Jones held them out and examined them. "You finished the neck edge by machine when you should have done it by hand," she said. "But you came after everyone else had received instructions, so I won't make you do it over." Tracy felt so relieved that she could have danced for joy. Maybe she understands the psalmist when he says, "I love the Lord, for he heard my voice; he heard my cry for mercy. Because he turned his ear to me, I will call on him as long as I live."

THE BAG MAN

Whoever turns a sinner away from his error will save him from death and cover over a multitude of sins. James 5:20, N.I.V.

Let's walk along the creek where I jog on Sundays," Lori's dad suggested. Eager to explore new territory, she and her sister Lana happily piled into the car. After parking the car beside an old mill, the happy trio set off along a wide pathway that hugged the edge of the creek bed. In one place the pathway narrowed as it approached a bridge. Walking single file behind their dad, the girls passed an old man clutching the handles of half a dozen paper shopping bags. "I wonder where he went shopping," Lori whispered to her sister. "He must have bought a lot of stuff."

"He hasn't been shopping, silly," Lana hissed. "The bags are old and dirty." A tree already dressed in fall colors caught their attention, and they forgot about the man until they retraced their steps back to the bridge. The girls raced ahead of their father, and as they ran into the shadow cast by the bridge they found the bag man making himself comfortable in a little wedge between the bank and the bridge. From one bag he had produced some food in a battered tin dish. Beside him he had spread some old rags. "He's going to sleep there," Lori whispered as they hurried by. "He'll spoil it for people who want to walk on the path."

"Grow up, Lori," Lana said with a superior air. "Think about the poor man. He probably doesn't have anywhere else to go."

Lori couldn't forget the bag man. She imagined herself driving him to a nearby motel and instructing the owner to give him a room. If only she had a charge card of her own so she could pay his expenses! And what if the room had two beds? She wondered. Would the man go out and find another bag man who needed the other bed? It would be wicked not to help rescue someone else from the frosty nights after someone had saved you. Then with a stab of realization Lori knew that, though she could do nothing for that bag man, she owed it to Jesus, who had died to save her from sin, to share His love with her neighbors and friends. For, "whoever turns a sinner away from his error will save him from death."

SOWING IN TEARS

Those who sow in tears will reap with songs of joy. He who goes out weeping, carrying seed to sow, will return with songs of joy, carrying sheaves with him. Psalm 126:5, 6, N.I.V.

Perhaps you have noticed that once in a while you feel like laughing and crying at the same time. Occasionally you feel raindrops falling even though the sun is shining. But usually rain clouds completely hide the sun during showers. And when you feel like crying you usually cannot think a single cheerful thought. Have you ever heard a parent or teacher say, "I'm really sorry to have to spank you, but you will be glad later that I did"? You didn't believe a word of it. But that's how it often is. A sad, unpleasant, or downright difficult experience often causes later rejoicing.

Del Tarr, a former missionary to West Africa, tells of Africans in the Sahel, a barren stretch of land just south of the Sahara Desert. All the rains come to the Sahel between May and August. So they must grow in four months all the food that they will need for a year.

September and October are months of plenty in the Sahel. The granaries are full. Everyone eats two meals a day. By December many families notice that their grain supplies are dwindling. So they prepare only one meal each day. By February even that one meal has shrunk. It's even worse in March. But April is the month of crying babies. Their mothers' milk has dried up. Parents dig roots and scrape bark from bushes to make a thin gruel. Dust fills the air and aggravates everyone's misery. Then it is that one of the small boys comes to his father. "Come see what I have found in the cowshed!" he says. "It's grain. Now we can eat." And the father is tempted to use it for food. But sadly he explains that this is the seed grain set aside for the planting in May.

It would be easy for that boy to doubt his father's wisdom. The evidence clearly seems to point to a serious lack of caring that the boy can't understand. But he will be glad at the harvest.

WITH FEAR AND TREMBLING

Continue to work out your salvation with fear and trembling, for it is God who works in you to will and to act according to his good purpose. Philippians 2:12, 13, N.I.V.

"I'm afraid you won't make it to Rotterdam in time for your boat," Theo called over his shoulder as the three pushed their cycles into the strong head wind blowing off the North Sea.

"Don't say that," Lyndelle replied. "We *have* to catch it."

"Do you suppose it would help to pray?" Anne asked. "When I'm in trouble I always pray." Lyndelle nodded in agreement. But Theo threw up his hands in a you-have-to-be-kidding motion.

Slowing to a stop, the two American girls poured out their problem in prayer and asked the Lord to help them make their boat in spite of the unexpected head wind. Theo waited until they finished before bursting into gales of laughter. "You'll never make that boat," he declared. "And no amount of prayer is going to change that."

"Praying helps me to do my best," Lyndelle quietly explained.

"And it keeps me from worrying myself sick," Anne added. But Theo seemed not to listen. The trio fell silent again and pedaled harder than ever.

By the time they reached the port and rushed breathlessly to the ticket window they were forty-five minutes late.

"What a coincidence," Theo commented, trying to sound unimpressed. "Your boat is still here." Lyndelle and Anne smiled. Had they listened to Theo they would not have made it. But God held up the boat while they pedaled harder. And together they had answered that prayer.

Getting out of tight spots and getting to heaven have something in common. They are achieved in the same way—by both you and God working. There's no telling what you can do when you team up with God like that.

PRESSED BUT NOT CRUSHED

We are hard pressed on every side, but not crushed; perplexed, but not in despair; persecuted, but not abandoned; struck down, but not destroyed. 2 Corinthians 4:8, 9, N.I.V.

Sandy leaned on the counter of the shooting gallery watching Dana expertly shoot "ducks" as they bobbed along in a line. She had missed the first two or three before managing to knock one over. Why do I feel like that duck? Sandy wondered. Life for me is like sitting on that moving belt and being pelted.

Do you view your problems as Sandy did? Or is life for you more like a roller-coaster ride—lots of ups and downs. When you are up you can't remember the downs. And when you are down you forget you haven't always been there. After the roller coaster of life plummets you to rock bottom, do you wonder, why me? You forget the rest of the ride—where you've been and how God has blessed you. You forget that you were warned that the ride has ups and downs. All you know is that you feel hard pressed, perplexed, even persecuted.

Whether you're in the shooting gallery or on a roller-coaster ride, the apostle Paul puts the whole thing in perspective when he says, "We are hard pressed on every side, but not crushed; perplexed, but not in despair."

When arthritis crippled Hattie Carthan she was tempted to jump from her fifth-floor window. As a farewell she shouted, "Why me, God?" Back came the answer clear and direct, "Why *not* you, Hattie?" The more she thought about it, the more sense it made. This life promises nothing for certain, except that sooner or later we will all experience disappointment and suffering. If God meant to hide anyone from trouble, wouldn't He have protected His own Son? But He sent Jesus to live and suffer with us. So instead of asking, "Why me?" Hattie now asked, "What can God and I do?" So far they have helped transform her Brooklyn neighborhood by inspiring people to plant trees. What might God and you tackle together today?

EXACTLY ON TIME

But mine eyes are unto thee, O God the Lord: in thee is my trust. Psalm 141:8.

Ever since God had delivered Manfred from the awful habit of stealing he had believed in prayer. And gradually he learned that, whether he had met a crisis or faced another ordinary day, his life went more smoothly when he took time to pray.

After he graduated from the seminary he reported to the conference office for his first preaching assignment. "Why don't you preach at the Lubeck church next Sabbath?" the secretary said. But early Sabbath morning Manfred found, to his surprise, that the conference had already assigned a preacher to that task. "I'm sure I'll learn a lot listening to your sermon," Manfred told the older man. But the pastor shook his head. "Wouldn't it be better if you went on to the next town?" he said. "The elder is scheduled to preach there, and I know he would rather listen to you."

At the railway station Manfred learned that the train would not leave until one-thirty. Thankful that he still had lots of time, he tried to hitchhike to the church. As he stepped to the curb and raised his thumb he prayed that God would find him a ride, but not a car stopped. After a while he wondered whether maybe God did not need him to preach that day. Perhaps the elder's sermon was better. "If You need me to preach," he prayed, "please send a car before ten past ten." But at ten after ten nobody had stopped. "Fair enough," Manfred told the Lord. "After this next car I will return home." And he felt a little disappointed that the Lord did not need him that day. But suddenly the last car braked beside the curb.

The driver dropped him outside the church just as the Sabbath school superintendent started to announce that the local elder had broken his leg and could not preach that morning. "Perhaps we should all go home," he said. At that exact moment Manfred walked into the church. God had brought him to it exactly on time. The Lord is interested in all the plans for your life—not just when you are in trouble. So ask for His help every day in the little things as well as the biggies.

UNFAILING LOVE

Many are the woes of the wicked, but the Lord's unfailing love surrounds the man who trusts in him. Psalm 32:10, N.I.V.

When Korean Airline's Flight 007 was shot down after straying across an unfriendly international border, 269 people lost their lives. Shortly before that, Robert Smith, who looks after the periodical department at the Review and Herald Publishing Association, had taken Flight 007 to Seoul, Korea. Fortunately, Mr. Smith did not fly a few days later. But sometimes Christians do find themselves in the wrong place at the wrong time. The wicked aren't the only people with woes. "But the Lord's unfailing love surrounds the man who trusts in him." When the Christian comes to a time of trouble he is not alone. God is there beside him.

"Look, a car didn't make the curve," Louis Hill cried as he pointed to the damaged guardrail at the top of a steep incline. By the time he had braked safely and raced to the edge of the ravine, he could hear terrified screams from below. "Someone call an ambulance," one of the shocked bystanders said. But nobody had gone down to the aid of the injured man. Without a thought for his own safety Louis ran down the narrow trail. After he reached the injured man, the screams stopped.

"I couldn't do anything for him," he explained later. "A huge boulder had pinned him down, and blood was flowing into his eyes. He thought he had gone blind. I just wiped away the blood and held his hand." Having someone there while he waited for rescue quieted the young man's fears. And so it is with the Christians who faces a scary situation. God takes his or her hand, and fear disappears. "The Lord's unfailing love surrounds the man who trusts in him." As you memorize today's text you are buying insurance against future discouragement and fear. Sometime later you really will feel the touch of God's hand and you will remember that "unfailing love surrounds" you. Then you'll know that whatever happens, with God there you'll be all right.

MOM'S "UPPERS"

I lift up my eyes to the hills—where does my help come from? My help comes from the Lord, the Maker of heaven and earth. Psalm 121:1, N.I.V.

Ed arrived early at the field to limber up before the game began. As the stands began to fill he found himself scanning the rows for the familiar faces of his parents. Sometimes they were the only parents who came out, and he felt a little embarrassed to see them. "Is your mom here yet?" one of his friends asked. Ed cringed. So the other guys had noticed how they always came!

"Last week your mom said she was counting on me to win tonight," the other fellow continued. "My folks can't come, so your folks are my substitute parents." Suddenly Ed glowed. He could hardly wait to tell his mom how important she was to the team.

"Yeah, I guess my mom's good at giving uppers," Ed said.

The other boy looked puzzled. "Does your mom deal in drugs?" he asked.

Ed laughed. "No, and she doesn't wear dentures, either," he explained. "You see, when she needs encouragement for some reason she looks out our living room window to the hills. And she repeats a verse of Scripture: 'I lift up my eyes to the hills—where does my help come from? My help comes from the Lord.' That tells her that no matter how big her problem is, God is bigger. And that gives her an 'upper.' Get it? Up—hills—God."

"I'll remember that when I look up into the stands and see her there," the friend said.

"She'll be glad," Ed replied. "Only she'd want you to look higher than the stands. It's God who gives the uppers."

Ed's mom would also have said that you shouldn't rely on uppers just once in a while when you are in a threatening situation. You should look to God and read His Word every day if you want Him to keep you upbeat. The Maker of heaven and earth has all the help any of us needs. But we must lift up our eyes and ask for it—all the time.

GOD'S SOLUTION

I cried unto the Lord with my voice; with my voice unto the Lord did I make my supplication. Psalm 142:1.

Lontar was through with God. "Where was He when my parents died?" he asked defiantly. "He really let me down!" His grandmother knew how lonely the boy felt. She tried to talk to him about the puzzling way life hands out sorrow and suffering seemingly at random. "You can't blame God," she often said. "He tried to warn our very first parents about evil. But once Satan gets in control, things only get worse. God is the solution to the bad things that happen—not the cause." But Lontar would not listen—he just hated God all the more.

When Lontar was 16 he went to live with a young pastor who loved God deeply. The minister did not preach at him, but every day he prayed, "Show Lontar how much You love and care for us, dear Lord." One day the pastor put his car up for sale and prayed that someone would buy it, as he desperately needed the money. A buyer did come and agreed on a price. "See, Lontar," the pastor said, "God has answered our prayer."

But before the completion of the sale a cam shaft broke on the car. "Oh, now I'm really in trouble," the pastor sighed at worship time. "I need the money from the sale of that car. And I can't sell the car until I have some money to fix the cam shaft. Let's ask the Lord for $400." After the minister's prayer Lontar smiled to himself. He didn't believe that God existed, and he pitied the pastor for being so childish.

The next afternoon Lontar was the first to get home. He heard the telephone ringing while he was still unlocking the front door. A reporter from a leading newspaper needed to talk to the pastor. It turned out that the young minister had written a poem for a contest sponsored by the paper and had won $1,000. "See?" the pastor said later. "We asked God for $400 and He sent $1,000. What a wonderful God to serve!" Don't worry if you can't solve your problems by writing a poem. The Lord has a different solution for you.

TREASURES IN HEAVEN

"Do not store up for yourselves treasures on earth, where moth and rust destroy, and where thieves break in and steal. . . . For where your treasure is, there your heart will be also. Matthew 6:19-21, N.I.V.

Most of us feel proud of our country. We want to help keep it great. And no matter who you are or in which country you live, you have a right to think that your country is best. Recently a professor at the University of Pennsylvania drew up a list of forty-four things that make a country great to live in. I wish I knew all the factors on his list. Then I could understand why he decided that the top ten countries of the world to live in are: Denmark, Norway, Austria, the Netherlands, Sweden, New Zealand, Australia, Ireland, Belgium, and Finland. He rated the United States forty-first and the Soviet Union forty-third.

If you were deciding the most important things in your life, what would they be? Name some of them before you read on. Are toys near the top of the list? If so, you should stay in the United States, because in this country people have the most money and things. But are those most important? If you are dying of lung cancer at age 12 as a result of breathing polluted air, what comfort will money or toys bring? Wouldn't you wish that you had pure air to breathe instead? And won't you feel the same way about pure drinking water and food that has no chemicals added? Could health be more important than fun and comfort?

Christians can afford to chuckle about studies that show which is the best country, because no country on earth can measure up to our heavenly homeland, where all races will be one people. The air, water, food, and money that we have are important only in terms of how they help us reach the heavenly kingdom. Anything that keeps us healthy enables us to better prepare for heaven. But *things* can keep us too busy to think about heaven. Maybe that's why Jesus says that we should store treasures in heaven. He means that we should use our money to tell others of His soon coming and help bring in God's kingdom.

BORROWING JACKS

"Therefore do not worry about tomorrow, for tomorrow will worry about itself. Each day has enough trouble of its own." Matthew 6:34, N.I.V.

As sometimes happens with secondhand cars, George's lacked an important piece of equipment—a jack. "If you get a flat tire you'll wish you had one," his older brother admonished. George remembered what he had said when he first felt the bumping of a flat tire while driving home from a date one moonlit night. By the time he stopped, the rim practically rested on the pavement.

George sized up the situation and in a jiffy set out back down the road to borrow a jack. As he walked he worried about what he would say to the man of the house he had passed ten minutes before. Suppose George said, "Excuse me, sir, I have a flat tire. Could you lend me a jack?" Angry at being awakened, the man would no doubt mention the inconvenience. Then George would reply, "It was our first date—we lost track of the time. Sorry to bother you and all that, but if you could just lend me a jack you'll find it on the porch in the morning."

But who would lend a jack without asking why the borrower needed it? George could explain that too. "My tire is as flat as a bad joke," he would say. "I cannot get home to bed without changing the tire. And for that reason I must borrow your jack." What if the man didn't trust him? People like that made George mad. "Can't you give a guy a break!" George growled as his heels ground into the gravel driveway leading to the house.

Suddenly a window flew up and a voice called from the darkness, "Who is it? What do you want?"

"You know very well what I want!" George yelled back. "Come on down and lend me that jack!"

Of course, you wouldn't do that. Or would you? Do you sometimes borrow trouble instead of jacks? Do you ever lie in bed worrying about your parents dying or robbers breaking in or the time of trouble? Jesus said: Don't fret over the future. That is in God's hands. Trust Him to walk beside you today and He'll be there when you need Him most.

LIKE HIM

Dear friends, now we are children of God, and what we will be has not yet been made known. But we know that when he appears, we shall be like him, for we shall see him as he is. 1 John 3:2, N.I.V.

"Why should one loudmouth make life miserable for everyone?" Nancy mumbled to herself. "I'm going to tell Patti what I think of her ugly outbursts." And she did. Nobody had ever spoken to Patti about how she embarrassed others.

"Well, that's the way I am," the girl spluttered. "If you don't like me that way . . ." But Nancy had already walked away. Once a loudmouth, always a loudmouth. But is that true? Or is it possible to change?

Scientists lured Imo, a Japanese macaque (muh-KAK) monkey, and her band into the open by dropping sweet potatoes on the beach. The monkeys did not like sand-covered food, but they had nothing else to eat. When Imo was 18 months old she discovered how to wash the sand from her food. One month later another young monkey began to clean her food as Imo did. Four months later Imo's mother followed. And after five years all but the adult males had changed their eating habits. So habits can be changed.

When Imo was 4 the scientists scattered unhusked rice on the beach, hoping that the monkeys would pick up each grain separately and allow the scientists more time to study them. But soon Imo scooped up the grain, sand and all, and threw it into the water. As the sand sank to the bottom the rice floated to the top, where the monkey skimmed it off and ate it. Soon the others followed her example.

But the adult males didn't learn to wash their food, as the others did. Why? Scientists think that they probably did not eat with Imo and the rest. So they did not see her example.

As children of God, we read our Bibles and pray every day. We show our love for Jesus by trying to please Him. And slowly but surely we grow more like Him. "When he appears, we shall be like him." That's His promise to you and me—and Patti. But we must stay close to Him so we can benefit from His example.

THINGS THAT ARE DEAR TO GOD

Seek ye first the kingdom of God, and his righteousness; and all these things shall be added unto you. Matthew 6:33.

"Have you noticed how worried Anita looks today?" Jody whispered to her friend Betty Jo. "I wonder what's the matter."

"Oh, some people like to look dramatic," Betty Jo replied.

But Jody wasn't satisfied. Between classes she slipped up to Anita and asked her if she was feeling OK. Anita nodded unconvincingly. "It's my dad," she whispered. "I'm worried about him. I'll explain it sometime." Hating to see her friend worried, Jody promised to pray that things would work out for Anita's dad. And both girls felt better as they hurried to class.

Jody reminds me of a minister in Pennsylvania who used to say that today's text means that if you take care of the things that are dear to God, He will care for the things dear to you.

A missionary to China took that promise as her own during the war with Japan. She and her husband worried about their children who were away in a mission school located in an area occupied by the Japanese. Helpless to reach her children, the mother prayed every morning for their safekeeping and claimed the promise of Matthew 6:33 as the minister had explained it. Every day she went about caring for those who were dear to the Lord, trusting Him to care for her children.

"How can you look so calm when you must be worried sick for your children?" people often asked. And she would explain her understanding of Matthew 6:33 and how she was caring for those dear to the Lord. And God did deliver the children in perfect health five and one-half years later.

Are you letting things worry you lately? Do you wonder how the bills will be paid? Or maybe someone close to you has been involved in a serious accident, and you aren't sure of the outcome. You could worry yourself sick or harden yourself and pretend you don't care. Or you could spend more time caring about someone dear to God and trust Him to care for your dear one.

AND IF I GO

The Lord will rescue me from every evil attack and will bring me safely to his heavenly kingdom. 2 Timothy 4:18, N.I.V.

Janee had a set of Dr. Seuss books that her mother read to her at bedtime. When her mother went out and bought a set of *Bible Story* books, Janee cried at bedtime because she preferred Dr. Seuss. But now she wishes that she knew all the Bible stories.

Her Sabbath school class had been studying about Elisha. Janee at first pronounced his name e-LISH-a because she had to read the lessons to herself and wasn't familiar with his name. She always enjoyed hearing Mrs. J. retell the story in Sabbath school class.

"What do you know for certain about you and God after studying about Elisha?" the teacher asked.

Janee waved her hand vigorously. "Jesus raises people from the dead," she said.

Death was right at the top of the girl's list of fears, and the idea that Jesus answers prayers suggested that if she asked Him, He would not let her die. What a happy thought!

"Can you name one thing that will eventually happen to every one of us?" the teacher continued. After many hints someone answered correctly, "We'll die."

"Why do people die?" Mrs. J. wanted to know. Janee knew that. She had heard about Adam and Eve.

"Because Jesus died you need not be afraid of death," Mrs. J. explained. "He will be there holding your hand. And when you wake from that sleep, you'll look into His face—and live forever." The idea of eternal life excited Janee so that she almost danced for joy.

"You have eternal life now when you have accepted Jesus," Mrs. J. added. Janee thought of all the beauties of heaven and the joy of living forever. Somehow sleeping the first death didn't seem so bad when you knew how it would be when you woke up. The girl sighed contentedly. She could cross the fear of death right off the top of her list.

GOD'S METEORITE

"A stone was hewn from a mountain, not by human hands; it struck the image on its feet of iron and clay and shattered them." Daniel 2:34, N.E.B.

Chunks of rock called meteoroids hurtle through space. If the meteroid enters the earth's atmosphere, the friction from the atmosphere makes it glowing hot and creates a streak of light. We can often see falling stars, as most people mistakenly call meteoroids, on clear nights. Most meteoroids burn up in the atmosphere, but occasionally one reaches the earth. Then we call it a meteorite. Long ago an enormous meteorite crashed into the Arizona desert, leaving a crater measuring about 4,100 feet across. The meteorite exploded on contact, thus gouging out the 570-foot-deep crater. The remaining fragments of the exploded meteorite scattered on the desert floor far outside the crater. Weathering soon breaks down meteorites until they look like ordinary rocks.

King Nebuchadnezzar once dreamed he saw an enormous rock, flying like a meteoroid, smash a towering image to pieces. The whole dream (read more about it in Daniel 2) troubled him until Daniel explained that each major part of the image depicted a world kingdom. The feet of clay and iron represented a mixture of strong and weak nations that wouldn't get along too well. Suddenly a meteoritelike rock struck the feet of the image, reducing the whole thing to dust that blew away in the wind. In the days of those kingdoms symbolized by the feet—our day—" 'the God of heaven will establish a kingdom which shall never be destroyed' " (verse 44). His kingdom will not begin like a new government taking over in Washington or London. But like the meteorite " 'it shall shatter and make an end of all these kingdoms, while it shall itself endure for ever' " (verse 44).

We who belong to God's kingdom of grace—who have accepted Jesus as Lord and who live by the rules of His kingdom—will feel at home in the kingdom to come. At last the whole earth will obey God's laws. Everyone will give honor and glory to the everlasting King. I can hardly wait! How about you?

UNDER THE MERCY

Surely goodness and mercy shall follow me all the days of my life: and I will dwell in the house of the Lord for ever. Psalm 23:6.

From the first day of school Wanda didn't seem to belong. The other children in the little one-room schoolhouse made sure of that. At every opportunity they taunted her for her hand-me-down clothes. They groaned when someone chose her for his team and fussed when asked to sit near her. For a little girl like Wanda, goodness and mercy seemed far away. In fact, she hardly knew what they are. Instead she withdrew into her own little world, sitting alone and drawing pictures. One recess as Wanda sat under a tree drawing, her teacher placed a little book in front of her. The pretty cover had written on it the name of a famous painter. Inside were paintings by famous artists. Her teacher said softly, "You can become a great artist with God's help. You draw well and you don't give up easily. I think you're special." After that, Wanda hardly heard the cruel taunts, because to her teacher and to God she was special.

God doesn't promise that being part of His kingdom of love will keep us from cruelty and disappointment on earth. In fact, when a weakhearted Herod beheaded John the Baptist, Jesus said, "Among them that are born of women there hath not risen a greater than John the Baptist" (Matt. 11:11). But in John's hour of need God did not intervene and rescue him. What had happened to goodness and mercy?

Jesus explained it this way: "And from the days of John the Baptist until now the kingdom of heaven suffereth violence, and the violent take it by force" (verse 12). At least they seem to. But we see only part of the kingdom of heaven in our lifetime. For, though we may suffer hurt and violence here, nobody may remove us from the goodness and mercy that span the grave and carry us at last into the kingdom of glory, where we "will dwell in the house of the Lord for ever."

FIRST AND LAST

Sitting down, Jesus called the Twelve and said, "If anyone wants to be first, he must be the very last, and the servant of all." Mark 9:35, N.I.V.

Eric B. Hare used to tell about the time Burma was about to fall to the enemy and the government evacuated all foreigners. Hoping that the war might soon be over so his family could return, Pastor Hare carefully packed away their belongings and gathered up the few things that he could carry over the long trails into India.

At the border he was thankful to find somewhere to rest. Government officials promised to arrange transportation to carry the refugees on their way to Calcutta. One morning several old army buses with hard seats pulled up before the camp. To those who had walked so far, any kind of vehicle looked good. And grabbing their belongings, people pushed and shoved to get on board. Those left behind waved politely, trying to feel glad for those fortunate enough to be leaving on the departing buses. After an hour or so more buses arrived, and again people stampeded to find a place.

Much later those who remained watched to their surprise as luxury buses drove into camp. Carefully they helped one another to find seats. Someone discovered soft pillows stowed above the seats, and they went first to those too old or too ill to get one for themselves. What a difference from the pushing and shoving of the earlier groups, Pastor Hare thought. Eventually the more modern buses passed some of the vehicles that had left earlier. Those on the newer buses noticed how tired the people looked, jammed in together as they were. The whole scene reminded Elder Hare of Mark 9:35, where Jesus said, "'If anyone wants to be first, he must be the very last, and the servant of all.'" This is especially true of the long journey into God's heavenly kingdom. The places of honor up there are reserved for those who think of the needs of others before their own. I want to be that kind of thoughtful person, don't you?

BLOOMS IN THE DESERT

The wilderness and the solitary place shall be glad for them; and the desert shall rejoice, and blossom as the rose. Isaiah 35:1.

Sand dredged from the sea floor by pounding waves gets thrown up on the beaches of the Great Australian Bight. The wind picks up the sand and blows it over the land, forming spectacular dunes that have inched their way relentlessly toward the little village of Ceduna. Standing there by the post office twenty years ago, I heard about how the sand had slowly encroached, covering homes and the schoolhouse. Over the years the dunes have buried the post office from sight and forced the highway to be moved farther north, away from the moving sand. Today the only signs of the old town are nearly buried ruins. About one third of the land on Planet Earth is desert or semidesert. One gets a rather dreary view of mankind in a desert where one's labors literally turn to dust.

In some parts of the world, deserts result from man cutting down forests and overgrazing his animals, thus removing the plant life that anchors the soil from the clawing wind. It takes four things to make a desert bloom: water, weather, wealth, and a will to work. Flying over Palm Springs, California, for instance, one may see clearly where the desert ends and a beautifully kept estate begins. The greenness testifies to the work and money invested to make the change. But in Egypt, where desert rules all but 4 percent of the land, and most farmers are pitifully poor, reclaiming the desert seems like an unrealistic dream.

The Mojave Desert's Antelope Valley blossoms with spectacular beauty every April. But the beauty vanishes with the onset of summer. The blossoms don't last because the water doesn't. But it won't be like that when God's kingdom of glory returns to an earth made new. Not only will the deserts "blossom abundantly," but they will "rejoice even with joy and singing: the glory of Lebanon shall be given unto it, the excellency of Carmel and Sharon, they shall see the glory of the Lord, and the excellency of our God" (verse 2). I'm looking forward to that day. How about you?

NOT TALK, BUT ACTION

For the kingdom of God is not in word, but in power. 1 Corinthians 4:20.

"There it is!" Tammie yelled as the large Disney World sign loomed above the highway. Breathlessly she waited as her dad maneuvered into the lane exiting from Interstate 4. When at last they parked the car she raced her brother to the tram. While her parents bought tickets Tammie studied the entrance where people were lining up to wait for the gates to open. To be honest, she had to admit that it did not look like the gateway to a magic kingdom.

Soon the gates opened and the family found themselves riding the monorail and surveying the kingdom from far above the ground. "When will it look like we're getting to Disney World?" she asked.

"What do you mean?" her father queried. "We've been here since we parked the car. At any rate, when we walked through the gate back there we were definitely on Disney World property."

"But where does it say Magic Kingdom?" Tammie persisted. "I didn't see a big sign."

"Oh, she wants to see a sign like 'Welcome to Disney World, 5,679 Inhabitants,' " her brother teased. "Well, look closely and you might yet see a marker for the city limits!"

Tammie missed a sign for Disney World. God's kingdom of grace has no sign either, because the kingdom begins in men's hearts—not in space that we can measure and mark. And neither has it a fence or wrought-iron gates. And as with Tammie at Disney World, you may not realize that you are there until you have been there for some time. Clifford knew he was there when he realized that he had not cursed since the day two weeks before when he had asked God to take control of his life and help him guard his speech. Lonnie realized he was there when he actually wanted to help his old grandmother enjoy herself. It isn't the words—the promises of future glory—that remind you that you are a part of God's kingdom already; it's the power—the difference He makes in your life when you give yourself to Him.

THROUGH MOTHER'S EYES

Then will the eyes of the blind be opened and the ears of the deaf unstopped. Isaiah 35:5, N.I.V.

The other day Traci Phelps said in exasperation, "Oh, my mother never sees things from my point of view." Dottie knew what she was trying to say but wanted to open *her* eyes. You see, when Dottie was 3 months old her mother woke up one morning and discovered that she was blind. She had known that it was coming, but that didn't help much. Fortunately she had a strong faith in God and she asked Him not to let her feel sorry for herself. As far as Dottie knew she never did.

Fifteen years later medical science caught up with the problem enough to help Dottie's mom regain the use of one eye. Before she went in for surgery the doctor made her promise not to cry until her eye was completely healed. For a few days she lay with her eyes bandaged. When the doctor said that she could see Dottie, the girl tried to act grown up and do nothing that would make her mother cry, for fear of spoiling her eyesight.

Dottie stood at the bottom of the bed, smiling. Her mother said, "Dottie, we've got to do something about those bangs." They both laughed. Then they let 3-year-old Pete in to see her. He stood like a little statue beside her bed for nearly fifteen minutes, just smiling while she looked at him. Then suddenly he realized that his mother was seeing him for the first time. "This is my elbow," he said, showing it to her. "And this is my shoe." Then he brought her the flowers, books, and cards lying about the room. He was seeing everything from his mother's point of view. Dottie looks forward to the resurrection morning, when Jesus will open all the eyes and unstop the ears. But she doesn't need to wait until then to let Him open her understanding of other people. She wishes someone would explain that to Traci Phelps.

HIGHWAY TO HEAVEN

And an highway shall be there . . . called The way of holiness. Isaiah 35:8.

I shall never forget the evening that my brother and I joined some friends at a church road race. No, we were not into running. It was a motorcar race. Each car received a map and a set of directions. Our car rolled up to the starting point, an official marked our record card with the starting time, and we were on our own. We had fun trying to read the road map because some of the streets depicted on the map had no signs identifying them as we drove along. But in spite of losing our way several times, we lost the least points at the first checkpoint. Most people forfeited points for arriving too soon.

"Lucky we lost our way so many times," I giggled. After that we calculated the approximate speed we were supposed to maintain. This helped us to figure out when to arrive at the next checkpoint. At one point we missed a turn. "Don't worry," I told the driver. "We'll also find the checkpoint if we continue on this way." But we were penalized for approaching the checkpoint from the wrong direction. We might have won the race had we followed the map exactly.

Don't you wish we had a map to help us figure out the route to heaven? Actually, the Bible is our map, and when we give our heart to Jesus we do begin the journey. Isaiah writes about a wonderful highway "called the Way of Holiness. The unclean will not journey on it; it will be for those who walk in that Way" (N.I.V.). Had the ancient people of Israel been faithful in following God, He would have built the highway for them. But by faith we look forward to such a road in the earth made new. All those who walk on it will be followers of Jesus, " 'the way and the truth,' " (John 14:6). And nobody, even the most simple-minded, will lose his way or be penalized for going in the wrong direction. Because all those who enjoy its use will have allowed Jesus to guide their lives here.

LIONS AND LAMBS

The wolf and the lamb shall feed together, and the lion shall eat straw like the bullock. . . . They shall not hurt nor destroy in all my holy mountain, saith the Lord. Isaiah 65:25.

Joanie loves to play softball. She plays hard to win. But although for the three years she played on the blue team they lost more games than they won, Joanie would not have traded for a place on the winning team. "Our team members try to encourage one another," she explained. "And our coach doesn't act like we're in a battle. He's a good sport."

When Joanie watches ice hockey with her mom, however, she defends the fights that break out. "Oh, that's half the fun," she says. "It adds excitement to the game." But the coach of the academy she attends doesn't agree. He hands out stiff penalties when a player throws down his stick, even if nobody is hurt. "You should learn to play as a Christian," he says. "Athletes need to learn how to lose—gracefully."

Dave Forbes likes to tell how he always thought of himself as a Christian. But he didn't realize his need of God until the night, overcome by anger, he almost killed a player from the opposing team with his hockey stick.

Ashamed of being suspended from the team while a grand jury examined his case, Dave turned to the Bible. After the court declared a mistrial, he went back to hockey a changed man. Instead of partying late after a win, he remained in his room, reading his Bible until he found forgiveness.

"The thing that bothered me most," he said, "was the realization that I was a violent person. I couldn't imagine anyone shouting angrily at the referee or acting violently on God's holy mountain."

But is it OK to hate the other team so long as you're not violent? Joanie's mom doesn't think so; neither does the academy coach. "You're right to want to win," he says. "But you have to keep the game in perspective. Winning isn't what's important, but how you play the game."

Like Dave Forbes, I want to make it to that holy mountain. How about you?

MY FATHER'S HOUSE

"In my Father's house are many rooms; if it were not so, I would have told you. I am going there to prepare a place for you." John 14:2, N.I.V.

Nina Donnelly is a chaplain in a large hospital. "Seeing children die is a rotten thing," she wrote in an article for *Leadership* magazine. Sometimes she meets children like 9-year-old Laura who will not get well again. She likes to sit and talk to the girl, rubbing the child's sore legs and knees.

"What's heaven like?" Laura asks. Laura has leukemia. Talking about heaven takes her mind off the pain.

"What do *you* think it's like?" Nina asks her.

The 9-year-old is sure of her reply. "It's no more pain. And having my hair long again. Running around—and looking pretty."

The chaplain says that she thinks Laura is still pretty, but the child can't agree. A photograph of herself with long dark hair proves her point.

"That's what heaven's like," Nina says. "And seeing God." For a while Laura remains silent. "Will He be mad at me?" she asks. "I haven't always been good."

"Are you sorry about that?" The woman asks. Solemnly Laura nods. "Then why don't you tell God that you are sorry?"

"I did," Laura says. "But I don't know if He heard me."

The chaplain assures the girl that although God sometimes feels disappointed with us, He doesn't get mad. And He's quick to forgive and forget. She wishes she could hug the girl or tickle her, but she can't—it would hurt her too much. Instead she describes God's house of many rooms and all the joys of heaven. Laura forgets her pain for a while as she listens in fascination.

For Laura, heaven is all the things that she misses. What is it for you? And how could you bring the happiness of heaven to someone like her today?

NEVER LOST AGAIN

And so we will be with the Lord forever. 1 Thessalonians 4:17, N.I.V.

One minute I was standing in the toy section of a large department store at Christmastime. The next, I was lost. In panic I searched the crowd of shoppers, looking for a familiar face. My heart leaped into my mouth—well, it would have if my throat had not been so painfully tight. I wanted to cry, but it would only have made things worse. As long as I live I'll never forget that feeling.

When I had children of my own I determined to make sure that they were never lost. But I shall never forget the morning in Poona, India, when I awoke and discovered my 3-year-old son missing. His bed was empty, and the front door was unlocked. A drum in a nearby village kept up an incessant, pounding beat. Had Terry marched to the beat of a distant drum? Had he gone in search of the drummer? Hurriedly my husband and I dressed and began searching. First we checked our yard, then called down the streets of the large college compound.

"Sister, what are you calling for?" the press manager asked as I passed his house. My explanation brought a look of alarm to his face. "A little child should never leave the compound alone," he said. "You must find him quickly." Suddenly my heart skipped a beat, and panic tightened my chest. After finding him I realized that losing my child hurt far more than being lost myself.

When the redeemed from this earth gather with their Saviour in the heavenly kingdom, what comfort we all shall feel. You and I will never again know that scary lost feeling or the terrible panic of knowing that someone else is lost. But what a tremendous relief it will be for God, for "we will be with the Lord forever." Never again will anyone be lost. The good news this morning is that you never need know the worst lostness of all—losing Jesus—if you keep your hand firmly in His by reading the Bible and praying before you start each day. Don't ever leave home without it.

THERE IS A RIVER

There is a river whose streams make glad the city of God, the holy place where the Most High dwells. Psalm 46:4, N.I.V.

When we agreed to accompany the Pathfinders from First church on a camping trip, we had no idea that they had chosen the hottest May weekend on record. All night I lay on my sleeping bag waiting for the cool breeze. It didn't come. By ten o'clock Sabbath morning I was too hot to enjoy a Sabbath walk. "Why don't we take this path down to the lake?" I asked. "We could sit in the water and sing and have Sabbath school undisturbed."

"Do you really want to feed the mosquitoes and leeches?" the leader asked. "Let's stay in camp until the heat has passed. Later we'll walk over to the beaver dam."

From the shade of the trees I watched the heat sizzling up from the white gravel roadway and recounted my coolest memories. I remembered wading in a mountain stream while rock hunting in faraway New Zealand. And I thought of a hot Sunday drive in India. We had constantly sighted mirages that promised a cool splash, but remained out of reach; then we found a river, far more inviting than the mirages had been. I thought of Psalm 46: "There is a river whose streams make glad the city of God."

I can almost see that river steadily flowing who knows where. And as I dangle my feet in its cooling waters, I marvel that some of the drops mingled there actually flowed from the heavenly city. Suddenly, I forget the heat and begin walking upstream until a smaller stream meets the river. Is this the one that flowed from the city? I wish that New Jerusalem streams joined a river on this earth. But it is enough to look into a lake or pool and know that somewhere there is that river. Someday I shall sit beside it and rest for a long while. But right now there's work to do.

ASK TOM!

Here is a trustworthy saying: If we died with him, we will also live with him; if we endure, we will also reign with him. 2 Timothy 2:11,12, N.I.V.

Sometimes the Bible makes no sense to those who have not discovered Jesus as their personal friend. For instance, who ever would think of death bringing life? But if you look at a tiny seed you have to admit that it looks dried up and as dead as can be. And yet, when you bury the seed in the ground it springs to life. But that new green shoot would not have come had you not buried the seed.

When Tom found Jesus at some tent meetings, he knew that he had found something important that he wanted to keep forever. And the more he studied the sayings of Jesus, the more he realized that he couldn't keep what he had found without giving up himself. That meant obeying Jesus, doing *His* will instead of what he felt like doing. One of the first things Tom gave up was drinking liquor and smoking. He figured that anything that made him feel dirty was not worth hanging onto anyway. Next he felt convicted that he should keep the Sabbath. But how could he risk losing a good job? How would he feed his family?

The minister tried to tell Tom that God would provide. But of course, he didn't know just *how* God would do it. And somehow he knew that Tom must make a leap of faith. Like jumping over a ditch in the dark. Even though you know where the bank is, it's scary not being able to see it. It took Tom a while to gather enough courage to ask his boss for Sabbath off. And it took more courage to quit rather than to continue working on Sabbaths.

Tom is an old man now, and he is still glad that he decided in favor of spiritual life, even though it looked like his little family might starve to death at the time. He believes that his life has been much richer for making that decision. His family thinks so, too. And by God's grace and much prayer and Bible study they have endured. They look forward to the time when Jesus will come back to earth and set up His kingdom of glory. For they know they "will also reign with him." Those little decisions made today may seem hard, but they will pay off someday. Ask Tom!

UP, UP, AND AWAY

Then we which are alive and remain shall be caught up together with them in the clouds, to meet the Lord in the air: and so shall we ever be with the Lord. 1 Thessalonians 4:17.

"It was a little scary at first," 13-year-old Robyn Alford said of her summer hot-air ballooning experiences. "We had to learn a lot all at once," she adds. Robyn joined fifty other Girl Scouts from twenty-eight States for a scouting program called Up, Up, and Away, where she learned everything from tying knots to predicting weather—skills she would need on a balloon trip.

Preparing a balloon for flight turned out to be quite a task, Robyn discovered. After she helped unload the thousand yards of sturdy nylon fabric that make up the balloon and spread it on the ground, she helped attach it by cables to the basket. She zipped padded leather sleeves over the fuel lines and upright supports for the propane fuel burner. Then she held the fabric part of the balloon as the pilot directed hot air into the balloon's body. As the inside became hot, the balloon began to rise. "At first when we went up, the balloons were tethered to vans or jeeps on the ground," Robyn says. "When the tethers were released we floated skyward. It seemed to me like we were staying still and the earth was moving."

Hot-air balloon pilots cannot steer. But by heating up the air, they send the balloon upward until they find air currents that carry the balloon in the direction they want to go. They let some of the hot air escape through a vent to bring it down.

Hot-air ballooning must be fun. But I'm sure it is nothing by comparison with that journey up through the clouds that Jesus has planned for us. And the clouds I'll be looking for on my super journey are the clouds of angels that surround Jesus. On that trip I won't be staring down at the earth. I'll be too busy looking for Him.

MARJORIE'S RAZZING

Lord, who shall abide in thy tabernacle? who shall dwell in thy holy hill? He that walketh uprightly . . . and speaketh the truth in his heart. He that backbiteth not with his tongue. Psalm 15:1-3.

If you ever had people poking fun at you all the time you probably know how Marjorie Felder felt when she entered the jeweler's to have her watch repaired. "Could you fix it by Monday?" she had asked. "I'm leaving for college."

"What are you doing that for?" the man demanded roughly. "Nobody raised in Harlem makes it through college."

The man's words angered her so much that she felt like snapping back. But instead she raised herself to her full height and politely explained how her brother Henry was already in college and doing well. "Ten kids graduated in my class," she explained. "And all ten of us are going to Oakwood College."

"I'm telling you that the statistics are against you. You'll never make it," the man snarled.

And again resisting the temptation to yell, Marjorie explained how she did not fit the statistics. "My mother sent me to church schools," she said. "When I graduate from college, I'll come back and show you my diploma." But the jeweler seemed unimpressed."

As the man had predicted, the going was tough for her. She worked long hours to pay her tuition. Sometimes the odds seemed all to be stacked against her. But whenever she felt like quitting, she thought of the jeweler and quietly kept on.

He wasn't at the counter when she entered the shop. But one of the clerks called him. "I wanted to show you this," Marjorie said as she unrolled her diploma. "All ten of us graduated just as I predicted."

A grin spread over the man's face. "I've had this waiting just in case," he said, handing her an expensive bottle of perfume. "Your mother brought you up in the house and not in the street. That must have made the difference."

What does he know about my upbringing? Marjorie thought. But he had noticed that through all his razzing she had never talked back. I can't imagine a loudmouth in the kingdom of heaven, or somebody who bites back, either. Can you?

THE MATCH

Ye are the light of the world. A city that is set on a hill cannot be hid. Matthew 5:14.

My husband and I once lived in a city strung out on a hill. Mussoorie is situated about seven thousand feet up in the foothills of the Himalayas. Most of the year it reminds one of a ghost town. The large high-ceilinged residences stand empty and boarded up. But in the spring, people from the plains would return, and the population would overflow into the sunny bazaar and fill the long, narrow streets with sounds of bargaining. But the biggest difference that the season brought to the hillsides could be seen rather than heard. At night the town shone with lights—streetlights, flashlights, torchlights, firelights, and lights flooding from windows and doorways of stores and homes.

Travelers riding the steep switchback roads up the mountainside felt the throb of the approaching town whenever they caught sight of its lights. The rays shouted a cheery welcome. But when the power failed, the blackness seemd more dense and threatening than usual because walking in the darkness posed a real danger in Mussoorie on the steep streets of the town. To miss the path in some places might mean a fall of several feet or much more.

I once read how a patient in a psychiatric hospital gave a woman a strange gift—a single match. A small child, forbidden to play with matches, might appreciate such a gift. But the woman, not knowing what else to do with it, put it in her purse.

That night at the church Christmas program, a little boy was supposed to open the program by lighting all the candles. However, he marched down the aisle without his matches. Realizing his predicament, the woman offered him her one match. And what an effect it caused as its flame began the lighting of one candle after another until the whole church shone with light.

The citizens of God's kingdom are like lighted matches. They share their light with others until the whole world seems brighter. But you can't spread the glow unless Jesus sets you ablaze with His love. Won't you let Him today?

HEARING EARS

Then the eyes of those who see will no longer be closed, and the ears of those who hear will listen. Isaiah 32:3, N.I.V.

Jason Lufkin, of Raleigh, North Carolina, has two pairs of ears. The pair he was born with don't hear too well. That isn't unusual for 10-year-olds, I know—especially during a backyard baseball game or around bedtime. But Jason couldn't hear his parents calling even if he wanted to. Have you ever thought how hearing can save your life? That's why school buses stop at railroad crossings and open their doors. And that's why cars have horns—to warn you of their presence when you forget to look. But since Jason cannot hear car horns and approaching traffic, someone has to accompany him everywhere he goes.

His other pair of ears is hairy and has legs. You see, members of a labor organization in North Carolina helped the Lufkins buy Ginger, a hearing-ear dog that accompanies the boy everywhere he goes. She hears the alarm in the morning and gently licks Jason's cheek to wake him up. When Jason's mother calls, the dog leads him to her. Ginger accompanies Jason to workouts for the neighborhood football team. They each look both ways when they cross the street, and, if the dog hears an approaching vehicle after they start across, he steps in front of Jason. When they get to the playing field, Ginger sits on the sidelines until the game is done.

Often when the Bible talks about people hearing or listening, it means that they take notice of what is said—they obey. And obedience is important to Jason. Should Ginger step in front of him on the street, Jason would not kick the dog aside and continue on his way. Otherwise she would soon stop listening for him and signaling what he can't hear.

I'm sure Jason looks forward to the day when "the ears of those who hear will listen." But you and I need not wait so long to make better use of our ears. Let's really try to listen today—to our parents, teachers, neighbors, and friends. And let's especially listen to God as we read His Word and do what it says.

NO MORE SEA

And I saw a new heaven and a new earth: for the first heaven and the first earth were passed away; and there was no more sea. Revelation 21:1.

Have you ever sat beside the sea on a summer evening and watched the great red sun slowly sink into the horizon? It may have seemed you could walk that path of red and gold that stretched from the sun to your beach. In such a setting a vision of the new earth with no oceans would seem puzzling. What would the earth be without the sea?

For Sandy and Joe Barker that question probably has deeper meaning. Sandy loved to sail around the friendly Florida Keys, but one June they drifted in their disabled boat into the open sea. Sandy later wrote, "I looked out at the most terrifying sight of my life. Water. Everywhere. Like a jagged gray blanket, it stretched on forever."

The mighty oceans at their best fill one with a sense of beauty and mystery, but at their worst they pose a stormy threat to man. The power of a curling breaker makes a surfer's day, but whipped into fury, those powerful waves smash mighty ships and cover many a lonely grave. Oceans are symbols of high adventure and of sorrowful separations.

The prophet Isaiah wrote to his disheartened countrymen recovering from the savage attacks of the Assyrians under Sennacherib: "There the glorious Lord will be unto us a place of broad rivers and streams; wherein shall go no galley with oars, neither shall gallant ships pass thereby" (Isa. 33:21). Galleys were the warships that carried invaders to the land of Palestine. So Isaiah's message promised peace and security. It also brings a special hope for us, for even though we cannot imagine a world without oceans, our wonderful God will more than take their place. Whatever He has planned for us in heaven will leave no aching and longing for something we once had on earth. And best of all, never again will we stand at a wharf and wave goodbye to loved ones, not knowing if we will ever meet again. Up there we will never say goodbye.

CHEAP ENOUGH

And I looked, and, lo, a Lamb stood on the mount Sion, and with him an hundred forty and four thousand, having his Father's name written in their foreheads. Revelation 14:1.

Ellen Harmon loved Jesus dearly. With other Adventists she was disappointed when Jesus did not come in 1844. But while some abandoned God, Ellen clung to Him more than ever. One December morning while she was praying with friends God gave her a wonderful vision. You may read about it in *Early Writings*. The Holy Spirit took Ellen far above our dark world. Above her she saw the Advent people climbing a straight and narrow path. A light shone behind them to light up their way. Just before them, leading the way to the Holy City far above, was Jesus, ever encouraging the little group. Some grew tired of the journey and doubted the light that had shone on their path from the beginning. They fell from the path and lost their way.

The group toiling ever upward was the 144,000. All along the way wicked men tried to keep them from following the path, but when in trouble they needed only to reach out to Jesus for help. The 144,000, perfectly united in the love of Jesus, were saved at last by the coming of Jesus on a cloud. A great silence filled the earth. Then Jesus said, "'Those who have clean hands and pure hearts shall be able to stand; My grace is sufficient for you.'"—*Early Writings,* p. 16.

Jesus sounded the silver trumpet and cried for those asleep in Him to awake. As the 144,000 recognized friends and loved ones who had slept in the grave, they shouted, "Alleluia!" The Lord took them up to a sea of glass where each received a crown and a white robe from Jesus. Then they all marched confidently to the city of God. As Jesus swung open the great pearly gate He cried, "'You have washed your robes in My blood, stood stiffly for My truth, enter in.'"—*Early Writings,* p. 17. The glories of the city with the tree of life and the throne of God overwhelmed the saints so that when they tried to recall the trials of earth they could not, but exclaimed, "'Alleluia, heaven is cheap enough!'" And heaven's arches rang with their singing.

THE PROMISE

Cast not away therefore your confidence, which hath great recompense of reward. For ye have need of patience, that, after ye have done the will of God, ye might receive the promise. Hebrews 10:35, 36.

As Ellen gazed on the beautiful fruits in heaven she asked permission to taste some. But Jesus told her she must return to earth and tell others what she had seen. Someday she would return to stay, He promised. But some people, hearing Ellen tell of her visions, declared that she had been mesmerized (hypnotized). One prominent physician explained to Ellen that she was an easy subject for mesmerism. He could easily hypnotize her himself, he said. So Ellen permitted him to try. For half an hour he attempted to bring her under his power, but finally gave up. Ellen's faith in God helped her resist the doctor's efforts. But people still insisted that her highly excitable nature, not God, caused the visions.

One morning as Ellen knelt in prayer she felt the Spirit of God rest upon her. Maybe it's mesmerism, she thought, and resisted the Spirit. Immediately she felt herself struck dumb, and her mind went blank as punishment for doubting. Then a card appeared before her with the chapter and verse of fifty texts lettered in gold. After she came out of the vision Ellen remembered the verses and looked them up in her Bible. The first was Luke 1:20: "And, behold, thou shalt be dumb, . . . because thou believest not my words." There followed other verses reminding Ellen that some people would never believe the words of God as revealed to her. Then came the lovely passage from Hebrews 10: "Cast not away therefore your confidence. . . . For ye have need of patience that . . . ye might receive the promise."

Ellen remembered the glorious city she had seen in vision. She remembered her Saviour's lovely face as He bade her return to earth. And she remembered His promise that if faithful she might one day stay there forever. Earth seemed dreary after her return. "Oh, that I had wings like a dove, then would I fly away and be at rest!" she cried *(Early Writings,* p. 20). Don't you wish you could see that heavenly land? Someday you will if you cling to God's promises and continue to take Him at His word.

ANOTHER HOME

He will wipe away all tears from their eyes, and there shall be no more death, nor sorrow, nor crying, nor pain. All of that has gone forever. Revelation 21:4, T.L.B.

A missionary friend of ours needed repairs to his stereo system. The young man who contracted to repair the machine insisted on delivering it to the house when he finished. When at last he found his way to the Spicer College campus and the home of our friend, he exclaimed over the beauty of the compound. He admired the fertile field of soybeans opposite the missionary's house and the tall shade trees lining the roadways. "Oh, how I would love to live here," he sighed. "I would never leave!"

His appreciation of our mission property led us all to open our eyes and realize its beauty. True, the unpaved roads were dusty, but the neatly trimmed hedges and the brilliant bougainvillea never lost their color. We were living in a tiny sanctuary and hardly appreciated its calm and beauty.

Many of us today enjoy a little of heaven on earth. Loving Christian parents surround us with every good thing. Sometimes we have to try hard to think how heaven could be better. But millions on this earth go to sleep every night hungry. Millions mourn the loss of loved ones. Countless boys and girls carry a continual ache in their hearts for parents that have separated, for brothers and sisters they no longer remember, for family members dying with cruel diseases.

Sooner or later pain and death strike closer to home, and we, too, long for the better land where sorrow and pain will be no more. Can you picture that happy day when those who cannot run and play here will gallop and fly around the New Jerusalem for the first time? Imagine yourself clasping Jesus' scarred hands and thanking Him. After that, even your favorite things down here would seem uninteresting. Your real home is with Him.

GREAT EXPECTATIONS

And he carried me away in the Spirit to a mountain great and high, and showed me the Holy City, Jerusalem, coming down out of heaven from God. Revelation 21:10, N.I.V.

Tonya waited months for her new baby brother only to find that he couldn't play with her for another two or three years. Waiting for Christmas and birthdays seemed endless too. And some of the packages looked more interesting wrapped than they did afterward. It turned out to be that way with roller coasters, too.

School had already started when the county fair came to Nashville. So Tonya's family went after the children arrived home in the evening. Reluctantly she accepted the majority decision to eat first. Then Tonya's father, who didn't particularly care for roller coasters, good-naturedly bought two tickets. Tonya squealed as the roller coaster climbed, but felt a little queasy every time the tracks fell away beneath her. When the ride ended, she had barely stepped down before her stomach rebelled—in front of all those people.

"How was the ride?" her mother asked. Tonya smiled weakly. "Not all that great," her father said. The girl agreed. The long-awaited treat had bombed in the end.

Maybe you have had your expectations dashed, as Tonya's were. And you wonder about the promises in the Bible. You wonder what will turn out to be the worm in the apple that is heaven. But that is one thing you may look forward to and know that your very best expectations will not be good enough. Heaven will never disappoint and the glories will never fade. The golden streets will not tarnish or form potholes. The angels won't grow tired of our company, nor will we become bored, for Jesus will be there. He is the source of all real pleasure. Without Him heaven would be nothing. So if things on earth don't live up to your expectations, set your sights on heaven and Jesus. He will never let you down.

HE WILL SAVE US

For the Lord is our judge, the Lord is our lawgiver, the Lord is our king; he will save us. Isaiah 33:22.

There was once a time when Jenny feared the judgment. She also feared dogs, strangers, and darkness. But she overcame all her fears the same way—through Jesus. As she learned to trust Him, she gained confidence in meeting new turns in the road of life because she knew He was with her. But every once in a while the fears popped up again in some new form. Thus she wondered whether the thief who struck next door would lurk inside her darkened house. On Sabbath she was too self-conscious to greet strangers and make them feel welcome at church. And she was afraid to keep a dog for fear that he would mess up the house. Even worse, her fear of the judgment took new forms. She worried that something she overlooked in her life might keep her out of heaven. Would God understand her weaknesses when it came time for Him to sit as her judge?

My father used to tell of a drunkard of the frontier who staggered one day from a saloon to drive his team of horses. Somehow after untying the reins, he lost his balance, and as he fell his foot caught on the wagon. The team bolted, dragging the helpless man along the ground. A stranger standing nearby quickly leaped forward and brought the team under control. He saved the man's life.

Many years later the teamster killed a man in a drunken brawl. As he stood in court waiting for the judge to pass sentence, he suddenly remembered where he had seen the man before. "Oh, judge!" he cried out. "Don't you remember me? You saved my life!" The official did remember, but sadly he shook his head. "Then I was your savior; now I am your judge," he said as he pronounced the death sentence.

It need not be like that for you and me in the final judgment, however. For Jesus, the Lawgiver, promises to teach us day by day to live life to the fullest with Him. As we acknowledge Him each day as our Saviour, we need never fear the future. Heaven will be ours, for He has power to save us.

A TIME FOR JUDGMENT

For as the Father hath life in himself; so hath he given to the Son to have life in himself; and hath given him authority to execute judgment also, because he is the Son of man. John 5:26, 27.

Some years ago a well-known television personality popularized the saying, "God will get you for that!" Whenever a neighbor or friend poked fun at her so that she could think of no way to get back at them, she would terrify them with the suggestion of God evening up the score. She made judgment sound awesome.

"It would be awful having everyone see all you ever did, and thought—even in private," Pam suggested in Bible class one morning.

"Well, it beats doing and thinking nothing," Paul joked, trying to make her angry. "Anyway, at least you can take comfort from the fact that everyone has to go through it."

At this point the Bible teacher intervened. "There is good news about the judgment," he suggested. Most of the class found that hard to believe. "First, think of judgment as a promise," Mr. Neilson said. "You don't need to keep score of the bad things people do to you, because God promises to take care of that. Also, you can let Him be the judge of those who hurt you. You need only remember that rightdoing has its own rewards.

"Second, think of the judgment as the time when you can afford not to say 'I told you so!' You won't need to say it, because the evidence will be plain for all to see.

"And best of all, you needn't fear the judgment, because as you get to know Jesus better by reading His Word, you will grow to love and trust Him. Who can lose with their Best Friend for the judge? He will stand by your side, reminding the Father and all the watching universe that His blood covers your sins. Whatever is lacking on your account He will make it up.

"Now that's good news!"

IN TOUCH WITH YOURSELF

For it is a good thing that the heart be established with grace. Hebrews 13:9.

I read recently of a teenager who was really different—he drove to school. That's not so unusual, I know, but Ron had a recycled school bus. Of course, everyone laughed at him! If Ron noticed their reaction, he just turned on all the flashing lights and took an extra turn or two around the parking lot. But that's only one of the unusual things he did. He carried a briefcase to school and wore all his pens and pencils and a collapsible baton in a clear plastic pocket organizer. He would whip out the baton and "direct" music every chance he got. Ron liked old-time march music. And everyone laughed at his collection of Glenn Miller records.

Ron enjoyed being himself. He wasn't afraid to stand out in a crowd. Everyone grew to respect him for his courage and originality. At graduation when Ron went forward to receive his band award, the band struck up a Glenn Miller tune. Instantly Ron whipped out his baton and conducted them. The audience laughed. And then they all gave him a hearty standing ovation that said, Hey, thanks for being yourself.

You don't need to drive a school bus or carry a briefcase to be different. But if you want to stay home Saturday nights with your family, stay home. If you are the only person who studied the Sabbath school lesson, don't pretend that you didn't. And don't wear Nikes if you prefer Adidas, or wear designer clothes just because of the name.

Even more important, don't be afraid for people to know that you really care about Jesus. Don't laugh at their dirty jokes just to be one of the fellows. Remember that this world needs men and women, boys and girls, who will stand for right even though everything collapses around them, who will be true to themselves no matter what. Jesus knows and likes your real self. After all, that is the only self that He can take into His kingdom. So ask Jesus to help you be yourself today—you'll like it!

THE WOLF AND THE LAMB

The wolf will live with the lamb, the leopard will lie down with the goat . . ., and a little child will lead them. Isaiah 11:6, N.I.V.

When you were small did you ever wish that you could make friends with the wild animals? I spent a whole afternoon trying to pour salt on birds' tails so I could tame them. It didn't work, of course. But it was fun trying.

I forgave the birds for being unfriendly when we found ourselves the proud owners of an unusual cat and dog. Pepe, the dog, was a half-grown black poodle (of sorts!). The cat was pure white except for its orange ears and tail. The two would chase each other around the house, only to flop down and rest together. The cat often took Pepe's face in her paws and licked him clean or fell asleep, her nose snuggled under Pepe's chin.

Once the whole family set out on a winter's walk after a deep snowfall. As we walked along the car tracks, the dog kept close to our heels, while the cat pretended that it had no intentions of accompanying us. Then when we weren't looking, she would rush up from behind and pounce on the dog. On our return journey a car with headlights blazing forced us all into a snowdrift beside the road. The cat rushed into the nearest driveway and hid beneath a car. In the darkness that followed we could not find her. We called and called, but to no avail. Thinking she might follow us, we continued on toward home. But by the time we were all ready for bed the cat had not appeared. Not wishing to get dressed again and worried for the safety of the cat, we laid the burden on Pepe. "Go find the cat," we urged him, pointing down the street. The dog rushed out. Later we heard his bark at the door and found both dog and cat on the doorstep.

If only all the animal world were at peace as those two were. Don't you look forward to the day when the lion will eat straw like the ox and the cow will eat out of the same trough as the bear? And children will play with snakes—cobras and vipers. The animals "will neither harm nor destroy on all [God's] holy mountain," "and a little child will lead them" (verses 9, 6).

HEALING THE NATIONS

And the leaves of the tree are for the healing of the nations. Revelation 22:2, N.I.V.

The apostle John describes the Holy City as having a beautiful stream of clear water flowing from the throne of God right through the center of the city. "On each side of the river [stands] the tree of life, bearing twelve crops of fruit, yielding its fruit every month" (verse 2).

I'm not sure whether the fruit is like anything that we know, and whether each crop has a different fruit. The important thing is that the tree bears continually. You remember that when Eve sinned, God had to drive her and Adam from the Garden of Eden so that they couldn't eat its fruit, because to continue to eat it was to live forever. But in heaven we will eat from the tree just as often as we wish. And not only will we eat the fruit, but we will use the leaves also. The leaves are for the healing of the nations.

Ellen White tells us that when you and I have that fruit and those leaves, we will "grow up as calves of the stall" (Mal. 4:2) until we have reached the height of Adam and Eve when they were first created (*The Great Controversy,* pp. 644, 645). And although God took that tree up to the heavenly city, its branches hang over the wall so that we can still enjoy some of its blessings today. Through Jesus we may eat of the life-giving fruit now.

Today I saw an unusual scene. A robin and a cardinal were sitting either side of the same nest in which the robin had laid four eggs and the cardinal three. Nobody knows why the two families shared the same nest. At first the four parent birds squabbled, but after the eggs hatched all four fed all six of the surviving chicks. As the babies grew, the parents fed only their own offspring until they learned to fly. Those birds give us a little glimpse of heaven on earth. Christian schools give us another. There we see different races of people getting along together. It's a sign of the life-giving healing that Jesus brings.

ROCKETS AND SEA BUTTERFLIES

Lift up your eyes on high and see: who created these? He who brings out their host by number . . . ; by the greatness of his might, and because he is strong in power not one is missing. Isaiah 40:26, R.S.V.

Have you ever lain on the ground at night and stared up into the sky? As you look for the familiar points of light you discover one that moves toward you. Is it a shooting star? You wonder. No, your dad explains, it's a helicopter coming in to land. And sure enough, the chopping sound carries on the night air. Then again you see a crawling point of light. But as it passes overhead you hear no sound. "Hey! that's a satellite!" you yell. And you wonder how it got up there in the first place.

It takes an enormous amount of power to launch a satellite into space. An ordinary car engine could never do it. But a rocket can produce three thousand times more power than a car engine the same size. To do this, during the first two and three-fourths minutes of flight it burns more than 560,000 gallons of fuel (enough to take an average car across the United States from coast to coast five thousand times). Of course, a car could not handle all the power of a rocket engine—it would melt! Which makes me wonder about the power God used when He set the worlds in space.

You need only to "lift up your eyes on high" to see who has created these things, who "brings out their host by number, calling them all by name; by the greatness of his might, and because he is strong in power not one is missing." And the same mighty God who understood the use of rocket power long before men discovered it, who understands the mysteries of outer space, also created and cares for the mysterious creatures of the ocean floor. There tiny one-inch semitransparent squid grab their meals with suction cups fixed to two long tentacles. And one-inch sea butterflies beat their "wings" as they swim. Surely if God took the time to plan for the delicate things of creation as well as the powerful, He cares about you and me.

AMAZING THINGS

"The Lord, the Lord, is my strength and my song; he has become my salvation." Isaiah 12:2, N.I.V.

The general of the army had been recalled, and overnight a new commander had been appointed. He well knew the troops under his command—how easily a show of strength from the enemy would demoralize them. Now was the time to strike before the foot soldiers had time to doubt his leadership ability. "Be strong and courageous," came the general's orders. "You will extend your territory from the desert and from Lebanon to the great river. Be strong and courageous—and obey all orders from higher up. Do not be discouraged, for the Lord your God will be with you wherever you go" (see Joshua 1:9).

The time for action had come. But before giving the command to break camp, Joshua sent two spies to check out the city of Jericho. " 'The Lord has surely given the whole land into our hands,' " they reported upon their return (chap. 2:24). With this good report to boost morale, Joshua issued orders for preparation to march. " 'Consecrate yourselves, for tomorrow the Lord will do amazing things among you,' " he said (chap. 3:5).

What sound advice that was! Many times when we have a big test of our abilities we ask God to help us, to give us strength. And then we go out there to do our own thing in our own power. But not Joshua. He knew in whose strength that army marched. His confidence did not rest in human might or wisdom. The Hebrew leader realized that his meager army could not batter down the walls of Jericho or figure a strategy to overcome the army of giants that they faced. But he never doubted that his great God would somehow provide the victory if they consecrated themselves to Him. And God used His power first to hold back the floodwaters of the Jordan, and then delivered Jericho into Israel's hands.

Later, you will remember, the army of Israel suffered defeat because one man in the camp was not consecrated to Him. Many people needlessly perished before the leaders discovered the problem. Whatever the challenges that face you today, do not try to face them alone. Give your life to Jesus. Trust His strength. He will not let you down.

STRENGTH TO THE WEAK

He gives strength to the weary and increases the power of the weak. Isaiah 40:29, N.I.V.

"Never listen to your fears," the late Hubert Humphrey, U.S. Senator from Minnesota, used to say. "I've gone through some things in politics and in my personal life that, when you think about them too long, could scare the socks off you. But in each tough situation, I have found myself drawing on the same power—the strength of a firm faith in God."

That faith came to Hubert Humphrey's aid the night his father announced that he was taking his wife away for a rest. The worries of how they would pay all their bills were too much for Mr. and Mrs. Humphrey. So they left the family drugstore in Hubert's hands.

"How will I know if I am making the right decisions?" Hubert asked his father in consternation. "Just do what you think is best," his dad calmly replied. Hubert wasn't sure how he would manage. He knew that one mistake could fold the drugstore for good. But he wisely decided to trust the power and strength of God.

Two nights later a distraught farmer whose herd of cows was sick awakened Hubert. He described the symptoms, and Hubert recognized that the dread disease anthrax was threatening to wipe out not only the farmer's herd but all the herds in the district. After finding some serum for the farmer, Hubert realized that he should order enough to handle an epidemic. But what if one didn't come, and the store was left with all that serum? That could ruin the family business for sure.

Then Hubert prayed. No thunder or bells answered his prayer. Just an assurance that he should order the serum. The epidemic came, and thanks to Hubert's foresight, the serum was available when needed. It saved most of the herds, and when the farmers came to town and paid their bills, they put the drugstore well on the way to financial recovery. Aren't you proud to know a God who "increases the power of the weak" when they trust Him?

THEY SHALL NOT FAINT

They that wait upon the Lord shall renew their strength; . . . they shall run, and not be weary. Isaiah 40:31.

"This is just a short race," Bill told himself as he set out on the twenty-kilometer (12.4-mile) Bethesda Chase. Bill had trained for the twenty-six-mile marathon and routinely ran ten or twelve miles on a Sunday morning. So to make it more of a challenge, he decided to start faster than usual.

For the first Sunday in March the weather turned out to be a warm 40 degrees. What better conditions could one ask for! The first five miles ticked away uneventfully. Bill kept up his speed and felt fine as the road gently dropped away to the Rock Creek Parkway and followed the bends of the stream.

The exhilaration of passing other runners, and realizing that he was not tiring with the extra pace, kept him humming along. The race was well named, he decided, and not at all like the excruciating crawl that overtook one during the last miles of a marathon.

Then he saw the hill. What a steep one. Had he known it was coming he would have begun slower. And what a place to meet it—near the end of the race. As the road climbed out of the parkway the runners really showed their stuff. Many stopped altogether and bent forward, trying to relax their tense muscles. But Bill didn't dare pause lest his muscles freeze up. They already felt like rubber, and his chest had tightened so that his breath came in short, sharp gasps.

Just then he heard two runners approaching. He knew he had passed them before the hill. How embarrassing for him if they now saw him conked out. But as they drew abreast they called encouragingly, "You're looking good. You're going to make it. We'll run with you for a while."

Bill straightened his back and looked to the top of the hill. It didn't seem so far now that he wasn't alone.

Somebody runs the race with me today. "Keep steady," He whispers. And I know somehow I'll make it, too.

EXTRA STRENGTH

See, the Sovereign Lord comes with power, and his arm rules for him. See, his reward is with him, and his recompense accompanies him. Isaiah 40:10, N.I.V.

Americans, like people the world around, are impressed by strength and power. If something is stronger, it must be better, we think. So we stock our supermarkets with extra-strength Tylenol, concentrated detergents, and extra-hold hairsprays.

Chemical tests given to athletes at the 1983 Pan American Games in Caracas, Venezuela, highlighted such craving for power. Young men and women competing for world records and hoping to get that extra edge on strength and endurance had resorted to the use of anabolic steroid drugs. Such drugs promote weight gain and speed the development of muscle tissue. Tests have not shown that steroids promote strength—in fact, the evidence indicates their use may cause serious damage to the body. That's why the International Olympic Committee bans the drugs and tests athletes for their use.

Nevertheless, some trainers and athletes took the chance of using the drug and shaving a tenth of a second from their time. They thought the tests could not trace the drug if they used it two or three weeks before.

But a new computerized system of testing picked up traces of drugs taken months before. Triple-medalist Jeff Michels reportedly said that the test pinpointed the date four months before when he had last had steroids. Nine medalists had to return their medals, and twelve other athletes skipped their events rather than risk being caught by the test. One powerful test had blocked their attempt to achieve fake physical power. Which reminds us all that one day the Supreme Power of the universe will administer His test to every man, woman, and child on earth. But those who have learned to rely on the true source of power and not on their own cunning need not fear. For their reward is sure.

ALL YOUR MIGHT

Whatever your hand finds to do, do it with all your might. Ecclesiastes 9:10, N.I.V.

Working out each day was one way Manfred chose to keep healthy. Soon the university coaches noticed his abilities and offered him serious training. His seven-foot frame helped him excel in the one-hundred-meter high hurdles. After some time he began winning and gradually worked himself within reach of his country's national university champions.

Manfred enjoyed a sense of achievement through the competitions he entered. But a conviction nagged at the back of his mind: He should not compete on Sabbath. "But how else can I be a hurdler?" he asked himself. The answer was obvious—he couldn't. For track meets always convened over the weekend. Yet he hated to give it up. When the national finals came up that year he heard that the national champion was injured and could not compete. As the second-best, he was assured of winning. Manfred did well in the qualifying heats and began well in the final event. But just after he cleared the last hurdle he felt his legs freezing up. Falling on his face just before the tape, he lost the race he should have won easily. In shame and humiliation he limped back to the locker rooms.

Suddenly he saw himself running in the greatest race of life. Effortlessly he cleared the hurdles and was heading toward the end of time. "Oh, no!" he said to himself. "Wouldn't it be awful to come so far and then fall short of the tape?" And the thought of missing the final reward brought a conviction to his heart—no more Sabbath track meets. Manfred still received invitations to compete in important hurdles races. But he politely refused unless the race was held on some other day. And many times the schedule was changed for him. "Being a Seventh-day Adventist is no excuse not to do my best," he says. "But I must put God first."

THE HOLLOW OF HIS HAND

Who has measured the waters in the hollow of his hand, or with the breadth of his hand marked off the heavens? Isaiah 40:12, N.I.V.

As an introduction to a math unit on measurement, Mr. Jones had his class measure the school gym with their hands. Pushig his thumb against the wall at one end, Joe stretched as far as his little finger would reach. Then he drew up his thumb and placed it right beside his little finger. He had counted one hand span. How many would it take to reach the other end? More than once Joe forgot the last number he had counted and had to start over. How would you like to measure the ocean that way? "I wouldn't even measure the Gulf of Mexico," Joe says. "It's much too far!"

Roger wouldn't either. He knows something about the size of the gulf. Once when he and his big brother Clifford were fishing out of Panama City, Florida, they ran out of gas, and the currents swept them out into the gulf. Roger hadn't realized the power of wind and water before. The boys were powerless to paddle against the current. When they woke up the second day and couldn't see land, they knew they were in big trouble. Once a helicopter flew overhead, and Clifford stood up and waved his yellow slicker. But nobody saw them in the vast blue sea. The fifth day out the boys were disheartened when another boat passed within 150 yards without anyone sighting them. A brief squall gave them only a mouthful of water each, but Clifford made Roger promise that he would never give up. In spite of their predicament, they talked about how close to God they felt. "I know He's right here with us," Clifford said, and they prayed that God would keep them alive. Next morning a boat picked them up. Almost all on board had been asleep; a mate who had decided to stretch his legs on deck spotted them. Clifford and Roger knew that their powerful God of the sea and sky cared enough about two boys to hold them in the hollow of His hand.

DO IT

Whatsoever he saith unto you, do it. John 2:5.

He had been gone from home more than six weeks, and now he was back again, bringing some friends he had met on the way. His mother had missed him and wondered if things at home would ever be the same again. Because he had returned, her whole world felt like one continuous celebration. Even the added burden of helping friends prepare for their daughter's wedding seemed like a joyous task—until at the reception the wine ran out early. Embarrassed for her friends, she wondered what to do. Then she remembered Jesus. After explaining the dilemma, she waited to see what He would do. But He didn't do anything—He told them to do it. So undramatic! she thought. Why fill clay pots with water? But she never doubted Him.

"Whatever he saith unto you, do it," she told the servants, and they busied themselves drawing water. What happened next some people argue about. When did the water turn to wine? As the servants poured it into the pot? Or as they poured it out? And was the wine grape juice or was it spiked with alcohol?

Fine Christian people sometimes claim that Jesus made fermented wine that night. "Obviously some want to believe that," Dr. Hardinge says. "So I ask them why they want an excuse to drink a little wine. Because of the taste? Or because of the way it makes them feel? They usually say, Because of the feeling, and that's the very reason they shouldn't touch it."

Wine and other such substances give one a false sense of strength, and they interfere with the mind's decision-making processes. They make it harder to obey God. You see, Scripture tells the story about turning the water into wine not to wow us with His creative power, but to gently remind us of the need to obey. "Whatever He says unto you, do it." Today, let's be careful to let nothing come into our lives that will hinder our ability to obey. Not pills, pot, or any other drug.

HINDS' FEET

The Lord God is my strength, and he will make my feet like hinds' feet, and he will make me to walk upon mine high places. Habakkuk 3:19.

Tim felt nervous. That night he would pitch for his boys' club team. And he had pitched only one game before. Usually he played first base. The extra responsibility made him tense. "Could we pray about the game?" he called to his mother. Readily Mrs. Connally put down the potato she was peeling and washed her hands. She was glad that her son had learned to rely on God rather than on his own strength.

"Why don't we claim some scripture," his mother suggested as she sat down beside him. "I read about an interesting text that helped a boy when he needed it most. It's about hinds' feet. Hinds are a type of deer that can climb up high rocky places. The pitcher's mound isn't real high, but it could prove to be higher than you think. 'The Lord God is my strength, and he will make my feet like hinds' feet, and he will make me to walk upon mine high places.' "

Tim smiled. That scripture was just what he needed. " 'The Lord God is my strength,' " he repeated to himself. Pitchers certainly need strength and endurance to last right through the game, he thought.

The other team looked strong from the beginning and took an early lead. Tim walked several players, and his team's fielding wasn't too good. As their score fell further behind, spectators began yelling advice to Tim. But before each pitch he dropped his head for a moment and reminded God about the hinds' feet. He held himself straight and tall and pitched calmly. At the end of the game he knew that God had answered his prayer. His team had not won, but God had given him the strength to walk calmly even through defeat.

PROVE IT

For since the creation of the world God's invisible qualities—his eternal power and divine nature—have been clearly seen. Romans 1:20, N.I.V.

Like most little girls of 8, I used to think little boys were a pain. But lately I've been thinking that it isn't easy to be a boy. You aren't supposed to cry, and so the other fellows don't know how rough they're getting with you. And take Corey Vandenberg. He has such a piercing voice that he must despair of it ever sounding like a man's. To make up for his voice, Corey tries to act tough all the time. He pretends that he hates girls, but I know that he likes me.

We aren't allowed to play games with shooting and guns at our school, but Corey points two fingers and pulls the trigger with his thumb. He tries to pretend he's a cowboy. And he keeps saying how he's tough like John Wayne. But he'd die if he read the Sunday paper. It says that John Wayne, the macho cowboy, collected dolls. In fact, the Cowboy Hall of Fame displays sixty-four of them. He used to keep his dolls in his trophy room, alongside the Oscar award he won for the film *True Grit*. Which just goes to show that it's not what you collect that counts, but what you are on the inside.

God didn't have to go all over our earth trying to show off His power at Creation either. Otherwise He wouldn't have dared to make butterflies and forget-me-nots. He didn't need to prove anything. The Creator had the whole universe at His command. In fact, every star is a powerhouse of atomic energy. You can't get much more powerful than that. But He didn't want to frighten everyone by going about Creation with a heavy hand. That's why beneath each majestic tree He planted grasses, moss, and wildflowers. And for every whale He fashioned whole schools of tiny angel fish. Not only did He figure out how to put speed into the lynx, but He gave the housecat its purr. So when we see God's power in nature, we also see His love and caring. Maybe there's a lesson in all that for Corey and me.

POWER FOR JACKIE

But he said to me, "My grace is sufficient for you, for my power is made perfect in weakness." 2 Corinthians 12:9, N.I.V.

"When I was 12, I was a good girl," Jackie says. "I didn't swear or dance or drink. I joined the church and attended every week." But just after her high school graduation the family home burned down, and a nephew accidentally poisoned himself. Instead of keeping close to God and asking Him to strengthen her faith, she blamed Him for her flood of troubles.

After one year Jackie dropped out of college and married. She found a good job in a bank, and she soon received a promotion to assistant branch manager. Many of the male tellers that she trained went on to become branch managers somewhere else. It didn't seem fair. If her training was good for those tellers, how come the bank didn't promote her to branch manager? The more she thought about it, the more unfair the situation seemed.

To get back at the injustice, Jackie began a plan of "creative borrowing," which was her way of stealing from the bank. She invested the money in an old plantation homestead that she began fixing up. Every month Jackie wrote herself a phony loan on the bank to pay the mortgage on the homestead. And each month she told God, "If You help me get away with this one more time, I'll quit." But she knew she didn't mean it. One month she forgot to make the payment, and her world collapsed.

The FBI investigated her and sent her to prison. She wondered whether she would ever rise above the disgrace. The first morning she found the prison chapel and joined in a worship service. Suddenly the love of Jesus began to melt the hardness of her heart. She discovered His all-powerful forgiveness. He changed her heart and helped her start over. And He used Jackie to reach other prison women. When she realized her weakness, God was able to show her His power. His power is made perfect in weakness.

THROUGH A TROOP

For by thee I have run through a troop; and by my God have I leaped over a wall. Psalm 18:29.

Barry liked to hear his mother talk about God's love, but he never learned to trust God. When his stepdad became desperately ill, he asked God to heal him. But his stepfather died. Angry and hurt because God had not answered his prayer the way he wanted, Barry drifted away from religion and joined the Hell's Angels motorcycle gang.

Barry liked the power he found there—powerful bikes and powerful friends. When his mother pleaded with him to give his heart to God, he would say, "Mom, there ain't nothing more powerful than the Hell's Angels!" But one day at a rally the Hell's Angels leader asked Barry to kill a rival gang leader. Barry refused. He had bloodied men in fights, but he was no murderer, he said. His refusal marked him for death.

The next day as Barry entered the Western Union office to pick up some money his mother had sent for him to fly home, he found himself surrounded by toughs in black leather jackets. Slipping into a phone booth, he called home. "Before I die I just want to say I'm sorry for all the bad things I've done," he told his mom. "Can you forgive me?" Quietly Mrs. Mason assured Barry of her love and forgiveness and urged him to turn to Jesus.

"But I can't," he insisted. "When Dad died I cursed God." Again his mother reminded him of God's forgiveness and undying love. Weeping there in the phone booth, Barry gave himself to Jesus and committed his future into God's hands. For two hours he talked to his mother until a tall blond stranger of massive build tapped him on the shoulder. "Come with me, Barry," he said. A Christian minister had come to help him escape the waiting gang. Now Barry travels around the country telling young people how God enabled him to "run through a troop" and "leap over a wall." At last he found a Power he can trust.

BLACK HOLES

For I am convinced that . . . neither height nor depth, nor anything else in all creation, will be able to separate us from the love of God that is in Christ Jesus our Lord. Romans 8:38, 39, N.I.V.

I was blissfully adding the finishing touches to a bulletin-board display on astronomy when Corey opened up a scary new subject for me. "Where is the black hole?" he asked.

"Where is it supposed to be?" I asked, trying to gain time.

"Oh, out in space—somewhere," he said. "I saw a simulation of one on TV."

"But they aren't close to our universe," I said, feeling sure that if they had been, I would have known about it. I looked up an article on black holes, and what I read was so frightening that I began to wonder what Corey had been watching on TV.

It seems that a black hole is a space big enough to swallow your neighborhood. But you needn't worry because they occur way off in outer space. Should a spaceship stray near a black hole, it would be sucked in and be absolutely crushed. Black holes are the very opposite of what God did to this earth in the beginning. He created it from nothing and gave it light and warmth from the sun. Black holes, on the other hand have absolutely no heat or warmth, just gravity.

When Paul asked, "Who shall separate us from the love of Christ?" (verse 35, K.J.V.), he might have wondered about black holes. They sound so scary that it seems as though nothing could save you if you were in one. But nothing can separate us from God's love—not life or death, "neither angels nor demons, . . . *nor any powers,* neither height nor depth, nor anything else in all creation, will be able to separate us from the love of God that is in Christ Jesus our Lord." Now that's comforting.

THANK YOU, MR. LINCOLN

"Jesus of Nazareth . . . was a prophet, powerful in word and deed before God and all the people." Luke 24:19, N.I.V.

Do you know any powerful people? Maybe you know a boxer. Nobody messes with him, out of respect for his strength. Or the mayor of your town. A majority of the people voted him into office, thus giving him power to make decisions for the community. He now has the power to hire and fire people and to spend the taxpayers' money. Do you know any other powerful people? Maybe your church has a powerful preacher or a choir leader with a powerful voice. Our church has a small boy who is a powerful influence. Because of his example, boys who sit next to him in Sabbath school tend to listen to what the speakers say.

"Jesus of Nazareth . . . was a prophet, powerful in word and deed." I wonder what Luke meant when he wrote that. When I'm anxious I read the words of Jesus, and they calm me. When I'm sad they cheer me. And when I'm embarrassed over something I have messed up, they encourage me. Jesus not only spoke with love and encouragement but also acted that way. That kind of power is not the least bit scary. People who love and obey Him learn to become like Him—powerful in helping others.

Some years ago a young man earned his extra money by doing small acting jobs. One day someone recommended him to represent Abraham Lincoln at a school ceremony. The actor, with his tall frame and deep-set eyes, looked surprisingly like President Lincoln, but he felt stupid doing the part. After the program a little black girl ran over to him and tugged at his coat. Looking up into his eyes, she sweetly said, "Thank you, Mr. Lincoln." For one joyous moment the actor felt like the real President, and he graciously accepted the little girl's appreciation for a great man who has influenced all our lives. Someday you may hear a thank-you for the way you have influenced somebody. And you, like Mr. Lincoln's look-alike, will know that the thanks don't belong to you, but to your powerful Lord.

BREAKING THE HABIT

"Everything is permissible for me"—but I will not be mastered by anything. 1 Corinthians 6:12, N.I.V.

If I could weave the words of today's text into a song, I would call it "Growing Up," for it sounds like the motto of a growing-up person. Paul says, "Hey, I can do whatever I like. But some things won't do me any good. So I'll not let myself be ruled by bad habits."

In his book *Killing Giants, Pulling Thorns,* Charles Swindoll tells how he used to bite his fingernails right down to the quick. For well over twenty years he carried around ten ugly stumps. He hated the habit and wanted badly to stop. But he couldn't. "In spite of the pain and the pressure, that habit, like all bad habits, had me in its grip," he said.

Now, habits bother almost everyone, and nail biting is just the type of habit that Paul was talking about when he said that he wouldn't allow it to master him. He'd feel the same way about overworking a slang expression, overeating, or always being late. Some habits—like alcohol, tobacco, and popping a pill every time you feel less than perfect—can trap you into depending on them physically. Such habits are awfully hard to break.

One way to overcome a bad habit is to *recognize it.* Tom can't sit down without opening a bottle of Coke. "I'm not addicted to caffeine," he says. "I just can't start anything without it." He can't overcome that habit until he admits it *is* a habit. The next step is to *take the problem to Jesus.* Admit you can't overcome the habit on your own, and recognize that He has the power to help. Then *plan some strategies.* Like keeping a record. Give yourself a star every time you refuse to give in to your habit. When you have twenty stars, treat yourself in some way. But start over any time you fail. Remember, work on only one habit at a time. And if it takes a long time, cheer up! Just *starting* is getting in control. And by God's grace you'll succeed.

IN YOUR HAND

"O Lord, God of our fathers, are you not the God who is in heaven? . . . Power and might are in your hand, and no one can withstand you." 2 Chronicles 20:6, N.I.V.

If you sometimes feel small and insignificant, today's text is especially for you. It reminds me of the tiny silky terrier that stood bravely yipping at a pack of stray dogs. One might have admired his courage had it not been for the fact that facing the pack beside him stood a massive German shepherd. The powerful ally bolstered the little dog's courage.

Of course, we who draw our security from the power of our mighty God should remember that we cannot stand for long on our own. Whether we are walking on the water or standing up to giants, we would do well to remember to whom the power belongs.

When Patrick tried to cross the Pacific in a rowboat, he felt sure that he could overcome the challenge of the sea. But after he endured two thousand miles of ocean, a freak wave capsized his boat nine hundred miles from Honolulu. Having lost all his food, he had to radio for help.

But Patrick didn't give up for long. He improved the sea anchor on his boat and vowed to try again. This time to his twenty-two-foot dory he attached a plaque that read, "O Lord, have mercy! For Thy seas are so great, and my boat is so small." This old fisherman's prayer puts the matter of power into proper perspective. But Patrick didn't realize the truth of that prayer until a terrible storm blew up after he had begun his second trip. Powerless against the heavy seas, the young man hung on for dear life and prayed the fisherman's prayer.

When everything goes well at school it's easy to take the credit yourself. But as soon as trouble strikes, we remember that the power to live a successful Christian life comes from God. And as we weather our storms we learn, as Patrick did, that the sea of life is so great and we are so small. And just as the storm lifted for Patrick so that he made it to Hawaii (in 111 days!), so it will lift for us. And when it does, let's not forget again that "power and might are in [God's] hand."

NOT FOR SALE

"But you will receive power when the Holy Spirit comes on you; and you will be my witnesses in Jerusalem, and in all Judea and Samaria, and to the ends of the earth." Acts 1:8, N.I.V.

Jesus' disciples had tasted the loneliness of being without Him. No longer did they waste precious time arguing among themselves about who would be great and powerful. Instead they cherished the advice that Jesus gave them. "'Do not leave Jerusalem, but wait for the gift my Father promised'" (verse 4). So after He returned to heaven, the disciples waited and prayed for the gift. And while they waited they did all that lay in their own power to prepare themselves. They gave up all selfish hope for their own personal power and prayed together "with one accord" (verse 14, K.J.V.).

Suddenly with the rushing sound of a strong wind the Spirit came into their upper room, and little tongues of fire rested on each head. Filled with power, they went out from there to witness, just as Jesus had said that they would. Not only did they speak in different languages and bring more than three thousand people to Jesus in one day, but "everyone was filled with awe, and many wonders and miraculous signs were done by the apostles" (chap. 2:43).

After persecution scattered the early Christians into Judea and Samaria, the power of the Holy Spirit went with them. "When the crowds heard Philip and saw the miraculous signs he did, they all paid close attention to what he said" (chap. 8:6). His power to cast out evil spirits and to heal the deformed and paralyzed brought "great joy in that city" (verse 8). But Simon, a man who had gained power over people through magic and witchcraft, coveted Philip's power. After his baptism Simon followed Philip everywhere. He even offered money to Peter and John if they would lay their hands on him and pray for the Spirit. But God's power cannot be bought. It is a gift He gives those who dedicate their lives to His service. You will feel that power in your life as you pray for it and spend yourself in doing His will.

THE BOMB

Not by might, nor by power, but by my spirit, saith the Lord of hosts. Zechariah 4:6.

Corey was the youngest of the neighborhood gang that played on his street. He enjoyed being part of the ball games and the tree climbing, but he especially liked having everyone play at his house. But usually the older children stayed only a short while before wandering off in search of something more exciting. As Corey prepared for his birthday party he wondered what games his dad should plan. He didn't want people getting bored.

"Leave it to me," his dad said. "I know just the ones. And to finish up, we'll let off some firecrackers I saved from New Year's." The boy remembered seeing a box of firecrackers in his father's closet. He could just picture all those sparklers—enough for two or three each—and the Roman candles, rockets, and one enormous thing shaped like a bomb. That should do it, Corey decided. Wait until everyone sees that bomb!

The party did turn out well. Only twice did Jerry complain that he was bored, and the change of games took care of that. Everyone enjoyed the food and the story around the campfire. And the firecrackers proved an instant hit. "This is *so* much fun," Jerry said as he lit his third sparkler. Corey nearly burst with excitement, waiting for the bomb. But his dad kept it until the very last. At first the bomb wouldn't light, and when it did, it burst with a mighty explosion that frightened everyone. All the girls and one or two of the boys went home crying.

Corey felt let down. He had pinned all his hopes on the excitement the bomb would generate. Instead, it had—well, *bombed* was the only word for it. "It's like that with power," his dad explained, trying not to laugh. "Powerful things can be awfully good or awfully bad. Sometimes you don't know which way they'll go. So it's best not to pin your hopes on power. If you want to make friends and keep them, a loving spirit can prove more effective—even more powerful—in the long run."

NO BOASTING HERE

"Let not the wise man boast of his wisdom or the strong man boast of his strength or the rich man boast of his riches." Jeremiah 9:23, N.I.V.

Three men in the Bible illustrate the truth of today's text. Each was famous for something he had plenty of. Two of them lost their gift, while the third wound up with everything.

The first was blessed with wisdom. And though he was the wisest man who has ever lived, he did some incredibly stupid things. (So take heart! Silly mistakes don't prove anything where intelligence is concerned.) Solomon foolishly trusted his own wisdom and forgot God, which was like having no wisdom at all.

The second man would have easily taken the gold for weight lifting at the Palestine Olympics. We don't know how hefty he looked, but he did surprise people with some of his feats. When he left God he lost both his hair and his strength. And just as Solomon came to his senses before it was too late, so did Samson. God gave him another chance to prove his loyalty, but not another chance at life—which might be a point worth pondering.

Scripture doesn't tell us the name of the third man—just that he went out and traded all his riches for the Pearl of Great Price, the Saviour of souls. And those who seek first the kingdom of heaven, which is what he did, wind up having the other two things—wisdom and strength—added (see Matt. 6:33).

When Rocky Bleier came back from Vietnam with both legs wounded, he vowed to continue his football career. But it took time for the shattered bones to mend. The first time he showed up for spring training he was too slow to make the team. The next year he pulled a hamstring, and the team doctor advised him to quit. But Rocky's pastor suggested that, instead of trying to make a career of football all by himself, he should ask God to show him what to do. Rocky did, and enjoyed a successful football career. But he knows that he could not have made it on his own any more than Solomon, Samson, or the rich merchant.

YOUR KNEE UPON THE GROUND

"But let him who boasts boast about this: that he understands and knows me." Jeremiah 9:24, N.I.V.

It was 1936, and Hitler had come to power in Germany, declaring that the German race was better than all others and promising proof of his boast at the Berlin Olympic Games. But the U.S. team with its record-breaking Jesse Owens threatened his pet ideas. Jesse Owens came from a poor but hardworking family. He believed in God, and he was black. Already Jesse had broken world records in the 100- and 200-meter dash. And he was a member of the record-breaking relay team. But the event at which the Germans most wanted to beat him was the broad jump.

Hitler's fair-haired favorite for that race was Luz Long. In his book *Jesse: The Man Who Outran Hitler,* Jesse tells how he wanted to beat Luz's qualifying jumps. But in his eagerness to show the German what he could do, he fouled. For the second qualifying jump Jesse decided to take it easy. But he jumped miserably. In sudden fear of not qualifying, he walked off by himself and, realizing that he needed God's help, knelt to pray. But before he could utter a word the official called his name to make his final jump. Suddenly Luz walked over to him and gave him some reassuring advice. "Start six inches farther back and give it all you've got." It was just the help Jesse needed to regain his confidence. And it also cemented a friendship between the two. In the broad-jump finals Luz set a new world record, but Jesse Owens immediately broke it. When his feet landed in the dirt, Luz darted to his side with congratulations.

For years the two friends wrote to each other. In Luz's last letter, written from North Africa, he confided, "That hour in Berlin when I first spoke to you, when you had your knee upon the ground, I knew that you were in prayer. . . . I believe in God [now] and I pray to Him." And Jesse knew that tests of strength and declarations of racial superiority mean nothing compared to understanding and knowing God.

GIANT KILLERS

So David prevailed over the Philistine with a sling and with a stone, and smote the Philistine, and slew him; but there was no sword in the hand of David. 1 Samuel 17:50.

If we think back far enough, almost everyone can remember somebody gigantic whom they feared. Ricky was scared of Big Dan, who strutted up and down his block boasting of how he could beat up the smaller kids. A big mean German Shepherd terrified Suzie.

David wasn't big for his age. But when David saw Goliath strutting his stuff in the valley, he wasn't intimidated, though his big brothers were. You see, all those lonely, boring Saturday nights watching the sheep while his brothers were having a good time had finally paid off. Sitting out under the stars and feeling God's presence had taught him to depend on God. So instead of feeling sorry for himself, he had learned to slay his first giant—loneliness. And his second—self-pity.

How did he do it? By relying on God's strength. So when Goliath challenged, he slew him—and "there was no sword in [his] hand." David knew that you don't slay giants by acting like one. Trying to scare them with a show of strength doesn't work. But courage in the Lord works wonders.

Daniel knew this when he refused to submit to the Babylonians. Esther recognized it when she went unbidden before King Ahasuerus. Paul remembered it during the shipwreck and afterward when the viper fastened itself to his hand. And you and I may depend on it as we face whatever makes us afraid or angry today. We don't overcome fear by whistling in the dark or by swinging with our fists. And we won't rid ourselves of anger by teaching someone a lesson or by getting back at them. You don't slay giants by trying to act like one.

Ricky thought he left the giants behind on Thirty-third Street. But when he arrived at academy he discovered a whole new set. Giants of fear, loneliness, and rejection. But he was prepared for them. He started every day by reading his Bible and praying for the courage to stand for the right. It will work for you, too. God guarantees it.

ANYTHING WITH GOD

"Do not grieve, for the joy of the Lord is your strength." Nehemiah 8:10, N.I.V.

Do you believe in miracles? I do. And I tend to agree with the saying that used to be printed on posters: "Miracles happen only to people who believe in them." Of course, miracles happen all the time to all kinds of people, but those who believe in them are more likely to notice.

The principal of a large eight-grade school once told me that she didn't relax at the beginning of a new school year until she heard that the first-graders were all reading. For her, learning to read was a miracle. And so is walking. But we take it for granted, because it happens all the time.

As a result of a childhood accident Les cannot use his legs. He gets around in a wheelchair. But he grew up determined not to be a weakling or depend unnecessarily on others. So he asked God to help him develop the muscles of his arms and upper trunk. He performs with a tumbling team that has built some of its most spectacular pyramids using Les as the key person. At the close of the program people often give him a standing ovation.

Then there was Carrie. Confined to a wheelchair and not expected to live a long life, she refused to stay in bed moping. Instead she came to school in a wheelchair and studied extra hard, asking God to help her keep up with her class. At academy graduation the class presented her with a brand-new wheelchair. After one of the boys lifted her into it, everyone cheered and applauded for several minutes. Incidentally, I thought it something of a miracle for fellows to care so much.

Nobody thought Kathy Miller would live after her car accident. She lay for three months in a coma and woke up to discover that she had to learn to walk and talk all over again. So determined was her faith in God and miracles that in another three months she ran a six-mile minimarathon with her dad. True, she came in last, but have you ever run six miles? Remember, the joy of the Lord can be your strength just as it was for Les, Carrie, and Kathy. And keep looking for those miracles.

THE POWER OF PRAYER

The prayer of a righteous man is powerful and effective. James 5:16, N.I.V.

"When I was 10," Sally MacMillan says, "I went swimming with my brother in a motel swimming pool. Charlie was dog-paddling without any problem, and I tried to imitate him. But I panicked and grabbed him, almost drowning us both. Neither of us mentioned the incident to our parents. I'm sure Charlie soon forgot it. But I began to fear deep water.

"The next summer when I went to camp I joined in the swimming lessons. The first day I prayed that Jesus would help me not to be afraid of the water. And I had no problem because we stayed in the shallows. Underneath I knew I hadn't overcome my fear.

"Every day of camp I prayed that I would lose my fear of deep water. Because I was taller than the rest I didn't get in over my head—or get over my fear. And though I appeared to be swimming, I always dragged a toe along the bottom.

"For several years I carried around my fear. Every summer I prayed to overcome it, but then stayed in the shallow water. When I was 17 we lived in an apartment complex with a swimming pool. The lifeguard offered to teach classes in senior lifesaving and asked me to join. I took a deep breath, said a little prayer, and signed up.

"The very first day of class he assigned us to swim laps. I knew how to swim; I'd been swimming for years in the shallow end of the pool. But when I started my laps I knew I had to either swim into the deep end or look like a total fool. So I said my prayer and started swimming. And when I touched the wall at the deep end I was surprised to find that I had crossed into the deep water without even realizing it."

Sally went on to complete her lifesaving honor and then to get her water safety instructor's license from the Red Cross. The next summer she returned to camp—as the swimming instructor. Sally believes in the power of prayer. But, she says, you have to trust it.

ALL EYES ON HIM

"For we have no power to face this vast army that is attacking us. We do not know what to do, but our eyes are upon you." 2 Chronicles 20:12, N.I.V.

"'A vast army is coming against you from Edom, from the other side of the Sea,'" the messengers told the king. "'It is already in Hazazon Tamar'" (verse 2). Alarmed by the news, King Jehoshaphat sent word throughout the land, calling men and women to come together "to seek help from the Lord." A large crowd gathered in "Jerusalem at the temple of the Lord in front of the new courtyard." The king himself led them in prayer.

"'O Lord, God of our fathers,'" he prayed, "'are you not the God who is in heaven? You rule over all the kingdoms of the nations. Power and might are in your hand, and no one can withstand you'" (verse 6). He reminded the Lord of His deliverance of the children of Israel and how He had given the land to them and their descendants forever. Jehoshaphat recalled how God had promised King Solomon that whenever a calamity befell the nation, they might stand in the presence of God at the Temple and cry for help. And with an invading army poised on their borders, the nation needed God's aid more than ever. "'For we have no power to face this vast army that is attacking us. We do not know what to do, but our eyes are upon you,'" the king concluded (verse 12). A mighty, heartfelt Amen must surely have followed as all the "men of Judah, with their wives and children and little ones, stood there before the Lord" (verse 13).

What good were their heroes and superstars now? Even the strongest soldiers and generals with their brilliant tactics were outmaneuvered and defenseless before the invading hordes. The people wisely turned to the Lord. And God answered through one of the Levites, "'"Do not be afraid or discouraged because of this vast army. For the battle is not yours, but God's"'" (verse 15). Next morning Jehoshaphat led his people, singing and praising the Lord, to the battlefield, where the invaders' dead bodies lay strewn on the ground. Of course, God doesn't often answer prayers by annihilating our enemies, but He does promise that day by day we may depend upon His power.

SEVEN-UP

At once Jesus realized that power had gone out from him. He turned around in the crowd and asked, "Who touched my clothes?" Mark 5:30, N.I.V.

Do you remember when you were in third grade and your class celebrated some special event with a party? Did your room ever play seven-up? Rhonda used to sit at her desk with her head on her left arm, her eyes closed, while she raised her right index finger above her head. How that finger tingled as she hoped one of the seven people who were "up" would touch it. Occasionally she sensed someone close, but he or she would pass her by and touch Jenny or Dale instead. What excitement she felt when someone reached out and touched her finger. When the seven had returned to the front of the room, someone called, "Seven-up!" and Rhonda and six others would stand and try to guess who had touched them.

Jesus wasn't playing games when He stopped one day and asked, "Who touched Me?" Power had gone out from Him, and He wanted to know why.

"How can You ask who touched You?" His disciples asked. "Look at all these people milling about. It could have been anyone bumping You accidentally." But the Master knew the difference between a thoughtless brushing by and the deliberate touch of faith. When the "culprit" stepped forward and bowed at His feet, Jesus assured her that she was healed.

Nita Schuh, of Dallas, Texas, remembered that story from Mark 5 one Christmas Eve as she sat in the intensive care unit beside her husband, a stroke victim. Sensing the presence of God surrounding her, she reached out her hand in faith. Just as the woman of Scripture found power in a touch, Nita found peace when she reached out in faith to God. She experienced a miracle that night—the miracle of God's power to calm her worries and to assure her that all would be well. Next time you are tempted to worry yourself sick, remember seven-up and reach out to Jesus until you feel His reassuring touch.

POWER AND THE DANDELIONS

Let your speech always be gracious, seasoned with salt, so that you may know how you ought to answer everyone. Colossians 4:6, R.S.V.

Two girls once knelt in the grass picking dandelions. When each had a large bunch they returned home. The mother of the one found an old jam jar and filled it with water for her posy of smiley faces and placed them by the kitchen sink. "Do you like them?" the little girl asked, but she knew the answer. After all, they were only plain old dandelions.

The mother of the other girl accepted her flowers with joy and arranged them carefully in her best crystal vase. She set them between the candlesticks in the center of the table she was setting for guests. Her daughter didn't need to ask if her mother treasured her gift—the girl proudly saw that she did. And though she is now grown up, she never admires a vase of flowers without remembering those dandelions and the power of her mother's acceptance.

Knowing this could give you considerable power with people—power to make them feel happy and accepted. By keeping a sharp eye open to notice little gestures of kindness and friendliness and showing that you accept and appreciate them, you may make someone feel wanted and worthwhile. You could make their day. So today if a little person offers you something, be it only a smile or a sticky piece of candy, accept it gratefully—not for the doubtful value of the gift, but for the thought that prompted it. And when Mother asks if you want chocolate pudding or banana cream pie for supper, don't brush her away, saying, "I don't really care." Thank her for caring about you enough to ask and tell her how much you enjoy her cooking. Then watch the difference your words of acceptance make.

POWER THAT PAYS

Remind them to be submissive to rulers and authorities, to be obedient, to be ready for any honest work, to speak evil of no one, to avoid quarreling, to be gentle, and to show . . . courtesy toward all men. Titus 3:1, 2, R.S.V.

Not only was it Mike's first day in a new school, but it was his first in public school also. His mother noticed his nervousness, but took it for excitement. He didn't have the heart to tell her. She drove him to school—"So you won't have to face a bus full of new faces all at once," she explained.

On his classroom door hung a "wanted" sign, like the sheriffs had put out in the wild West. Mike's name was on the list that was near the bottom of it. "You're the first one I've corralled," his teacher joked. "You get to help identify the others."

Mike didn't know for sure what he was looking for that first morning. "I probably wanted to identify the class bully," he says now. "Several people came into the classroom strutting their stuff, but they were also looking for friends." Charlie had the build of a bully, but he giggled a lot—like a girl. Donnie was quick with his fists, but he fell in love with the teacher and pushed people around only in fun. But trying to act tough was big with Steve, and at first most of the kids were scared of him.

Had someone suggested today's text as advice on how to gain power, Steve would have laughed at them. But Mike took his mother's advice: "A good example can be a power for good." So he tried to be friendly and courteous. And not only did he win a classroom full of friends, but he soon noticed Steve following his example. "It wasn't easy," Mike says. "Fighting and pushing people around is often easier. But being patient and polite pays in the long run."

MORE GLORIOUS THAN GOLD

There is that maketh himself rich, yet hath nothing: there is that maketh himself poor, yet hath great riches. Proverbs 13:7.

Nancy had wanted a watch for years. She had not even owned a toy one before. Her slim wrist would look good with a watch. Finally she thought her dream had come true when a woman at church gave her one that no longer worked. Hoping that nobody would know the difference, she wore it. One day a friend looked closely at the watch. "How come your watch says eleven-thirty?" he asked. Nancy felt foolish. Suddenly her watch looked terribly cheap, and she never wore it again. She had thought to make herself look rich with a worthless watch.

"Never mind," her mother had soothed that evening. "Not everything in life is as good as it looks. There has to be a lesson there somewhere." Then Mother told Nancy about the tarnished flute.

Long ago there was an old reed flute that had been passed down for many generations. No other could match its richness of tone. But an ugly brown stained the old flute. It appeared tarnished and cheap, but its music lifted men's souls to heaven. "The flute doesn't look as good as its music sounds," people said. "Let's overlay it with gold." And that is what they did. The flute shone in the sunlight filtering through the stained-glass windows. But the flutist, when he raised it to his lips, could produce only flat metallic tones. The gold overlay had ruined it. The poorer looking flute had given the richer tone. Suddenly people valued the rich sounds produced inside far more than the gold lavished on the outside.

And that's how it is with people. It takes real growing up to value them for what is inside and not for what they wear or how they do their hair. The good news this morning is that Jesus values you for who you are inside. Your simple self walking with Him is far more glorious than gold.

A CARGO OF GOLD

How much better is it to get wisdom than gold! and to get understanding rather to be chosen than silver! Proverbs 16:16.

On September 4, 1622, two Spanish ships laden with treasure left Havana, Cuba, for Spain. Two days out the vessels ran into a furious storm and sank with all their cargo. Over the next fifty-six years divers searched for and recovered some of the treasure. The rest lay at the bottom of the sea for 350 years.

A bundle of worm-eaten documents discovered in Spain enabled Melvin Fisher and his salvage team to locate the wrecks. One day in 1971, after years of searching, a diver noticed a yellow glitter on the ocean floor. The *Atocha* had been found. But it took another nine years to locate the *Santa Margarita.*

The divers mapped out the wreckage and began to retrieve the treasure systematically. They found a dull, lumpy mass of silver coins that the seawater had eaten into. But the gold coins looked just as bright as ever. Mr. Fisher said that he would never forget the sight of an ocean floor carpeted with gold coins. One of the most valuable objects found in the wreckage of the *Santa Margarita* was a solid-gold plate covered with an intricately etched design and valued at $1 million.

Another diver discovered a pile of gold chains that he said looked like "a hive of golden bees." Apparently people used to wear golden chains instead of carrying traveler's checks. If they needed ready cash, they could remove a link and use it as money.

Wouldn't you like to have been one of those divers picking up treasure from the sea floor? Even if you couldn't keep any of it, just helping to count the pieces would be fun. The wise man says that getting wisdom is better than finding gold. All the seawater of life's tough experiences cannot dull wisdom—it shines all the brighter in hard times. The beginning of wisdom is getting to know God. And you discover the genuine twenty-four-carat variety when you take time each day to read your Bible and pray.

FOR HIS GLORY

"Bring every one who is called by my name, all whom I have created, whom I have formed, all whom I have made for my glory." Isaiah 43:7, N.E.B.

When Raquel graduated from high school she determined to attend a Christian college with two of her girlfriends. But how would they earn the necessary money for the tuition? After putting their heads together they decided to sell Adventist books door to door during the day, and missionary magazines on the street corners downtown at night. The first week Raquel did well. She enjoyed the work and sold many books. If she kept it up all summer she would surely make it to college in the fall.

One night during the second week her father discovered what she was doing. Since he was not an Adventist, he did not understand her yearning for a Christian college and forbade her to sell books. Suddenly her plans were dashed. "So much for the star saleswoman," she told her friends. "My career ended before it began." And she spent the rest of the summer helping her mother at home and trying to think of some other way to get to college. In the fall her friends left without her.

Raquel might easily have blamed God for deserting her. But her faith clung to the promises. "All right, so I was trying to get to college on my own," she admitted. "I gloried in my newfound talents." And she promised God that she would trust Him the rest of the way and wait patiently for Him to work things out.

And He did. A week after college began, the conference president and the local church pastor visited her. "Why aren't you at college?" they asked. She explained her financial problems. Her parents could not possibly provide all the money, and the girl had found no work that her father approved of. "Well, we think you should go," the men insisted. And they financed her trip. Raquel completed a two-year course and met a fine young man whom she later married. "I learned a good lesson," she says. "I could miss out on heaven by glorying in my own efforts. But whatever I do, I let it be for the glory of God."

TOP OF THE CLASS

And the harvest of righteousness is sown in peace by those who make peace. James 3:18, R.S.V.

"In our family everyone made good grades in school," Cathy says. "Laura was valedictorian of her eighth-grade class, and MeriLee has made all A's in academy." Cathy herself makes mostly A's. But good grades do not guarantee wisdom. James observes in chapter 3, verse 13: "Who is wise and understanding among you? By his good life let him show his works in the meekness of wisdom."

Max made no claim to either wisdom or a clever brain. He did, however, by much hard work make second trumpet in the school band, which nobody on his family tree had managed before. Mrs. Miller was proud of her son's humble efforts and encouraged him to keep up with his practice every day.

At the end of the first semester the director required each band member to play a short solo. Max chose a simple melody that he had been practicing for weeks. He didn't do too badly, and the band leader said that he should keep working to produce a clearer tone. But Bobby Miller, who played first trumpet effortlessly, leaned over and said, "How do you do that? It sounds like a coughing foghorn."

People who learn easily sometimes show little concern for other's people's feelings, Max concluded. Is it possible to be so ambitious for grades and popularity—for the honor these things bring—that we forget real people like Max who work equally as hard just to pass?

If you want to be top of your class, look into your heart. James says, "If you have bitter jealousy and selfish ambition," don't boast that you are smart, because the kind of wisdom that counts with God is "pure," "peaceable," "gentle," and "full of mercy . . . without uncertainty or insincerity." For "the harvest of righteousness is sown in peace"—in kind and thoughtful acts (verses 14-18).

NEW, BUT NOT BETTER

Lord, you have been our dwelling place throughout all generations. . . . From everlasting to everlasting you are God. Psalm 90:1, 2, N.I.V.

In our "throw away" society we come to expect that new things are better. Old things are to be thrown away. Thus we have disposable dishes, spoons, forks, cups, tablecloths, and napkins. We throw away pie pans, shopping bags, diapers. After reading stacks of magazines, newspapers, catalogs, and paperbacks, we throw them into the trash. A wheel comes off a toy—we throw away the whole thing. We fill in the blanks of our workbooks, and nobody else can use them. And always new articles will replace the old.

So when Mother repapered Rani's bedroom and made a new spread for her bed, Rani's best friend couldn't understand why Mother didn't buy a new bed, too. "My mom slept in that bed until she was married," Rani explained. "And anyway, we couldn't throw it away; it's an old friend."

But Rani's friend wouldn't give in. "That bed's not a person, and it looks old-fashioned," she said. Rani had to admit that perhaps she hadn't cared for the bed as well as she might have. The next day she offered to help her mother take the old bed apart and sand it. They filled in the cracks and added a new coat of varnish. Next morning Rani sanded it again before her mother waxed and polished it to a glorious shine.

The next time Rani's friend came to visit, its beauty stunned her. "You must have worked for hours on it," she said. "Wouldn't it have been easier to buy a new one?"

"Easier," Rani agreed, "but not better." By the light of Rani's bedside lamp the cherry wood glowed more gloriously than ever. And her friend had to admit that old is not bad. Old can be glorious, tried-and-true. And that's how it is with God. He has "been our dwelling place throughout all generations"—and that's a long, long time.

BORN LEADERS

"The Lord does not look at the things man looks at. Man looks at the outward appearance, but the Lord looks at the heart." 1 Samuel 16:7, N.I.V.

"I'm home," Randy yelled as he slammed the back door and walked up to his room. Normally he liked to tell his mother the best and worst things that happened, but not today. He needed to think awhile first. How come people let you down when you're counting on them? With his fist he thumped his pillow. Greg looked like a really good fellow. He enjoyed a joke, but he really said a lot of serious things in Bible class. And appeared like just the type who would help Randy, Kelly, and Ron lead out when the eighth-graders entertained the old people at the nursing home. Before they added his name to the program, they checked with him. "Sure! Be glad to help," he had said. But when his turn came to offer the prayer he just sat and giggled with Phil and refused to participate. So Randy had to pray. Greg was good-looking, confident, and ready with words—a born leader, Randy mused. So why wouldn't he at least pray?

When Randy finally felt like sharing his thoughts with his mom, she didn't look surprised. "It's hard to understand," she consoled, "but it happens." She reminded her son about the time Samuel went to the house of Jesse, carrying a horn filled with oil. God had told him to anoint one of Jesse's sons. When he saw Elias, Samuel knew he had found his man. He could already see a glorious new reign with this pleasing young man on the throne of Israel. "But the Lord said to Samuel, 'Do not consider his appearance or his height, for I have rejected him. The Lord does not look at the things man looks at. Man looks at the outward appearance, but the Lord looks at the heart.'" And of course, on that basis God had already chosen David—the kid brother. Which shows that the people God uses to His glory are those with humble, willing hearts.

WHEN GOD SENT RAIN

"I will not give my glory to another or my praise to idols." Isaiah 42:8, N.I.V.

A terrible famine had spread into parts of the back country, and Nurse Louise, along with two friends, had gone to keep the little Adventist clinic open. On the first day after their arrival they visited the sultan in his palace. He seemed pleased that the Christian missionaries had come to help his people, and promised to do all he could to help. For days he and the leading sheiks in his territory had prayed for rain. They had knelt on their prayer mats in the courtyard of the palace and bowed their heads low as they chanted the sacred prayers for rain. But nothing happened.

Every day hundreds of people died from starvation and the cruel diseases that accompany it. With the help of the sultan's secretary the three women vaccinated thousands of people against cholera. Soon the results were felt and the disease checked. But people sat out in the relentless sun and dust with empty stomachs. "What could be done?" the nurse asked as she walked along the banks of the almost-empty river. "Pray," the answer came. "Pray for rain. Pray that the river will fill up and crops may again be planted."

Knowing that God will not give His glory to another, that before she prayed for rain the people must know that she was praying, Nurse Louise again approached the sultan. "Would you like me to pray for rain?" she asked. "Would you come to a prayer meeting?" The sultan agreed to send some of his leading men to the prayer meeting, but at the appointed time they did not come. But the three Christian women prayed anyway. The Lord sent rain and filled the river. Waterfowl returned to nest along its banks. Grass began to grow, and the people planted crops. "Why did you not send the sheiks to pray for rain?" Nurse Louise asked the sultan one day.

"We couldn't find the head sheik," he replied. "And anyway, we knew the Christians were praying for rain."

"To God be the glory," Nurse Louise whispered. The sultan knew whose prayers were answered.

THE LOSER GLORIFIED

"Father, the time has come. Glorify your Son, that your Son may glorify you." John 17:1, N.I.V.

Jay did not grow up in a churchgoing home. But he knew there is a God in heaven, and he liked the Christmas story. The idea of a little baby coming to earth as a gift to link God with man fascinated him. But the rest of the gospel story didn't make much sense. "Jesus must be a loser," he said to himself. "What kind of person would let Himself be crucified?"

"What kind of person would let himself be picked up using stolen credit cards?" he asked himself the day he was caught. And Jay had to admit that he felt like a loser. But while in jail he discovered Jesus. For the first time he read about His life and death in the Bible. For the first time he understood why Jesus came to earth—to save Jay. And he began to grasp why Jesus died. For the first time he realized how the crucifixion of Jesus became a glorious symbol to Christians.

The Bible uses the word *glory* in two different ways. One meaning has to do with brilliance and light. The glory of the angels at Jesus' birth was one kind. But although darkness surrounded the cross when Jesus died, Jesus' death brought glory of another kind—honor and esteem. Thus glory describes the honor and majesty of royalty, or the esteem that great wealth brings a person. Glory also means praise for God from His worshipers, as well as those characteristics of God that we admire. When Moses asked to see His glory, God said, " 'I will cause all my goodness to pass in front of you, and I will proclaim my name . . . in your presence' " (Ex. 33:19).

At the cross Jesus' perfect life became an example for everyone. And the cross became the symbol of Christ's loving sacrifice for us. He who knew no sin died in my place and yours so that we might share eternal life with Him. And because He had known no sin, he arose from the dead. That kind of glory is good news indeed. It promises a new life for you and me and Jay.

TAKE AIM

So whether you eat or drink or whatever you do, do it all for the glory of God. 1 Corinthians 10:31, N.I.V.

Ruth Graham tells of a friend, a deputy sheriff who prided himself on being the best shot in the county. The law-enforcement authorities announced new and stiffer requirements on the firing range for deputies, and he felt confident that he could fire just as well from twenty-five yards as he formerly had from fifteen.

The new test required each man to fire twelve shots in eighteen seconds. The deputy had no difficulty in drawing a bead on the target, but just when the signal came for him to fire, his glasses fogged up and he couldn't see a thing. He could have panicked, because his job depended on his passing that test. But instead he remembered the words of his old Navy instructor: "If you ever lose sight of the target, remember your position."

So the deputy held his position and pulled the trigger just as fast as he could. When he was done he took off his glasses and wiped them. To his relief he had hit the bull's eye twelve times.

As a Christian you are on the firing range today. Sometimes you may be tempted to think that you are the target. But you aren't. You are the deputy aiming for the target. And what is the bull's-eye? Today's text says the aim of everything we do is to glorify God.

Sometimes your vision may become fogged by the suggestions of other people. Some tell you to do this or that, and others disagree. Many may present most convincing arguments to persuade you to disobey. But you must hold your position. And your position is beside Jesus. If you keep in step with Him, He will see that you hit the target and bring glory to His name. Don't panic, thinking that God's glory depends on you. Don't try to find the target on your own. For as you humbly live in obedience to God's will, others will see His glory because you held your position.

RUN FOR THE PRIZE

Do you not know that in a race all the runners run, but only one gets the prize? Run in such a way as to get the prize. 1 Corinthians 9:24, N.I.V.

"Like a band of barefoot brothers they ran along the beach at sunset. A phalanx of young Olympians clad in white, they matched one another stride for stride, splashing sand and saltwater onto their immaculate shorts. Fists clenched and faces grimacing, their pace quickened. . . . Gradually the . . . team angled off toward a seaside hotel." * The 1924 British team had trained intensively for months and was now ready for the Paris Olympic games.

Eric Liddell, a young Christian training for a career as a missionary, loved to run. But he ran, not to bring glory to himself—not because he thrilled to the roar of approving crowds—but because he hoped to bring glory to God. Eric was well aware of today's text. He knew that only one person would win. And he planned to "run in such a way as to get the prize." With this goal in mind, he had endured the strict training. But he did not mind the restrictions it placed on his social life. The simple diet, early bedtime, and early rising to work out on the track—all prepared him for the greatest race of his career, and they also kept him healthy and fit and in tune with God.

In Paris, when the Olympic organization posted the schedule for the qualifying heats, Eric saw to his disappointment that the 100-meter race was to be run on his Sabbath. And since his one aim in running was to glorify God, he refused to break his Sabbath and thus dishonor God. Instead he entered the 400-meter race. Many scoffed at his chances of winning the longer race, for which he had not trained. But Eric trusted God. As he lined up to start the race, someone slipped into his hand a note that read, "I will honor them that honor Me." With that assurance ringing in his heart, he led all the way to the finishing tape. With satisfaction Eric savored his moment of triumph as he received the gold medal to the strains of his national anthem and the fluttering of the Union Jack on the tallest flagpole. For the glory of the moment belonged to God.

---

* James L. Fly, "Like a 'Chariot of Fire,'" *Adventist Review,* May 5, 1983.

THE FAME GAME

"For whoever exalts himself will be humbled, and whoever humbles himself will be exalted." Matthew 23:12, N.I.V.

Have you ever wished you were famous? I mean really well known. People right across the country would know your name and recognize your talents. As Judy practices the piano she often imagines herself on the stage of Carnegie Hall playing her piece to a packed house. Why does she care how many people hear her play? Because she wants the deafening applause when she is done. "But I usually mess up somewhere," Judy says. "Then I'm glad that nobody can hear me."

Ed often fantasized seeing himself as a motorcycle stunt rider. So when his class needed something spectacular to dramatize their success in a fund-raising drive, he jumped his motorcycle onto the stage in the gym. "Why did you risk wiping out in front of everybody to do this?" a reporter from the school paper asked. Ed grinned. "How many fellows my age have had their bike in the yearbook?" he replied. Next he tried to capture fame by jumping a river. "This one will really make me famous," he promised. But though the jump began well enough, the bike did a half loop in midair and almost drowned him in the water.

Why do people like Judy and Ed want to see their names in lights? "Basically because they want to be loved," says Noel Paul Stookey. But fame usually leaves them as lonely and empty as before—unless they find Jesus.

That's how it is with fame—if you look for it you probably won't find it. But when you do your best to be successful in your own eyes and in God's, you don't really care if you're famous or not. If fame comes with success, that's fine! When Jesus said, " 'Whoever exalts himself will be humbled, and whoever humbles himself will be exalted,' " He probably meant that fame and glory come to those who least expect it. Have fun today doing your best for Him.

LOOK FOR THE GLORY

Then your righteousness will go before you, and the glory of the Lord will be your rear guard. Isaiah 58:8, N.I.V.

I used to read in the Bible about Moses and how his face shone after being in God's presence. What kind of glory lit up his face so that after he hiked all the way down the mountain and into camp people almost needed sunglasses to look at him? I suspect that the glory on Moses' face wasn't quite the kind you measure in candlepower, because I have seen some wonderfully lit-up faces lately. I'm not talking about the way Penny's face shines when Jon walks into the room, or the way 2-year-old Todd glows when his daddy comes home. What I have seen is more than that.

I first saw it at a crowded train station in New Delhi. Since our train would not resume its journey for another hour, my husband had gone in search of warm food. But I needed his help. A crease on my brow must have alerted a kind man to my need. "Is there anything I can do to help?" he asked. That was when I noticed the love of Jesus radiating from his face. I wondered if lots of practice at forgetting himself and helping others had made the difference.

Then there was the man at the little church high in the mountains near Mackay, Australia. When I heard the singing—nobody could play the organ, so they didn't even turn it on—I wondered what kind of blessing could possibly come from worshiping there. The Sabbath school teacher, a man without a college education but full of God's love, showed me. His face glowed. And the more he talked, the more I wanted to know God the way he did. Now that I'm looking for it, I see God's glory reflected in all kinds of people. You may see it for yourself in some unexpected places. And you might even see it on the face of one of your friends. The most important thing, however, is to let God light up *your* face with His glory. Maybe Isaiah 58 explains how this happens.

SHELLEY'S BOOTS

The brother in humble circumstances ought to take pride in his high position. James 1:9, N.I.V.

Sally stamped the snow from her boots before opening the back door. "How was your day?" her mother called from the kitchen, where she stood peeling potatoes.

"Oh, Mother, I hate these boots!" the girl complained as she began pulling them off, unaware of her mother's question. Suddenly the indignity of having to wear such plain, serviceable footwear overwhelmed her.

"Shelley Matson wears shiny white boots, and she acts as if she were in high school. Everyone thinks she is so grown-up. The girls do whatever she does, and all the boys hang around her. They treat Jeannie, Julie, and me like we don't belong in sixth grade. Sometimes I feel so miserable!"

Mrs. Cremeens put down a potato and dried her hands. "Sally, have you done graphs in math?" she asked. Her daughter nodded. "Well, growth is like an upward swing on a graph. When you stop growing, I suppose you have stopped living."

"Well, what happened to you?" Sally laughed. "You stopped growing at 15." Mrs. Cremeens smiled. She wasn't talking about that kind of growth. "Your character and personality keep on growing," she explained. "Your good looks slowly bloom and peak. You wouldn't want to peak in the sixth grade, would you? You still have academy and college."

Sally thought of the fun she had at recess time with Jeannie and Julie, dreaming about horses and reliving some of the horse stories they read. When I look at life like a piece of graph paper, I do have time to enjoy the sixth grade and not worry about white boots until later, she decided. She would glory in childhood as long as she could, remembering that the Christian "in humble circumstances ought to take pride in [her] high position." After all, she recalled, "life is what you make it." Sally wanted hers to be long and joyful. And her snow boots didn't look so bad after all.

WHAT IS GOD LIKE?

Like the appearance of a rainbow in the clouds on a rainy day, so was the radiance around him. Ezekiel 1:28, N.I.V.

Kris was attending an impressive popular church for the first time. In spite of the fact that her mother had cautioned her not to talk, the little girl, overcome by her first sight of what she thought was God, whispered, "Does He always wear a shirt and tie?" Her mother explained that the man in the pulpit was not God. For although God was present and could see Kris, she couldn't see Him.

A little later the girl noticed her mother's eyes closed. "Are you asleep?" Kris hissed, breaking the quiet of the presermon meditation. Her mother shook her head and explained how she was praying. But that only puzzled the little girl further because her mother's lips had not been moving.

"They don't have to," her mother explained again. "God hears when you pray in your heart."

"Wow!" Kris was impressed. "God must have big ears!"

How do you explain God to someone who doesn't know about Him? Perhaps you could explain Him as a force. We all recognize power that is stronger that human might. But force as in blind fury could scare people away from God. That's why God revealed Himself to Elijah, not in fire, earthquake, or storm, but by a still small voice. And to Ezekiel he appeared surrounded by a rainbow.

When Kris's mother tried to explain how God lives in heaven and watches over people on earth, she emphasized His love by mentioning how he sends the sunshine and the rain. That afternoon after a summer shower a rainbow appeared. "See," the girl said, "God did that."

I imagine that God was pleased that Kris noticed His handiwork that day. And He hopes she will continue to look for evidences of His love. Have you ever thought how your life reveals His signature when you walk closely with Him? People like Kris may learn to love Him when they see what He means to you.

GLORY THAT LASTS

So we fix our eyes not on what is seen, but on what is unseen. For what is seen is temporary, but what is unseen is eternal. 2 Corinthians 4:18, N.I.V.

"Do I really have to wear this dress tonight?" Cheri moaned aloud. "It needs plum-colored shoes, and the nearest I have are navy."

"You have other outfits you could wear tonight," Mother gently reminded. "And anyway, that dress goes very well with navy shoes."

Cheri bit her lip. She hadn't meant to sound so hard to please. But her friend Lori always dressed exactly right and had a way of noticing when someone else's clothes did not quite match. She was glad her father had not heard her fussing, though. His favorite comment for such occasions was "Clothes don't make the man; the man makes the clothes." She had to admit that was certainly the case with Carl. He could make even his brother's hand-me-downs look elegant. In fact, you hardly noticed his clothes. It was his warmth and wit that everyone enjoyed.

When we are wrapped up in ourselves, we find it easier to notice other people in terms of their outward appearance. We label them according to what they wear, how old they are, how fashionable, or how out of date. This is convenient and saves a lot of time getting to know people. Later when someone says something about Beth, you think of her label. "Oh, she is that mousy piano player," you say. And you need remember nothing else about her.

The problem with this system of labeling is that often you don't get to know the people. And you dislike them because you don't know them. As we mingle with people today, let's look past their clothes and try to find out how they feel about things. Let's really listen to their replies. By focusing on the unseen—what is not immediately obvious—we'll discover many truly worthwhile and lasting friends.

GLORIOUS MORNING

"When the Son of Man comes in his glory, and all the angels with him, he will sit on his throne in heavenly glory." Matthew 25:31, N.I.V.

Can you picture that "great gettin'-up morning" when Jesus will appear with His angels? The glory of that scene dazzles even through sunglasses. It is a special brightness of a vast sinless throng. The brilliance of the scene will blind some people so that they hide from it. But those who have lived every day as though they are in the presence of Jesus will not be afraid. They have the assurance that He has forgiven their sins and cast them into the deepest sea. And because God doesn't remember their sins, neither do they.

In describing that moment, Jesus pictures "'all the nations . . . gathered before him'" (verse 32). From His throne God separates the sheep from the goats. The sheep, representing the righteous, He places on His right, and everyone else on His left. Then Jesus calls the righteous to Him. "'"Come, you who are blessed by my Father; take your inheritance, the kingdom"'" of glory (verse 34). But the people are puzzled. On what basis have some been saved and others not?

"'Then the King will say to those on his right, " . . . take your inheritance, the kingdom prepared for you. . . . For I was hungry and you gave me something to eat, I was thirsty and you gave me something to drink, I was a stranger and you invited me in, I needed clothes and you clothed me, I was sick and you looked after me, I was in prison and you came to visit me"'" (verses 34-36).

Then comes the surprise: the chosen ones do not know when they did these things. They don't remember seeing Jesus a stranger or taking Him in. But "'the King will reply, " . . . whatever you did for one of the least of these brothers of mine, you did for me"'" (verse 40).

I want to be a part of that glorious morning, don't you? Ask Jesus to help you share in His work of unselfishly helping others today. When your parents or teachers ask you to do something difficult, set to work cheerfully. That way you are sharing the coming glory.

FOREVER IS A LONG, LONG TIME

He that overcometh shall inherit all things; and I will be his God, and he shall be my son. Revelation 21:7.

"Ali, I'll race you to the edge of the garden and back!" Tende called as he braced himself for the run. But Ali did not accept the challenge. "I don't feel like running," he said in a tired voice. Wondering what was wrong, Tende walked over to his friend and asked him.

"My mother died," Ali said sadly. "And I won't ever see her again." Tende didn't know how to say he was sorry for what had happened to Ali's mother, so he just kicked a rock with his bare toe. If his friend had been a Christian, Tende would have reminded him about the glorious reunion day in heaven. But what was the use of mentioning it to a Moslem? Tende sighed with frustration. Ali looked up, expecting the other boy to explain his sigh.

"Oh, nothing," Tende said as he kicked another rock. "It's just too bad you aren't a Christian!"

The other boy sat up sharply. Nobody had ever told him, the chief's favorite son, that it was too bad that he was not something or other.

"If you were a Christian, you would know about heaven," Tende explained. "Our Bible teaches that Jesus is coming to take those who love Him to heaven. It's too bad that you don't know about heaven."

Right there and then Ali decided that he would persuade his father to send him to a Christian school. And although Ali only professed a sudden interest in book learning that could be satisfied only by attending the best school in Kampala, he never lost that burning desire for heaven. When he later heard about the seventh-day Sabbath, he readily accepted it. He wouldn't let anything stand between Him and his newfound Father in heaven. By God's grace Ali is an overcomer. He knows that overcomers shall inherit all things forever. And forever is a long, long time.

YOUR NAME FOREVER

I will praise you, O Lord my God, with all my heart; I will glorify your name forever. Psalm 86:12, N.I.V.

When Manfred was little he used to sit on his father's knee at worship time and stroke his left hand. Father never talked about his hand, and Manfred didn't like to ask what happened to it. You see, much of the palm was missing, and the fingers curved like stiff claws. And when Manfred stroked his father's thumb a large lump separated from the bone and moved back and forth.

One night Mr. Krauss explained to Manfred how he had been a soldier on the Russian front. Often he crossed the Russian lines on a dangerous mission. Once he felt sorry for himself having to do such dangerous work on his birthday. When he stopped to get out his sandwich, which he carried in his knapsack in an aluminum box, Mr. Krauss discovered that a bullet had passed right through the can and the sandwich. "It might have gone through me," Mr. Krauss said. "Had it come two or three inches to the left, it would have struck a live hand grenade that I always carried. And that would have been even worse.

"And so," Mr. Krauss concluded, beaming, "that turned out to be the best birthday I ever had. I didn't remember the aches and pains of my mission—only the joy and thankfulness of being alive."

Manfred stroked his father's thumb in silence for a while. His voice sounded quite serious when he finally spoke. "Don't you just *love* God for watching over you like that?" he asked.

When Manfred sees the glories of heaven, his first thought will be to find Jesus and thank Him for His love and care. Like his father on that long-ago birthday, Manfred will forget the aches and pains of the difficult times on earth. He will feel a surge of happiness and thankfulness to be alive. Wouldn't you gladly honor and praise God's wonderful name forever—and ever?

CONFIDENCE FOREVER

The fruit of righteousness will be peace; the effect of righteousness will be quietness and confidence forever. Isaiah 32:17, N.I.V.

Melissa Sue Anderson, the actress who played Mary Ingalls on the Little House on the Prairie television series, felt annoyed by the fact that the part she played would soon change. The scriptwriters had Mary turning blind, and the actress wondered if the character would loose its challenge. Knowing that she could not influence the direction of the series, she decided to accept the transformation and do the best she could with it. And that's when the part opened up a whole new world for her. Melissa discovered what it meant to be blind.

I have read of people who lost their eyesight and how angry it made them. Nobody wants all of a sudden to lose his or her independence. You have probably noticed that—especially if you have to ask permission before you leave your yard. Or if you are accustomed to jumping onto your bike when you need to get something from your friend's house, you feel helpless when your bike is out of commission. But those are temporary inconveniences and quickly forgotten. They don't begin to match the frustration of blindness.

In order to play her part well, Melissa had to close her eyes tightly and walk without help. The first two or three steps didn't feel too bad because she knew where she was. But by the fourth step her self-confidence had vanished. And she could not force herself to take another step.

Today's text tells us that if something ever happens to shake completely our self-confidence, we should look to Jesus, who is the source of all true righteousness. One of the fruits of following Him is peace and confidence. He doesn't promise to remove our difficulties, you'll notice, but to quiet our troubled spirit, take away that knot that worry ties in our tummies. And He doesn't merely untie it—He takes it away forever.

THE GLORY FOREVER

For thine is the kingdom, and the power, and the glory, for ever. Amen. Matthew 6:13.

What do you think of when you think of *forever?* Old Father Time with his long white beard? Or wintertime that seems to last forever? I hope not. You see, when sin brought old age and wintertimes, it took away forever. Jan lost her mother in a car accident when she was only 10. She knows very clearly that she could not stand a forever that does to people what it did to her mother. But she can't wait for Jesus to bring in a new forever. Sometimes she lies on the grass and tries to wrap her mind around the idea of forever—eternity.

Mr. Campbell tells his science class that forever is like walking on a treadmill. Every step you takes keeps it turning. And its turning keeps you treading. It could go on endlessly if you didn't step off. Lots of people try to set up perpetual motion, he said. He showed Jan's class a jar of chemicals. When he dropped in some naphthalene moth balls, the chemical reacted with the naphtha to form little gas bubbles that clung to each ball. The gas bubbles lightened the weight of the balls. So the balls rose to the top, where the gas bubbles disappeared. That left the moth balls heavy again, and they sank to the bottom until more gas bubbles formed to push them slowly to the top. But the moth balls couldn't go on rising and falling in the jar forever, because each tiny gas bubble reduced the amount of naphtha in the balls. Eventually the balls would have been used up.

One day Jesus will release our world from the reign of sin and death. He will introduce us to a bright new eternity. A time when day is always at the morning. When the year is always at springtime. When Jan and her mother will be always youthful. "They will run and not grow weary, they will walk and not be faint" (Isa. 40:31, N.I.V.). And they will discover that God, their heavenly Father, is the most youthful one of all. That's glory forever, and Jan can hardly wait. How about you?

SCRIPTURE INDEX